D1807280

Armed Political Organizations

Armed Political Organizations

From Conflict to Integration

BENEDETTA BERTI

The Johns Hopkins University Press
Baltimore

Printed in the United States of America on acid-free paper
2 4 6 8 9 7 5 3 1

The Johns Hopkins University Press
2715 North Charles Street
Baltimore, Maryland 21218-4363
www.press.jhu.edu

Library of Congress Cataloging-in-Publication Data

Berti, Benedetta.
Armed political organizations / Benedetta Berti.
pages ; cm
Includes bibliographical references and index.
ISBN-13: 978-1-4214-0974-0 (hardcover : alk. paper)
ISBN-13: 978-1-4214-0975-7 (electronic)
ISBN-10: 1-4214-0974-7 (hardcover : alk. paper)
ISBN-10: 1-4214-0975-5 (electronic)
1. Political violence. 2. Hizballah (Lebanon). 3. Harakat al-Muqawamah al-Islamiyah. 4. Irish Republican Army. I. Title.
JC328.6.B478 2013
322.4′2—dc23 2012040979

A catalog record for this book is available from the British Library.

The Johns Hopkins University Press uses environmentally friendly book materials, including recycled text paper that is composed of at least 30 percent post-consumer waste, whenever possible.

To Avi, Eliana, Lily, and Milo

You can do anything with bayonets except sit on them.

Charles Maurice de Talleyrand-Périgord

CONTENTS

ACKNOWLEDGMENTS

This book could not have happened without the encouragement, support, and assistance of a large number of people—to whom I am profoundly indebted.

I first began thinking about this writing project in 2005, while I was completing a graduate degree at the Fletcher School. At the time my academic advisor, Professor Richard Shultz, encouraged me to pursue a doctorate to develop this project further. Professor Shultz's academic mentorship and support have been instrumental in both preparing my PhD dissertation (on which this project is based) as well as in writing the manuscript. Along with Professor Shultz, I also thank Professor Andrew Hess and Professor William Martel—both at the Fletcher School—for their guidance, support, and very constructive comments.

I express my gratitude to my colleagues and friends at Tel Aviv University and at the Institute for National Security Studies (INSS) for the strong institutional support and backing I have received since moving to this part of world. In particular, I would like to acknowledge Dr. Anat Kurz for her invaluable academic, professional, and personal advice.

Next, I want to thank the entire editorial team at the Johns Hopkins University Press, especially Suzanne Flinchbaugh. This is the second book I have written with Johns Hopkins and I could not have wished for a better experience.

It goes without saying, but I'll write it down nevertheless: I could not have written this book without the support, encouragement, and help of my family, specifically my husband, Avi. Thank you for putting up with my hectic life.

Finally, I need to thank the many (many) people—in Beirut, Ramallah, London, Dublin, Belfast, Tel Aviv, and Washington, DC—who have been kind enough to talk to me, to answer my many (many) questions, and who have helped me get a better understanding of the groups I am studying.

Armed Political Organizations

Introduction

The Challenge of Understanding the Dual Logic of Armed-Political Organizations

In recent decades, armed groups have shown an increased interest in creating political parties to take part in institutional politics. By using these political wings to participate in elections and to win public office, some armed groups have gained enormous political and decision-making power.

Even though this trend has been scarcely researched and analyzed, the influence of such hybrid political and armed organizations can be substantial. Consider two events that took place in 2006: the sweeping electoral victory of the Palestinian Hamas, an armed group and a political party, followed by its takeover of the Gaza Strip in 2007, and the July 2006 war between Israel and the Lebanese Hezbollah, an organization that also operates both as a sophisticated quasi-army and as a powerful domestic political party. More recently, with the Arab Awakening shaking up the status quo and the political landscape in the Middle East, the crucial question has been how to understand and integrate armed groups into institutional politics.

The book approaches this subject by seeking to answer two main questions: (1) Why do armed groups decide to establish political wings to compete in elections? (2) What conditions lead the political wing to become the primary means of expression of the armed group, ultimately leading to the relinquishment of the group's weapons?

Armed Groups and Political Wing Formation: The Dynamics behind Political Participation

The existing literature on the dynamics of political involvement of armed groups is scarce. The focus is on either what accounts for a group's relinquishment of violence and its transition toward adopting an unarmed strategy,[1] or on what factors shape the organizational behavior of a given armed group once it has fully transformed into a political party.[2]

Much less attention has been devoted to analyzing the internal dynamics and external factors that lead armed groups to create a political wing—defined as a special subunit within an armed group that engages in aboveground institutional political activities through contending elections and assuming office if elected.[3] Less research has also been conducted on participation in institutional politics of "hybrid" organizations that operate simultaneously as armed groups and political parties.

Among the most significant examples of scholarly works that deal with the process of political wing formation, it is important to mention Anisseh Van Engeland and Rachel Rudolph's study on armed groups' transition "from terrorism to politics," and Leonard Weinberg, Ami Pedahzur, and Arie Perliger's book exploring the relation between terrorist groups and political parties.[4]

Both examples serve as a useful starting point for further research. Van Engeland and Rudolph focus their analysis of political wing formation dynamics on defining the parameters that indicate an armed group's commitment to politics. In their work, a given armed group has a high potential to shift toward institutional politics if it has a concrete commitment to participate in the governance system ("political will"), a political ideology and electoral program, together with a concrete set of policies and relations with other domestic and international political actors. The political transition is also facilitated by a high degree of internal cohesion and leadership commitment toward politics.[5]

Weinberg, Pedahzur, and Perliger's research is even more comprehensive, focusing not only on the internal factors that can shape a group's transition toward institutional politics but also on how the group's environment can contribute to this shift. They identify four main factors that can lead to a group's transition toward institutional politics. These are a transformation in the political system toward democracy, an amnesty from the government, an increase in the military repression of the group, and an internal desire to better communicate with the group's social basis and thus better compete with other political organizations.[6] The book focuses less on addressing the relation of relative causal importance between these factors.

This book builds on the existing literature, expanding its scope and deepening the level of analysis. First, although it considers the importance of a group's internal commitment to change, the book argues that this factor is necessary but not sufficient to ensure a political transition. Second, the study tries to create a more complex model that accounts for the decision to create a political wing. This draws from Weinberg, Pedahzur, and Perliger's research but considers other important institutional and external causes of political transition.

The assumption of the study is that an armed group's decision to create a political wing is based on a rational calculation. The working hypothesis—which will be explained in chapter 2—states that the creation of such a political wing is the result of the interplay of four necessary but by themselves insufficient factors. These are an internal commitment to change, an institutional pressure to expand, a strain in the availability of mobilization resources, and an "opening" in the political opportunity system.

Drawing on Rudolph and Van Engeland, the research expects that a political wing will be formed when a dominant coalition within the armed organization supports the entry into institutional politics, thus ensuring a high commitment to change. The choice to create a political wing is also triggered by the group's institutional development and its related push to grow through expansion. In turn, the need to acquire power and stability while maintaining relevancy and organizational legitimacy motivates the aspiration to grow.[7] What's more, an organization's transition toward institutional politics can be seen as an adaptation mechanism that a given group implements to respond to a decline in the needed available resources to ensure organizational survival.

Finally, armed groups opt to form a political wing and to engage in institutional politics when the political opportunity structure within which they operate generates opportunities to maximize their influence and relevancy. Unlike other works on the subject—including Weinberg, Pedahzur, and Perliger's study—this research does not necessarily correlate such an opening to an increase in the overall democracy of the political system, nor does it make it conditional on an amnesty or on the establishment of a postconflict negotiation process and direct settlement talks.[8]

The research expects that the interplay of the organizational pressure to expand, the need to respond to the decline in the capacity to mobilize resources, and an external opening of the political system, will lead armed groups to set up a political wing to compete in elections. This outcome is impossible without an internal commitment to change. Understanding the internal power dynamics within armed groups and their commitment to political participation is also useful as it helps to assess the consequences of the group's decision to develop a political wing. More specifically, it allows the study to address the following question: When do political wings lead to broader acceptance of the rules of the political game and disarmament?

The Impact of the Political Wing: Strategic versus Tactical Change

A second characteristic of the existing literature on political activism of armed groups is that it tends to treat political participation as a sign of a group's future transition from armed militia to "legitimate" political actor. In other words, an armed group's desire to establish a political wing is seen as the beginning of a "linear transition" that will eventually lead the politico-military organization to relinquish its antisystemic and violent means. The group's participation in institutional politics is taken as prima facie evidence that the group regards "political institutions as the only legitimate framework for political contestation and adherence to the democratic rules of the game."[9]

Under this framework, violence is considered a by-product of the group's exclusion from accessing the decision-making and power centers of a given political system. Once the system "opens up" and allows participation, armed groups will choose to take part in the political process, and this in turn will lead them to pursue pragmatic political means in lieu of violent ones.[10]

This model draws from a classic understanding of the evolution of revolutions and revolutionary movements that links the presence of an armed revolutionary movement with the type of regime in power. The framework asserts that closed or exclusionary authoritarian regimes are most vulnerable to the growth of mass-based protest movements.[11]

The ballot box is seen as the "coffin of revolutionary movements,"[12] an argument further developed by Samuel Huntington, who asserted that democracies were not particularly vulnerable to revolutions, and that providing channels for the participation of opposition groups offered the best chance of lowering the potential for political violence.[13] Ted Gurr also referred to a given society's level of institutionalization as inversely correlated to that society's potential for internal strife, focusing on the stability and broadness (inclusiveness) of the political institutions and on the role of political parties to "provide the discontented with routinized and typically non-violent means for expressing their discontents."[14]

A number of scholars have also argued that the process of creating and joining violent groups is related to governmental exclusionary practices, such as social and political repression, exclusion from electoral competition, fraudulent elections, and manipulation of the electoral system resulting in gerrymandering.[15]

This framework has been also applied to terrorism studies. Martha Crenshaw, for example, identified the existence of concrete grievances and the lack of concrete access to the political system as the main variables that explain the birth of terrorist groups.[16] A corollary of this interpretative framework is that creating more democratic and open political systems will result in diminishing political violence and increased integration. Once armed groups are granted real access to representation through fair electoral competition, their need to rely on armed force will gradually wean out.

A related argument to strengthen the "linear armed-to-political group paradigm" suggests that regardless of the initial strategic intentions of a given armed group that joins institutional politics, the group's involvement in both elections and governance will gradually and incrementally lead the organization to transition to mainstream political organization.

By participating in the political process and becoming accountable to their constituencies as well as other political actors, armed groups are less likely to rely on violent means and more likely to regulate and restrict the use of violence within their ranks.[17]

Elections allow armed groups to be directly accountable to their constituency, as well as to the impact of public opinion in general.[18] More specifically, to attract more votes, the newly created political wings may be forced to drift to a less ideologically extreme or violent posture. Marina Ottaway at the Carnegie Institute summarizes this by stating, that "there is ample evidence that participation in an electoral process forces any party, regardless of ideology, to moderate its position if it wants to attract voters in large numbers."[19]

Participation in elections is also believed to have both an "integrating" as well as a "socializing" function.[20] First, by becoming integrated in the political system, previously excluded opposition groups can gradually develop a sense of ownership in the system. As such, they become more interested in its preservation and in establishing positive relations with the other political actors, both key ingredients to shift from violent confrontation to political dialogue.[21] Second, by being actively involved in the political system, armed groups and their leaders can gradually absorb and internalize the values and practices of democracy. Thus, they can begin an attitudinal change toward accepting to act as ordinary political actors and to "play by the rules." Finally, the involvement in institutional politics may encourage an armed organization to transition by empowering the political "moderate" leadership of the group, stirring the organization toward relying exclusively on mainstream politics.[22]

This linear understanding of the effects of political involvement has serious flaws. Treating political participation as an effective means to deter armed groups from engaging in violence wrongly assumes that these two different forms of political struggle are mutually exclusive. On the contrary, history shows a trend of recurring convergence between terrorist activities and political parties, and a systemic and reciprocal relation between armed and political organizations.[23] As the rest of this study will describe in detail, groups such as the Palestinian Hamas or the Lebanese Hezbollah have been able to operate simultaneously at both the political as well as at the military level, and increased inclusion in the political process has not resulted in a shift and a linear transformation into institutionalized political parties and demobilized armed groups. Even when looking more in-depth at the transformation of a group such as the Provisional Irish Republican Army, commonly thought as a primary example of a linear transition from armed to political, it appears obvious that political participation alone did not lead the group to choose between its Armalites and the ballot box.[24]

The assumption that political participation and inclusion provide an alternative outlet to armed struggle disregards the empirical evidence that links terrorist and violent activism to democratic and participatory political systems. On this subject, Eubank and Weinberg have shown that open and democratic systems have a higher risk of being targeted by terrorist groups, thus questioning the assertion that political participation in fair and free elections is enough to prevent the proliferation of political violence and terrorism.[25]

While it is undeniable that taking part in elections makes any armed group more accountable to its constituency and to the fluctuations in public opinion, it is an unwarranted assumption that the public will *automatically* choose to penalize violence and armed struggle. Armed struggle need not be detrimental to the political advancement of an armed group, as the public may support it, a topic that the study analyzes more in detail in the chapters on Hamas and Hezbollah. Furthermore, a political wing also has a series of political tools to create a separation between its own activities and those of the armed wing, and to make its electoral support not contingent on the level of approval for the armed wing's operation. For example, a group may heavily invest in providing social services and other political and social goods, thus creating a network of supporters-clients whose political backing is not linked to their approval of the group's military activities. Again, the analysis of the electoral strategies of both Hamas and Hezbollah will further substantiate this point.

The claim that a positive involvement in the political system leads to a progressive transformation into an ordinary political player fails to account for the fact that armed groups can join the political system and even act as mainstream political actors without necessarily having to forfeit their violent struggle, or undergo a strategic transformation. On the contrary, hybrid politico-military organizations may exploit the democratic system to increase their strength and solidify their position in the domestic context, thus making it harder to constrain the group and force it to disarm.

This is not to deny that political participation has an effect on an armed group and its strategic outlook, or that elections can be an important tool to integrate armed groups into the political system and perform a postconflict peacemaking function.[26] Still, while competing in elections introduces the logic of "accommodation through institutional politics" to a previously antisystemic armed group, such logic does not automatically replace the "armed struggle" rationale.

The existing scholarly works that describe the political development of armed groups under such terms risk presenting an oversimplified and quasi-deterministic picture. Other works, such as Jeroen de Zeeuw's analysis of postwar political transitions of armed groups, recognize that political evolution is hardly a linear process toward disarmament. De Zeeuw's volume includes a series of important insights into the factors that may ease such transition. The study for instance stresses the positive role of political reforms (proportional and power-sharing arrangements), security reforms to convince that disarming will be safe for the military wing, as well as the importance of large popular backing for the group's political wing, and international support.[27]

This research's findings support these conclusions, while stressing the importance of a previously unexplored factor: the internal balance of power within the group. The working hypothesis suggests that the internal power distribution and the type of relationship existing between the group's political group and its military apparatus are a key variable in understanding whether the organization is headed toward a political transition.

In other words, there is no deterministic certitude that political participation will lead to a linear transition from armed to political organization. Armed groups will embark in a complete transition and become "ordinary" political parties if—within the organization—the logics of armed struggle and that of political accommodation begin to be perceived as mutually exclusive, creating an intense internal disequilibrium. When these two logics are perceived as opposite, leading to an internal competition between the political and the military leaderships, then the organization is at its ripest for strategic change and "moderation." The following chapter will develop this concept further and explain when such a situation is more likely to occur, and what main factors need to be present to lead toward such "moderation." An important corollary of this theory is that armed groups' participation in institutional politics does not automatically lead to a linear transition toward demobilization. Instead, armed groups' involvement in politics will lead to cycles where the political strategy is given primacy within the organization, to be followed by cycles where armed struggle becomes the preferred option.

In the research, a complete or successful political transition is equated with a process of "moderation." Other scholars, like Van Engeland and Rudolph, define a successful transition as one where the armed group is able to take part in elections and win seats.[28] The problem with setting the bar to define a successful transition so low is that it prevents from distinguishing cases where a political wing operates in parallel with an armed one, as in the case of Hezbollah, with cases where political participation led to complete disarmament.

In this study, a successful transition leads to "moderation," inferring that the group relinquished its armed strategy in favor of an unarmed one. Together with disarmament, this process must also lead to the progressive integration into the political system.

Political integration is not merely defined by competing and winning seats; it also includes the acceptance of rules and constraints of institutional politics, as well an increased interest in bargaining and negotiating with other political actors. This process should also produce a gradual shift in the group's violent ideology, giving way into a more accommodating one, and eventually renouncing violence as an acceptable means to bring about the desired political change.

Case Studies Selection and Research Outline: Comparing Apples and Oranges?

The study uses comparative case studies to derive a general framework of armed groups' political involvement and to test the hypotheses on political wing formation. Given that this is a small-n study, the main purpose of the research is not to arrive to an all-encompassing model to predict political behavior of all existing armed groups. The study's portended contribution is far more modest: to provide a critical analysis and to question the dominant linear armed-to-political model, while proposing a possible new angle of research.

A historical-institutional comparison[29] of the chosen groups and their political strategy makes it possible to assess the role of external factors and internal changes in shaping a given group's discourse and strategy, as well as to analyze the effect of these factors on the groups' recourse to violence.

To test the hypotheses, the study looks in particular at the political development of three very different armed and political organizations. These organizations are the Palestinian Hamas, the Lebanese Hezbollah, and the Irish Republican Army in Northern Ireland.

The first criterion for selection of these cases was their high-profile nature. The second was their prominence, and that they offer a wealth of relevant data and information.

The IRA was chosen as a case study because it is most often cited in the literature to illustrate a linear institutional progression from armed group to political party. It offers one of the best examples of an armed group that permanently gave up violence to join the political process. The case is also used to generate hypotheses that address the question of policy responses to armed groups' activism.

Hamas and Hezbollah were chosen as "least likely" case studies to test the hypotheses' validity on political wing development as an alternative framework to understand the political participation patterns of armed groups. In other words, because these cases appear least likely to follow the proposed model of development of armed groups, based on the shifting internal relations between a given group's armed and political wings, they are particularly well suited to test and verify that model.

Both organizations have reached a highly formalized and institutionalized stage of their political development and have become formal, hierarchical, sophisticated, and integrated political machines. According to the "linear development model," as de facto prominent political actors, these organizations should have the highest chance of embracing the "accommodation through political participation" paradigm, while rejecting the logic of confrontation. Therefore, looking at whether these organizations' political development has indeed been linear and, if not, analyzing whether it has been characterized by alternate cycles of accommodation and armed struggle, allows probing the "cyclical model."

Comparing these three very different groups may seem problematic. At first glance, these groups could not be more different. They are located in separate areas of the world, grounded in different religious and political ideologies, and presently at substantially distinct stages of their military and political development. When taking a closer look, these differences, despite being real and substantial, do not constitute insurmountable obstacles in comparing the groups, especially after factoring in the common elements between them.

Organizationally, despite having different structures, the groups are all characterized as bureaucratic hierarchies with strong vertical chains of command and the presence of a strong leadership. The organizations differ in their degree of internal unity and integration at the leadership level, a factor that is highly significant when analyzing their varying levels of political development. Hezbollah is a group with a high degree of internal unity among its leadership, with its military and political activities integrated in ongoing strategic cooperation. Hamas's leadership structure, in contrast, is more geographically dispersed and at times overlapping. Although Hamas's military and political activities are generally integrated and the group is generally cohesive, internal conflict along the politico-military line does occur cyclically. In the case of the "republican movement," there has always been a formal separation between its military and political wings, the IRA and Sinn Féin, with distinct leaderships and structures. In reality, there was also a level of integration between IRA and Sinn Fein, especially in the first decades of operation of the group, wherein the Army Council de facto oversaw all political and military activities. Furthermore, double-membership within the IRA and Sinn Féin, including at the leadership level, ensured unity of purpose and organizational cohesion.

All three groups analyzed in the study can be characterized as complex politico-military organizations, which defeat the stereotype of the clandestine, alienated terrorist cell with no grassroots support. Particularly in the cases of Hamas and Hezbollah, the groups not only are armed and political organizations but also are important providers of social services, making them to some extent larger welfare and social movements. In contrast, the IRA never maintained a welfare network. This important difference might have resulted in a more volatile Sinn Féin–supporting base and electorate than that of Hamas and Hezbollah.

Last, each of the groups has benefited and still relies on external support—either from diasporas or from ally states—although the partnership between Hezbollah and Iran is greater in scope than any of the relationships Hamas or the IRA ever held with other third parties.

Although the context in which these groups evolved and operate presents obvious regional and cultural differences, there are a few interesting commonalities. The first similarity is that the groups were created in reaction to or within the context of a foreign territorial occupation. Each group holds a strong national-liberation dimension. Furthermore, each organization has been involved in "intractable conflicts (. . .) characterized by high levels of intergroup violence that has not been amenable to reduction through negotiation."[30]

The political wings of the three groups all operate in highly polarized societies where problems of societal cohesion and political instability are rife.[31] In the case of Lebanon and Northern Ireland, the groups developed within an ethnically divided and stratified society, characterized by high social separation, socioeconomic gaps overlapping with ethnic identities, and a political system that both institutionalized and enhanced the societal and ethnic stratification.

In contrast, the political systems, the domestic policies, and the international responses to these groups present substantial differences. The final section of the book, which looks into the policy implications of the study, analyzes this point further.

The Power of Politics

Party Formation and Armed Struggle

Traditionally, non-state armed groups, especially those that employ terrorist tactics, and political parties are perceived as representing the opposite extremes of a spectrum: the former obstruct and hinder the democratic political process, while the latter are key actors in promoting democracy and the rule of law. Such a dichotomous framework is highly problematic, and it fails to appreciate the similarities between these two types of organizations.

Both armed groups and political parties are, at their core, social organizations, defined as organized, collective efforts on the part of a number of people to bring about or resist social change.[1]

Both political parties and armed groups share the same manifest and existential goals. At the most basic level, all organizations share a common vital interest in survival and in the preservation of their power, and both political wings and armed groups share this existential concern and core survival interest. Also, political parties and armed groups act on the basis of a general internally shared weltanschauung and ideology, and they both have political goals and portend to transform a given society.

Political parties focus on institutional politics as a means to achieve their political goals, while armed groups tend to operate in the extrainstitutional, extralegal domain. Therefore, while political parties invest a large part of their political capital in electoral activities and conventional politics, armed groups' repertoire of action is more similar to the acts and initiatives conducted by social movements, including protests, disruption, and armed struggle. The extralegal, extrainstitutional reliance on violence emerges as the distinctive element that sets armed groups apart from political parties, despite similar organizational goals.

What's more, although the institutional configuration of both political parties and armed groups tends to be fluid and flexible, it is still possible to identify a number of structural elements generally shared by these two types of social organizations.

Both political parties and armed groups represent types of non-state actors, serving as intermediate institutions located between the individual and the state.[2] Political parties are a sui generis type of non-state actor because of their defined role within the state and the political system, albeit distinguishable from both. Moreover, both political parties and armed groups represent models of social organizations that bring together a group of people with a common weltanschauung and similar collective goals, along with a shared interest in bringing about social change. For both organizations, ideology and nonmaterial incentives play a substantial part in both recruiting and maintaining a membership base, a characteristic that sets these groups apart from private, profit-seeking organizations. At the same time, both political parties and armed groups tend to alternate between material and nonmaterial incentives to acquire, to preserve, and to increase their supporting bases, and both groups can be voluntary, professional, or hybrid organizations.

Finally, as social organizations, both political parties and armed groups tend to be more centralized and hierarchical than social movements. They seem to constitute intermediate institutions, with a fairly fixed internal organizational structure and formal membership criteria but maintaining the capacity to adapt and to evolve. Because armed groups engage in extralegal activities, they generally tend to operate at the clandestine level, and therefore, they usually prefer a stricter internal organization and membership structure.

While these organizations are commonly perceived as antithetic, a closer look at their functions and structural characteristics emphasizes their substantial shared similarities and characteristics. Accordingly, a given social organization could act respectively or even simultaneously as a political party or as an armed group, according to its shifting organizational goals and evolving institutional development. Keeping in mind the blurred boundaries between armed and political groups, the following section of the study examines what factors account for an armed groups' decision to create a political wing and begin to participate in institutional politics, while retaining its armed apparatus.

Institutionalization and Change: Armed Groups and Institutional Politics

An armed group's decision to create a political wing with the capacity to participate in institutional politics can be read as a function of a given group's institutional development, of its internal distribution of power and existing internal competition, and of its political and security environment.

Degree of Institutionalization

First, the decision to invest in creating a political wing—defined as a special subunit within an armed group that engages in aboveground institutional political activities through contending elections and assuming office if elected[3]—is related to the process of development, or institutionalization, of a given group. Institutionalization describes "the emergence of orderly, stable, socially integrating patterns out of unstable, loosely organized, or narrowly technical activities."[4] It refers to the process through which organizations become stable, with embedded values and predictable or recurring behavior.[5] This process serves a number of important functions within an organization, and it constitutes simultaneously a reason for change and a reactionary element.

According to a "classic" explanation of a political organization's development, the process of institutional growth tends to have a "moderating" effect on organizations, pushing them to seek accommodation with their environment. Under this paradigm, organizational growth's imperatives constitute an important incentive for armed groups to create "legitimate" political fronts, better suited to negotiating and attempting to reach an accommodation within their political contexts.

Angelo Panebianco provides a convincing paradigm of this "ideal self-moderation paradigm."[6] He asserts that political organizations tend to shift from a more fluid, open model to a closed and bureaucratic structure as they institutionalize. The model observes that organizations tend to go through three phases of institutionalization (genesis, institutionalization, and maturity).

At the outset, political organizations tend to be nonbureaucratic groups based on the notion of a community of equals and organized around a common social and political goal, along with the objective to transform society. As time passes the same groups tend to become increasingly bureaucratized and hierarchical, and they become more concerned with preserving power and surviving. Accordingly, they tend to pay significantly less attention to their original objectives and ideologies and are prone to seeking to adapt to the environment to minimize the chances of conflict and to guarantee their organizational survival.

Organizations are also simply groups of individuals, and as such, they also constitute micro-social and -political structures. Social structure, specifically, refers to the "patterned or regularized aspects of relationships existing among participants in an organization."[7] For all organizations, preserving the social and organizational structure represents a core interest of the group, and, as time progresses, self-preservation and survival interests turn into crucial strategic considerations.

Panebianco's model is a useful starting point to discuss the institutional development of armed groups that seek to become involved in institutional politics, although several important changes need to be made for this model to be relevant. First, armed groups' development from their formative to their mature stage is less substantially characterized by a progressive "bureaucratization" of the group. These groups tend to be hierarchical and tightly organized from their outset, mostly due to their need to operate underground and under conditions of secrecy. Regardless of this difference, it is still true to say that as armed groups institutionalize they tend to place increasing importance on their self-preservation and are subject to the pressures of organizational inertia, as postulated by Panebianco's model.

Second, the model correctly captures organizations' tendency to expand and become more complex and articulated with time, but it portrays this growth as a linear process. In armed groups, the tendency to become increasingly institutionalized, less ideology driven, and more prone to accommodation can be renegotiated and reversed, leading to a phase of "institutional regression." The institutional logic of "accommodation through political participation" that can originate within an armed group during its institutional development phase—provided the existence of exogenous factors that facilitate this transition—does not necessarily develop to replace the "confrontation through armed struggle" institutional imperative. On the contrary, the organization can shift between these distinct institutional rationalities based on exogenous inputs or accept them simultaneously within its overall strategy.

The development of a logic that encourages political participation is connected with the institutional development of armed groups, as this phase is characterized by efforts to grow, often through expansion. Growth and expansion are both sought as means to improve a given group's stability, relative power and autonomy, and internal cohesion and leadership's control and prestige.[8]

As an organization institutionalizes, it seeks to expand to fulfill its increasingly predominant interest in survival. Expansion is a survival strategy that the group adopts to stay relevant.

Organizational legitimacy can be undermined once the armed group's "novelty" has faded, and similarly its distinctiveness can be equally compromised with the passing of time and the creation of more look-alike groups. Under these conditions, non-state armed groups face the pressure to reassert their autonomy and legitimacy, and they can respond to these institutional pressures by either expanding or escalating militancy.[9] While the second option will lead the group toward a phase of different institutional development and toward the adoption of a distinct institutional logic, developing through expansion often leads to the formation of a political wing.

Therefore, the choice to create a political wing is triggered by the group's institutional development and its related push to grow through expansion, motivated by the group's desire to acquire power and stability, while maintaining relevancy and organizational legitimacy.

A Strain in the Availability of Mobilization Resources

Creating a political wing is instrumental to achieving expansion as it facilitates an increase in a given group's constituency and supporting bases. A political wing increases both the consensus and the level of participation in the organization by creating an aboveground, legal venue through which it can channel supporters. In other words, it provides an institutionalized means to lower the risks and costs of participation and thus raises the potential number of supporters.[10] The political wing allows the group to create solidarity and purposive incentives for participation that increase the number of potential supporters. At the same time, the political wing option preserves the existing militant supporter basis because it does not reject the institutional logic of the armed struggle.

Social organizations such as armed-political groups heavily rely on purposive incentives to maintain their supporting basis, and therefore, they are openly reluctant to abandon their original revolutionary goal to embrace the logic of political participation and compromise that dominates institutional politics. Instead, a separate political wing allows the organization to stress the continuity of its goals, while adopting radically different tactics to achieve those objectives. The political wing allows the coexistence of two contradictory institutional logics while preserving the original purposive incentives for participation.

Moreover, a political wing triggers expansion while protecting the solid "solidarity incentives" associated with a group's military wing. The organization preserves the prestige, power, and tight relationship associated with the members of the military wing by creating two levels of membership: the political and the military one.[11] The political wing can be seen as a tactic to increase the group's human resources, while maintaining the original solidarity and purposive incentive system.

An organization's transition toward institutional politics through the creation of a political section is hence also a function of the group's need to continue to obtain material and nonmaterial resources to ensure its survival.

More specifically, organizations meet this "initial survival threshold"[12] when they are able to guarantee "organizational maintenance." The concept of maintenance is broader than the notion of mere survival as existence, and it includes the capacity to secure a minimal level of resources and contributions, to maintain a membership base and a communication structure, to have a specific organizational purpose or raison d'être that justifies their existence, and to preserve internal unity.[13]

The decision to invest in institutional politics occurs as a result of change in the group's access to mobilization resources due to either a decline or a potential decline in the access to such resources, resulting in scarcity, or in a need to diversify or increase the available incentives in order to expand. More specifically, in the course of its institutional development, an armed group will be more inclined to create a political wing when the *group's access to resources is threatened by the organization's loss of autonomy or legitimacy, or when the available sources deeply conflict with the strategic need to grow.* This situation can arise for a variety of reasons.

First, interorganizational competition and the proliferation of groups dedicated to the same cause put a strain on the group's capacity to monopolize mobilization resources. Indeed, organizations, far from operating in an interorganizational void, belong to *multiorganizational fields*, defined as a network of organizations with which a given organization can establish connections.[14] Intraorganizational conflict generally arises due to two main factors: the competition for resources and the struggle for autonomy.[15] Resources refers to moral and cultural resources, including legitimacy, support, and popularity, social-organizational and human resources, and material resources. They tend to be scarce and finite within any given environment.

The more an organization depends on certain resources to survive, the more it needs to compete aggressively over them. The more an organization relies on a given resource to function, and the more the access to that resource is discretionary and controlled, the more the organization will be considered as dependent on it and will thus make competition over that resource a priority.[16] Also, the greater the number of organizations competing for that resource, and the larger the number and degree of heterogeneity of the existing organizations, the more competition and uncertainty a given organization will face.[17] Under these circumstances, an armed group can invest in the creation of a political wing as a powerful tool to diversify the armed group's dependencies and to ease its interorganizational competition.

Autonomy, on the other hand, has more to do with developing a distinctive area of competence and drawing boundaries between one's own organization and the competitor's.[18] Organizations that possess a high degree of autonomy ("distinctiveness") have a better chance at competing for resources, as this distinctiveness factor provides the organization with a reasonably stable and relatively unchallenged claim to resources.[19] In the context of armed groups, a prolonged stalemate, without any significant moral or practical victory, can threaten the group's distinctiveness and put a strain on its group's capacity to acquire resources, especially when the "grievances" of the given group are addressed at the political level. Also, in this context, the creation of a political wing will improve the situation by renewing the distinctiveness of the organization and diversifying its funding and supporting bases.

Shifts within the Political Opportunity Structure

Institutional development and resource mobilization theory partially account for an armed group's interest in having a political wing, but these two factors need to be integrated with a more detailed analysis of the role of the political context in influencing this transition. Armed groups opt to form a political wing and to engage in institutional politics when the political opportunity structure within which they operate generates opportunities to maximize their influence and relevancy. This can either happen through a series of changes within the political structure or by exploiting favorable preexisting conditions to political participation. *The capacity to participate is a function of the degree of openness or lack of openness of the political system, which includes the permeability of the structures of power, the characteristics of the electoral system, the presence of mediating institutions within society, and the cultural-institutional power dynamics in place. Shifts in the electorate equally affect the calculation to join the political system.*

First, institutional participation is encouraged when the structures of power are permeable—when the newly formed political wing can gain influence and access to the formal political institutions of a given country. Permeability is facilitated by the degree of decentralization, implying a multiplication of the opportunities to access decision-making power, and by the degree of separation of powers, also a tool to generate additional points of formal access to political power.[20] Another element that contributes to determining the level of permeability of the system is the actual degree of turnover within power structures.

Political systems perceived as "blocked" because the same contestants repeatedly gain access to power, excluding all other actors, do not encourage the creation of political wings.[21] Permeability is also related to the concept of stability, as countries with frequent and unpredictable regime changes will likely discourage political participation even when their power structures are relatively permeable. Extreme regime volatility can prevent political parties from translating political access into political power, thus lowering the incentives to invest in the political system.

Second, political participation will be encouraged by the electoral system's structure and characteristics. According to Arend Lijphart, an electoral system can be defined as "a set of essentially unchanged election rules under which one or more successive elections are conducted."[22] The main variables in understanding an electoral system include the used electoral formula, the magnitude of electoral districts, the number of available seats within a given assembly, and the electoral threshold (the minimum number of votes needed for a party to gain representation).[23] The emergence and participation of new political parties is especially encouraged in electoral systems that adopt an electoral formula that guarantees a "consensus-based model" based on proportional representation—which in turn is a key variable in promoting multiparty systems that share the executive through coalitions.[24] Smaller electoral districts also contribute to providing more proportional results, avoiding the underrepresentation of small and minority-based parties. Moreover, participation is also facilitated when a given country has a large number of available seats and a low threshold for gaining political access. Under these conditions, the direct involvement of an armed group's political wing in institutional politics will be facilitated—provided that the electoral system guarantees at least a minimum level of stability and durability of the existing political institutions. In addition, the incentive to participate in institutional politics will be also a function of the electoral system's fairness and transparency, and it will be correlated to its ability to avoid frauds or other electoral pathologies (such as malapportionment of gerrymander) that could deter groups from participating.[25]

Third, political participation is also encouraged in countries where the state provides mediating institutions in which the different competing political and ethnic-religious groups within a given country can find a political arena through which they can address existing cleavages. The state and its institutions, far from being a neutral arena where the different political actors compete to outperform one another, are key variables in explaining the structure of intergroup competition and the strategic choices of the involved parties.[26] If mediating political institutions exist and have the capacity to take and to implement decisions, then armed groups' political wings will have a vested interest in participating in the political process to gain access to these effective decision-making structures.

Political participation is also facilitated when the cultural-institutional strategies to deal with "dissenters" or new challengers are perceived as integrative rather than exclusionary.[27] For example, the introduction of a new governmental policy of amnesty and forgiveness can change a group's perception of the political arena and trigger an interest in forming a political wing.

Finally, as a new political party competing in institutional politics, a political wing will be more prone to participate when it perceives the opportunity to gain votes due to a shift in the distribution of the voters along the political scale. This trend can originate because of the ongoing decay of an older party that the new party can exploit to gain voters from its constituency, because of a rapid shift in public opinion, which existing parties are unable or unwilling to adjust to, or the progressive moderation of formerly "extremist" parties, giving the new armed-political group the opportunity to replace that party and gain a share of the "militant" electorate.[28]

Internal Unity and Commitment to Change

The previous sections emphasize how an armed group's internal power dynamics are subject to shift according to changes within the institutional development model, resource dependencies, and political opportunity structure. These sections also covered how an alignment between the need to expand and continue to mobilize resources, together with a political opportunity, can create a political wing and lead to its direct involvement in institutional politics.

In addition, the nature of the political commitment and the degree of emphasis placed on the newly formed party also depend on the internal power distribution within a given armed group.

Although it is clear that the creation of a political wing will induce a given armed group to undergo some degree of internal change, the magnitude and effect of the change produced within a given organization because of its official entry into institutional politics can vary widely. Specifically, organizational change resulting from the creation of a political wing can be defined as either radical (strategic) or convergent (tactical) depending on whether it aims at completely or partially transforming the existing structure and configuration.[29]

Organizations, like all other types of micro-social systems, are hardly ever internally homogeneous or static. On the contrary, they include different interest groups and opposing coalitions. Organizations can be described as complex systems "for arriving at collective decisions through bargaining and influence processes amongst a set of power- and influence-holding units."[30] Internally, each organization is composed of different subunits that compete to assert influence on one another.

Organizational subunits tend to differ not only because they fulfill distinct organizational functions and structural roles but also because the technical–functional boundaries between different units also lead to the creation of cognitive boundaries between the subgroups.[31] Accordingly, each subgroup develops a specific set of suborganizational interests and a related view of the organization's purpose and strategic functions. Organizational units are also dissimilar in terms of allocated resources and, above all, capacity to exert authority and influence.

Organizations are generally defined by a "dominant coalition" composed of those members in charge of the group's formal structure and thus allocated the maximum degree of structural power.[32] The dominant coalition holds the highest level of authority-based power within the organization because it is formally in charge of the decision-making processes. The executive group relies on this privilege to attempt to control other organizational subunits. All other internal niches, not just the dominant coalition, employ different bases of power to maximize their relative strength as compared with other subgroups. For example, organizational subunits can rely on "functional power" that is distributed among different members of an organization according to an individual's own level of job specialization and the essentiality of that job to the proper functioning of the organization at large.[33] Also informal mechanisms and shifting alliances and interest-groups within a given organization can determine and shape organizational relations and can balance formal power distribution through an influence-based power—"relational power." In the end, organizational control is a function of both the degree of authority assigned by the organizational structure and influence obtained through informal bargaining and coalition-building.

Applying this notion to political parties and armed groups enables the analysis of these social organizations as "opportunity structures" that allow the fluid participation of different organizational subunits whose choices, goals, and strategies are not fixed and preprogrammed, but arise out of opportunities (either externally or internally created) to maximize power. [34] Organizational change can then be read as an important tool employed by different subunits within the same organization either to maintain or to gain additional authority and influence, or, in other words, to shift the internal power dynamics in their favor.

Accordingly, in a largely cohesive and unitary group, where authority is highly concentrated within the hands of a dominant coalition, the formation of a political group can be largely seen as a convergent type of expansionary change, where the different units focus on self-reinforcing activities. By contrast, a more internally divided organization could use the political wing as an additional way to channel internal pressures and demands for change and increased power. Although the leadership will still conceive the political unit as a subordinate, supportive agency, the chances that the newly formed political wing will tend to compete with the older military apparatus are very high. These dynamics of internal competition are also self-reinforcing, as both the political and the military wing of the organization will develop distinct expertise and priorities. Thus, the larger the preexisting level of internal fragmentation, the more the military and the political units within the armed organization will tend to compete.

Applying this focus and studying armed groups by emphasizing their internal divisions and organizational complexity is a useful lens, because, as rightly noted by Bruce Hoffman, "all terrorist movements throughout history have presented themselves as monoliths: united and in agreement over fundamental objectives, aims, strategies, tactics and targets. Too often their opponents succumb to such fiction."[35]

Understanding the internal power dynamics within armed groups investing in institutional politics is also useful, as it helps to assess the consequences of the group's decision to develop a political wing. It allows us to address the question: under what conditions does the political wing develop to become the primary means of expression of the armed group, thus producing radical change and ultimately leading to the relinquishment of the group's weapons? In other words, *when do political wings become a source of "moderation" and lead to disarmament?*

As discussed previously, the process of institutionalization with a given social organization should not be read as a linear process toward increased accommodation and "moderation." While it appears that organizations' institutionalization and expansion introduce the institutional logic of "accommodation through institutional politics," it is also true that such logic does not systematically replace the "armed struggle" rationale *ex toto.* On the contrary, the development process does not happen deterministically, and the process of the growth of the political wing is determined contextually. A series of factors affect the development of a given group's political wing and influence whether the group is likely to undertake political transition of the type discussed earlier.

Specifically, the internal power distribution and the type of relationship that exists between the group's political wing and its military apparatus is a key variable in understanding whether the organization is headed toward a political transition and "moderation," as defined in chapter 1.

Kevin Siqueira identifies three types of relationships between an armed group's political and armed wings: (1) a situation of cooperation and strategic complement, (2) a competition-driven relationship, and (3) a "mixed" case in which the actions of one subsection support the other subunit's activities, while the actions of the latter detract from the first group's capacity to operate successfully.[36]

The first type of relationship described by Siqueira, where the actions of the armed wing and the political wing complement each other, is the least likely to produce a strategic type of organizational change, as the two institutional logics of accommodation and resistance are integrated within the organization's strategy, creating an equilibrium between the two factions. An extreme case of this scenario is the "pseudopolitical option," when the political group is an ad hoc creation of the armed faction designed to attract new members and galvanize the internal constituency, without portending to affect policy. A pseudopolitical wing is generally a product of a highly cohesive organization, with a high level of equilibrium and very low levels of autonomy or influence granted to the newly formed wing.

In contrast, radical change is more likely to happen in an ongoing competition between the two political and military organizational subunits, where alternative institutional logics of violence and adaptation begin to clash and are perceived as competing and mutually exclusive. Political and military leaderships within a given armed group are likely to develop a different set of skills and expertise, and, as such, they are also likely to develop a different vision of organizational goals and priorities. This is especially true if the two leaderships develop separately and with little intraorganizational cooperation. Furthermore, a competition-driven relationship also encourages both groups to become more entrenched within their own positions and to escalate their activities, potentially leading to an open conflict to outperform each other.[37]

Strategic change also can be pursued by an organization's political wing in a "mixed case" scenario, when the group's activities are consistently undermined by the ongoing armed struggle. In both cases, the chances for deep strategic change are connected to a perceived disequilibrium between the two factions that leads to a questioning of the legitimacy of the competing faction's institutional logic.

This situation of strategic internal competition is likely to be intensified according to exogenous factors. First, competition is more likely to arise in a situation of scarcity or deep uncertainty over available resources, leading a group's political and armed wings to fight over resource allocation. Second, the competition is also more intense whenever the two faction's recruitment and financing strategies are similar, while competition is lessened when each subsection maintains a certain margin of autonomy over raising material and nonmaterial support to finance their operations. The more the two factions rely on a diversified pool to recruit and finance themselves, the less resource scarcity is likely to lead to an open competition to dismantle the competing faction. Third, whenever the resource mobilization strategy of a faction detracts from another faction's capacity to operate, competition and competing institutional logics are likely to arise. For example, if the armed wing of a given organization insists on conducting a terrorist campaign to assert its power and please its constituency, even if this results in substantially alienating the constituency of the group's political party and hindering some of the group's sources of financial support, a split can arise between the mobilization strategy of the two subunits. If this situation persists over time, the political wing of the hybrid politico-military organization might have an incentive both to escalate its activities and to attempt to outperform and control the armed wing's operations.

Finally, while all organizations endure a certain degree of internal divisions as well as internal dissonance—meaning that all organizations are to a certain extent internally inconsistent to please all their different internal and external audiences—it seems that internal quarrels over tactics and strategies can be extremely damaging (even more than disagreements over long-term goals and definition of the enemy).[38]

Once a situation of prolonged competition arises, and once the logics of political accommodation and armed struggle begin to be perceived as mutually exclusive, a given armed-political group becomes more likely to be headed toward radical change. The chances for this transformation to take place in turn depend on the duration, intensity, and organizational pervasiveness of the internal conflict.[39] This can result in a number of outcomes, including a permanent split between the two halves of the organization, where the members who support either the "armed struggle" or the "political participation" option exit the group; a temporary reconciliation of the two factions' interests and the creation of a new equilibrium; and the reinstitutionalization of the group, either by regressing to its original armed-terrorism model or by establishing the primacy of the political party.

This last scenario is only likely to occur when the political faction possesses a high degree of autonomy and the capacity to spearhead internal change, along with organizational legitimacy and relevance within the political arena. The political faction must be perceived within the organization itself as "high status," which is in turn determined by resource sufficiency, authority, deference accorded to its leaders, popular legitimacy, and real-world impact.[40] Moreover, in terms of external factors, without a political structure that is open and permeable enough to grant the group the potential for political influence and relevance, it is unlikely that the political party option will prove strong enough to outbid the armed struggle strategy.

There is then no deterministic certitude that once a political wing has been formed and a given armed group has begun to participate in institutional politics this development will lead toward a linear development leading to "moderation" and disarmament. On the contrary, the relationship between a group's political and armed wings tends to produce exogenously determined phases of cooperation and competition. This leads to a cyclical development model, when waves of institutional proximity within the factions are replaced by open competition. The organization will alternate phases wherein the political strategy is perceived as dominant, with phases in which armed struggle regains primacy within the organization.

Whenever the competition along the political-military line escalates to where the two main institutional logics of armed struggle and politics are perceived as antagonistic, the organization is at its ripest time for radical change, and the political group has its greatest chance to establish its leadership over the military wing, given a favorable resource availability and political opportunity structure.

Hypotheses: Summary

This book looks at a given armed group's decision to form a political wing by testing the hypotheses advanced previously. A political wing will be formed as a result of the interplay of the following four factors:

1. Degree of institutionalization: the choice to create a political wing is triggered by the group's institutional development and its related push to grow through expansion, motivated by the group's desire to acquire power and stability, while maintaining relevancy and organizational legitimacy.

2. Availability of mobilization resources: a political wing is created as a tool to diversify mobilization resources to expand, while diminishing dependencies. A given group has the maximum incentives to form a political wing when access to resources is threatened by the organization's loss of autonomy or legitimacy—raison d'être—or when the available sources deeply conflict with the strategic need to grow.

3. Shifts within the political opportunity system: the political alternative is also a function of the degree of openness or lack of openness in the political system, which includes the permeability of the structures of power, the characteristics of the electoral system, the presence of mediating institutions within society, and the cultural-institutional power dynamics in place. Shifts in the electorate equally affect the calculation to join the political system.

4. Level of internal unity and commitment to change: political change depends on the existence of an internal commitment to reform the organization.

These factors are related to three different levels of analysis: (1) the environment, (2) the organization, and (3) the individual.[41] The focus of the study rests predominantly on assessing the impact of external constraints and opportunities and organizational dynamics. The role played by individual leaders and the impact of personality-driven conflicts, although relevant, is considered insufficient to explain larger trends. Another factor that is deliberately downplayed in the study's analysis of armed groups' decision to create a political wing is ideology. Ideology is seen more as a facilitating factor,[42] rather than a leading causal explanation to understand organizational shifts in strategy.

Political and social organizations in particular rely on ideology as a core tool to boost their legitimacy. Ideology, as "a verbal image of the good society and of the chief means of constructing it,"[43] is seen more as a key tool to provide internal cohesion and attract support. At its core, it is a communication device and a legitimacy-building tool. Ideology is also a powerful informal constraint on behavior, and, as such, it helps an organization to minimize the transaction costs related to information and compliance.[44]

By imposing a standardized expectation of what is both accepted and acceptable, ideology significantly reduces the chances of individual deviance, thus lowering the need for monitoring. A coherent and accepted ideology will not only serve internally, by increasing standardization and stability, but it will also allow an organization to communicate effectively with its external environment, thus increasing its legitimacy and its competitive advantage with respect to other organizations. Seen in this light, ideology is malleable and can be changed to meet different organizational needs. In other words, although important, ideological considerations rarely trump organizations' perennial quest for power and legitimacy and, as such, it should not be seen as the leading determinant of organizational behavior.

In contrast, this study focuses on both environmental and organizational factors. The hypothesis is that these four factors must be present for an armed group to decide to create a political wing to compete in elections.

The relation of relative causal importance between these four factors is necessary (these four factors have to be all present) and reciprocal (none of them is sufficient alone). Through this lens, an opening in the political opportunity structure is seen as the exogenous enabler of the political transition, while organizational commitment to change is seen as the endogenous enabler to the creation of a political wing.

Similarly, while institutional pressures to expand and grow are seen as providing the internal motivation to pursue political participation, a shift in the resource mobilization structure is seen as the externally driven incentive to seek a role in institutional politics.

Once a given group has begun to participate in institutional politics, the research expects, on the basis of the reasons discussed, that the relationship between the group's political and armed factions will not be a linear progression toward the affirmation of the former. The research predicts a series of waves of convergence and competition between the groups' military and political leaderships and postulates that the potential for radical change is related to a prolonged perceived disequilibrium between the two factions that leads to a questioning of the legitimacy of the competing faction's institutional logic. This leads to a cyclical development model, where phases in which political participation is given primacy are alternated with phases in which armed struggle is perceived as the most effective tool of the organization.

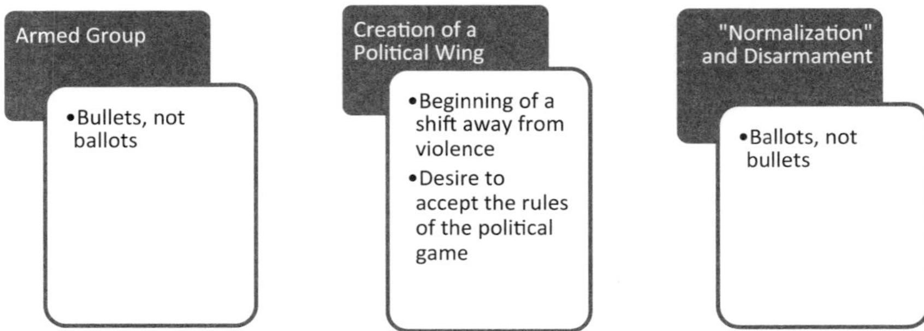

The Linear Development Process: Politics = Moderation

Shifts between politics and armed struggle are adaptation mechanisms to the changing political opportunity and resource mobilization structure, interorganizational competition, and internal dynamics.[45] In most cases, these shifts are not "radical." Groups find a way to invest simultaneously in both politics and armed struggle as, for the most part, this hybrid nature represents an asset rather than a liability. Maintaining a hybrid armed-political apparatus is advantageous from the organization's point of view. Indeed, this allows the group to grow, to better diversify its supporting bases and its funding strategy, and to better convey different messages to its specific audiences (respectively, the internal members of the group, the external constituency, the societies where the group operates, the "enemy" and its society, and the international community and the media).[46]

Strategic change and "moderation" should not be expected unless the group

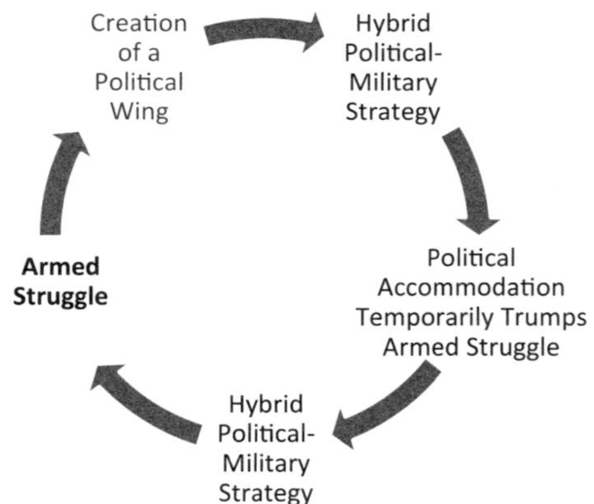

The Cyclical Development Model: Hybrid Political and Military Development

is forced to choose between bullets and ballots, due to an irreconcilable internal division between the political and the armed leaderships. Under these circumstances, the organization can undergo a strategic deinstitutionalization phase and, ultimately, modify its institutional configuration. The chances for the political option to acquire primacy will then depend on the level of autonomy and capacity to spearhead internal change of the political wing, along with its organizational legitimacy and relevance within the political arena. Conversely, absent a preexisting disequilibrium and open competition between the two political and armed subunits, the organization is unlikely to undergo strategic change, even in the presence of a favorable political opportunity structure and incentives.

The Lebanese Hezbollah

Armed Struggle and Political Integration

Hezbollah (The Party of God) is a Shia Lebanese organization composed of a military branch, sociocultural institutions, and a political party. This group was chosen as a case study because of its critical dimension, its high-profile nature, and its cultural uniqueness. Hezbollah, a highly institutionalized organization with a powerful and sophisticated political wing, also represents a "least likely" case to test the validity of the cyclical development model and the hypotheses on political wing formation. The group was also selected because of its relevance: Assessing Hezbollah's political development process has real-world policy implications, because the international community has been split over whether the group should be classified as a terrorist organization or a political party.

At the one end of the spectrum, some have labeled the Lebanese group a terrorist organization because of its involvement in both domestic and international attacks, including two deadly operations against the Israeli embassy and the Asociación Mutual Israelita Argentina, the Jewish community center in Buenos Aires, in 1992 and 1994, respectively.[1] Canada, Israel, the Netherlands, and the United States are the only Western nations currently labeling Hezbollah as a terrorist group.[2] In the United States, Hezbollah has been classified as a terrorist organization since 1995. It was designated by the US State Department as a Foreign Terrorist Organization in 1997;[3] with the additional designation Specially Designated Global Terrorist, given in October 2001, further underscoring the American government's belief that Hezbollah is a terrorist organization with a global network and reach.[4] In the aftermath of September 11, Deputy Secretary of State Richard Armitage captured this perspective by declaring that "Hezbollah may be the A team of terrorists," while "Al Qaeda is actually the B team."[5]

At the other end of the spectrum, other countries, like Australia, have considered Hezbollah's "external security apparatus" to be entities separate from the political wing of the organization, a position that enables them to relate to the group as a legitimate political party. The European Union has, to date, also not classified the organization as a terrorist entity, although several individual members of the group have been placed on the European terrorist list.[6] Several individual European countries have been reluctant to designate Hezbollah. For example, the United Kingdom has proscribed Hezbollah's armed militia since 2003 but views its political wing as a legitimate political interlocutor.[7]

A fundamental problem with both of these approaches is their reliance on a binary classification system—"political organization" or "terrorist group." As the next sections extensively illustrate, no definition of the organization that relies on these dichotomous terms can grasp Hezbollah's more complex organizational reality and accurately account for its development process.

Background
Origins and Early History

According to the received history of Hezbollah, the Lebanese Shia movement was founded around 1982 to respond to the Israeli invasion of southern Lebanon. However, the birth of this organization must be understood in the broader context of the rise and politicization of the Lebanese Shia community and in its ongoing postindependence struggle to achieve greater political participation and power.

The Shia community has been a religious minority within Lebanon since Shiism first was established in the area in the tenth and eleventh centuries as a result of the expansion of the Egypt-based Fatimid Empire. The history of the Lebanese Shia, like the history of Shia Islam in general, is one of persecution and marginalization: As early as the thirteenth century, during the Mamluk conquest, this community found itself persecuted and driven into the south of the country, and the later Ottoman occupation led to no dramatic improvements.[8] During the centuries of Ottoman rule (sixteenth to twentieth centuries), the Shia community saw the rise of a small number of political bosses (the *zaims*); building on their extensive ownership of land and on their Ottoman-based concessions to collect taxes, they became the de facto rulers of their community.[9] As a result, the Lebanese Shia lived for centuries in a quasi-feudal and clientelist system, kept largely dependent on the *zaims,* deprived of individual power, and alienated from the other sectarian communities.

It is not surprising that, when the Ottoman Empire collapsed in the aftermath of World War I and France took over the administration of the area corresponding to modern Lebanon and Syria, the Shia community was the most socially and economically deprived group within the newly established French Mandate. At the time, in the 1920s, the Shias were geographically segmented in the villages of the Jebel Amal area (in the south) and the Bekaa Valley, economically depressed, tied to the land either as sharecroppers or as subsistence farmers, and mostly uneducated.[10]

The newly founded Lebanese state, created by the French administration by carving up "Greater Syria" and ratified by the 1926 constitution, was borne out of a desire to protect the Christian minority, largely located in the areas of Mount Lebanon. However, since the area inhabited by the Christians was not considered large enough to constitute the basis for an independent and defensible state, France decided to include other traditionally non-Christian areas, like Jebel Amal, and Bekaa, to the state. The inclusion of traditionally Shia areas in the newly founded "Christian safe heaven" only contributed to the second-class citizenship of the Shia minority within the new country.[11]

Despite the unfavorable political circumstances, the first seeds of the politicization and rise of the Shia community as a crucial Lebanese political actor were sown in the years of the mandate, when religious clerics started to demand permission to celebrate the Shia festival of the Ashura (awarded in 1924), the official recognition of their sect (obtained in 1926), and the creation of a Higher Islamic Shia Court that would apply Islamic law according to the Shia-based Jafari School (a battle that would last until 1961).[12] Although this movement was neither politically organized nor cohesive, it nevertheless helped increase the self-awareness of the Shia community.

The 1943 proclamation of independence continued the political marginalization of the Shias, as they were left out of the Christian Maronite and Sunni government and were awarded only an insignificant 3.2 percent of all higher posts in civil service,[13] despite representing one of the three largest sectarian groups in Lebanon, along with the Sunnis and the Maronite Christians.[14] But the living conditions of the community began to change for the better during the 1950s, as wide economic and social reforms were introduced in Lebanon and economic conditions slowly improved.[15] At the same time, a large number of Shia families began to settle in urban areas, including the suburbs of Beirut, while others emigrated to both the West and the Gulf.

As a result, cracks emerged in the quasi-feudal *zaim*-based society: The old political bosses partially lost control over the community, and the newly urban Shia population started to look at existing political parties as a means to participate in Lebanese political life.[16] The disenfranchised urban Shias joined secular political groups, such as the Lebanese Communist Party, which offered them an escape from the pariah status assigned to them and their community by the confessional political system. Simultaneously, other sectors of the Shia community started to look inward, turning to local leaders to both empower and to unite their community.

This second group found its charismatic leader in the cleric Musa al-Sadr. Born in Qom, Iran, and educated in the major Shia theological centers of Qom and Najaf (Iraq), al-Sadr arrived in Lebanon in 1957 and became the religious leader of Tyre, in southern Lebanon. From the time of his arrival, al-Sadr sought greater political representation and power for his community.[17] With that objective in mind, he founded the Highest Islamic Shiite Council in 1967, a religious institution designed to support and advocate for the Shia community within Lebanon.[18] A few years later, al-Sadr also founded the first Shia sociopolitical movement within Lebanon, the Movement of the Dispossessed (Harakat al-Mahrumim).[19] The movement's armed wing, Harakat Amal, was created in 1974 on the eve of the civil war; under the leadership of Nabih Berri and together with Hezbollah it would become the main Shia political movement within Lebanon. [20]

Meanwhile, as al-Sadr's movement immediately gained loyalty and support from a vast sector of the Shia community, another element helped politicize and mobilize the Lebanese Shia: the increasingly powerful presence of the Palestine Liberation Organization (PLO). Following the September 1970 Jordanian military campaign to drive the group out of Jordan, southern Lebanon had become the site of the main operational and strategic headquarters of the PLO. Operating from the for all intents and purposes autonomous Palestinian refugee camps, the PLO leadership exploited the weakness of the Lebanese government to transform the south into a military base from which attacks could be launched against Israel, escalating its activities in the months preceding the 1975 civil war. As the PLO's armed gunmen proliferated in southern Lebanon, they were at first ostracized by part of the Lebanese Shias, and their presence pushed that community to become more united and better organized, both politically and militarily. After the civil war broke out in 1975, clashes between the PLO and the Shias did occur, especially as the war escalated. Although Amal had originally sided with the PLO as a strategy to weaken the Maronite Christians, it shifted sides by 1976, following the Syrian intervention to stop the offensive against the Christians. [21]

The Lebanese civil war inflicted disproportionate suffering on members of the Shia community, most of whom were concentrated in southern Lebanon, one of the main battlefields of the internal war, as well as the main theater of operations in the Israeli–PLO conflict. The radicalizing force of the trauma inflicted by the civil war and by the 1978 occupation of part of southern Lebanon by the Israeli Defense Forces (IDF) following their military operations was amplified by another watershed event: the "disappearance" that same year of Musa al-Sadr during a trip to Libya.[22] The loss of its leader left the Shia community without direction and increasingly divided between the secular leadership within Amal and elements more focused on religion, which included the Highest Islamic Shiite Council and a myriad of small movements and individuals.

Another important event for the Lebanese Shia was the 1979 Iranian Revolution, which supplied a renewed revolutionary ideology and ethos both to empower and to unite them. The dramatic changes in the Iranian political landscape and the rise of Iran as an Islamic Republic under the guide of Ayatollah Khomeini had a profound affect all across the Middle East, and it especially influenced the thinking and actions of the Shia communities outside Iran. The Shia community in Lebanon was no exception. On the contrary, the Iranian Revolution had a particularly strong effect on the local Shias, also due to the depth and strength of the preexisting relationship between the Iranian and the Lebanese religious communities. These bonds, which dated as far back as the seventeenth century, allowed for the ideology behind the revolution to spread within Lebanon and guaranteed the existence of extensive contacts between some of the clerics in Lebanon and those in Iran. Within Lebanon, the movement spurred by the Iranian Revolution was led by a loose group of young clerics who drew massive inspiration from the Iranian experience. Many of them had just returned from religious seminars in Iraq, and they had been members of the Shia revivalist and anticommunist party Hizb al-Dawa.[23]

After leaving Iraq, this group of young clerics, including Hezbollah's first and second secretaries-general, respectively, Subhi al-Tufayli (1989–1991) and al-Sayyed Abbas al-Moussawi (1991–1992), continued their preaching and political activism in Lebanon. Some of these clerics opted to join the secular Amal and attempt to transform it from within, while others contemplated the creation of a new movement. [24] Their ideology differed from al-Sadr's vision in a number of important ways, including their transnational and revolutionary orientation—in contrast with the reformist and Lebanon-focused agenda of Amal.[25]

With all these components already in place, the 1982 Israeli invasion of Lebanon provided the spark for the creation of the Lebanese Hezbollah. At the outset of the "Peace for Galilee" operation in June 1982, part of the Shia community welcomed the Israeli presence, hoping it would effectively drive out the PLO commandos.[26] However, as the military operation turned into a full-scale occupation and the Israelis ignored the Shia community while strengthening their relations with the Maronite Christians, the initial support of the Lebanese Shias turned into open resistance.

In addition, the arrival of a stable foreign international presence (the Multinational Force) in Lebanon provided the already-radicalized sectors of the Shia community greater incentive to organize themselves and fight back.[27] Disappointed by Amal's secular orientation, its political role, and its open confrontation with the PLO, many Lebanese Shias naturally gravitated toward the leadership of the Iranian-backed clerics who had emerged after 1979. Not surprising, a large number of Hezbollah's early supporters came from the Bekaa Valley, an area where Amal traditionally was relatively weak.[28]

In this context, Iranian help, in the form of material and logistic resources (including direct assistance from the Iranian Revolutionary Guards), was crucial in allowing the newly created movement to develop and gain momentum. This assistance was just the natural consequence of the Iranian emphasis on exporting the Islamic Revolution abroad, along with the ideological affinity between the Iranian clergy and the newly formed group in Lebanon.

Against this backdrop, Hezbollah was born as an umbrella organization encompassing a group of clerics and their followers, individual militants, and smaller factions, united in their common struggle against the IDF. According to Hezbollah leader Naim Qassem, in this constitutive stage of the organization a committee of nine members (representing the Bekaa Valley, the existing Islamic committees, and a splinter faction of Amal) came together to write a "manifesto." The document was then approved by Ayatollah Khomeini, and it was subsequently adopted by a number of smaller Islamic movements, which all merged to form "The Party" (Hezbollah).[29] By the mid-1980s, Iranian backing had become both broader and more substantial, as the newly founded group received political support, training, and weapons. At the same time, the movement was transforming into a highly structured organization—Hezbollah as we know it today.

The Narrative of Resistance versus the Narrative of Accommodation

In describing and analyzing Hezbollah's development since its founding, most available literature seems to embrace one of two diverging narratives, focusing on either the "resistance and armed struggle" aspect of Hezbollah's operations or its processes of "political accommodation and Lebanonization."

The resistance narrative stresses that from its inception the organization was built around its armed military components and its "resistance ethos" against the Israeli presence in Lebanon. Martin Kramer, for example, adopts this perspective to claim that the organization's power depends not on its political or financial resources but on rather its reliance on sustained violence, which is essential to maintain visibility and strength.[30]

Hezbollah's first decade of operations (1982–1992) was its most violent. It was a time of dire internal divisions and overall weakness in the Lebanese state: Lebanon's ongoing civil war had led to the proliferation of confessional militias, and the Lebanese Armed Forces (LAF) had proved utterly incapable of controlling such groups and ending the bloodshed.

With Iranian assistance, Hezbollah's military apparatus was able to become powerful enough to fight four simultaneous campaigns. The group's goals were to fight the IDF; to assert its military power over its Shia rival, Amal; to challenge directly the Lebanese government; and to expel any foreign presence from Shia areas of Lebanon and from the rest of the country.[31]

The struggle between Amal and Hezbollah dates back to the early 1980s and Hezbollah's founding: Amal's refusal to join ranks with the new Iranian-backed group led to increasing animosity and rivalry between the two Shia movements. The secular Amal and the religious Hezbollah began to clash regularly during the last decade of the civil war as they struggled for control of the Shia community. Moreover, Hezbollah disagreed with Amal's so-called war of the camps against the PLO and vehemently objected to its policy of neutrality with respect to the United Nations Interim Force in Lebanon (UNIFIL), which Hezbollah considered a foreign and hostile presence.[32]

These sporadic clashes and ongoing tensions finally exploded into a mini-war after a Hezbollah ally, the "Believers Resistance," kidnapped Lieutenant Colonel William R. Higgins, a US Marine serving with UNIFIL in southern Lebanon. The kidnapping went against the conciliatory strategy of Amal, which attempted to rescue Higgins; the subsequent confrontation between the two groups escalated the conflict and led to the 1988–1989 war for control of both southern Lebanon and the Shia-inhabited suburbs of Beirut.[33] While fighting Amal, the Iranian-backed Hezbollah was also openly challenging Lebanese sovereignty by attempting to drive all state authorities, including the LAF, out of the Hezbollah-controlled areas.

In addition, the organization was battling in the 1980s to expel Israeli and Western forces from Lebanon, relying on tactics that ranged from conventional attacks against the Israeli army to asymmetric warfare, including car bombings, suicide attacks, and kidnappings of Israelis and other foreigners. Between 1983 and 1984, Hezbollah's proxy organizations repeatedly attacked the French and American peacekeeping troops in Lebanon, finally managing to force their departure. These attacks included the April 1983 suicide operation against the US embassy in Beirut and the infamous barracks bombing in October 1983 that killed 241 US Marines.[34] Most experts on Hezbollah agree, despite the group's denial of responsibility, that both operations were undertaken by Hezbollah's proxies and allied organizations. At the same time, the group was involved in an armed conflict against the IDF. Here, Hezbollah adopted a strategy of attrition, trying to drive Israel out of Lebanon by inflicting a high number of casualties, especially through a series of "self-martyrdom" operations.

The resistance narrative thus stresses Hezbollah's reliance on domestic and international terrorism as a defining feature of the group's strategy and raison d'être. In addition to the attack against the US embassy, other infamous terrorist attacks tied to Hezbollah include the December 1983 operation against the French and American embassies in Kuwait;[35] the June 1985 hijacking of TWA Flight 847, which led to the assassination of the US Navy diver Robert Stethem and was later credited to the deceased leader of Hezbollah's External Security Organization, Imad Mughniyah;[36] and the Buenos Aires bombings of the early 1990s. The organization also has been allegedly involved in a series of both foiled and successful operations worldwide.[37]

After the civil war ended and Hezbollah began its involvement in the Lebanese political system in 1992, the group's military wing did not cease to engage the IDF in southern Lebanon, where it had established an extended military network following the partial withdrawal of Israeli forces in 1985. The attacks continued until and beyond the military withdrawal of the Israeli army in 2000. During the 1990s, Hezbollah's military operations against the IDF were generally confined to the "security zone," and after 2000, most armed activities likewise took place only around so-called disputed areas, such as the Shebaa farms, an area under Israeli control that Hezbollah and the Lebanese government claims as Lebanese.[38] Meanwhile, Hezbollah attacks against non-Israeli foreign targets within Lebanon stopped altogether in the 1990s, although the group's involvement in the Buenos Aires bombings and its role in several international plots ever since make clear that the organization had not renounced the use of violence and international terrorism.

The resistance narrative also stresses that the group's continued fighting with Israel—which escalated into a full-fledged war in the summer of 2006—is evidence that, at its core, Hezbollah remains predominantly a military movement. In this light, the parliamentary activities of the Lebanese–Shia movement are secondary to and dependent on the organization's military strategy, and thus supporters of the resistance narrative deny that the political party has "moderated" the group's behavior.

Finally, this perspective emphasizes the extensive military apparatus of the group, which includes several thousand rockets, missiles, and antitank weapons: Its arsenal, not its political or ideological appeal, represents Hezbollah's center of gravity. The organization's ongoing arms procurement strategy underscores this point, for even as the group has become increasingly integrated into the political system, it has not ceased to augment its military strength. Hezbollah is always seeking more sophisticated and lethal weapons, which it acquires from a number of countries, including Iran, Syria, and North Korea.[39]

Analysts who emphasize the "Lebanonization" and moderation of the group present a quite different reading of Hezbollah's institutional development. They divide Hezbollah's history into a "constitutive phase" (1982–1992), when the group's main asset was its military prowess, and a later period of gradual moderation and progressive reliance on social services and political activism to maintain its power and legitimacy. As a by-product of this shift, the group has been integrated into Lebanese society and transformed into a mainstream political party.

This second "political accommodation" phase is signaled by the group's decision to take part in the 1992 parliamentary elections, which initiated a trend of growing openness toward the Lebanese state, as shown by Hezbollah's repeated participation in municipal elections and in the country's executive (since 2005). These decisions are interpreted as a sign of growing pragmatism, as is the political platform chosen by the organization to compete in electoral races: Its program emphasizes nonpartisan social issues, as well as economic and social development.[40]

Through its political activism, Hezbollah began to develop relations with other sectarian groups within Lebanon, entering political alliances, embarking on social and cultural exchanges, and creating a (limited) network of supporters outside the Shia community. Those who advocate the Lebanonization perspective point to these changes in claiming that Hezbollah has become an "ordinary" political actor and has relinquished its early ideal of establishing an Islamic state within Lebanon.[41] Similarly, this moderation narrative draws on such behavior as the group's abstention, by and large, from bloody reprisals against members of the Christian community and others who had collaborated with or been allies of Israel during the years of the military occupation in southern Lebanon. This restraint was read by many scholars as a sign of Hezbollah's transition from an antisystemic to an accommodationist political organization.[42]

The group also conspicuously invested in creating a vast social network to offer a number of welfare services to Shia communities in Lebanon. Through its welfare system, Hezbollah developed strong social ties with the general population. In addition, the movement focused on public relations and on building a media empire, effectively targeting the global media through the Internet and through its satellite television channel, al-Manar.

Hezbollah similarly focused on improving its international image, first by stopping all public involvement in attacks against foreign targets. Moreover, the group insistently cast itself as a local "resistance" movement rather than an international terrorist group, repeatedly denying any involvement with any international terrorist attacks, especially in the aftermath of 9/11, when the group vehemently rejected all United States' "attempts to de-legitimize Hizballah's right to resist the Israeli occupation."[43]

While engaging in this international effort to boost its legitimacy, the group continued its military activities against the Israeli presence in Lebanon, but in conducting such attacks, it was generally guided by restraint and a logic of reciprocity. More specifically, before the IDF withdrew from southern Lebanon in 2000, Hezbollah followed (for the most part) detailed rules of engagement in dealing with Israel, which were later translated into a written, though unsigned, memo of understanding: The IDF would abstain from targeting civilians or civilian targets in exchange for Hezbollah's restraint in attacking Israel proper.[44] Following the Israeli pullout, similar rules of engagement were established according to which Hezbollah would focus its attacks on the "disputed areas."

Because they each emphasize only one kind of activity, the resistance narrative and the moderation narrative lead to fundamentally different perspectives that provide radically different readings of the same group. In particular, they answer the question of whether Hezbollah should be labeled "terrorist organization" or "political party" very differently. By integrating these two analyses into a comprehensive, holistic description of Hezbollah, we can obtain a more realistic portrait of the organization and its complexity. On its own, neither paradigm captures the high degree of integration in the group's organizational structure, which defies attempts to disentangle and separately analyze the activities of its political and military wings.

Organizational Structure and Ideology

Internal Organizational and Leadership Structure

Hezbollah is tightly organized in a pyramidal hierarchical structure. It is headed by the seven members of the Majlis al-Shura, or Consultative Council, which is elected by the Majlis al-Markazi (Central Council) and currently led by Secretary-General Hassan Nasrallah, who has held the position since 1992.[45] The Consultative Council, through its ideological, financial, military, political, judicial, social, and information committees, supervises and coordinates the activities of the entire organization, and its binding decisions control all activities.[46] Among its key responsibilities are electing the secretary-general and his deputy, appointing five out of the nine members of the Executive Committee, and directly overseeing the Combat Bureau, the "resistance" organ of the organization.[47]

At the outset, the Shura Council had no fixed number of delegates, nor was any one member elevated above the others.[48] But as early as 1989, the organization established that the main leaders within the group would appoint a Shura Council composed of nine members, each of whom would serve for a one-year term, who would choose a secretary for the organization.[49] In the following two years, Hezbollah reduced the council's size to seven members and extended their time in office to three years, giving the group its current form.

These organizational adjustments, which took place on the eve of the Hezbollah's formal entry into politics, were intended to improve internal efficiency and to maximize internal unity and cohesion. Indeed, Hezbollah's central organizing principle is the preservation of cohesion: The organizational structure is highly hierarchical and the Shura Council's decisions, whether unanimous or consensual, are imposed on all branches of the organization, strongly discouraging internal dissent or opposition.[50]

To prepare for involvement in institutional politics, Hezbollah also implemented another series of changes to make the organization and its structure more open and transparent. In 1989, the organization expanded its decision-making structure by adding a subordinate executive apparatus made up of an executive council, an advisory organ (the politburo), and the parliamentary, judicial, and jihad councils.[51]

The executive council oversees Hezbollah's regional and district operations as well as its day-to-day activities. It is composed of five members appointed by the Shura Council and four regional representatives, one each from Beirut, the Bekaa Valley, the al-Dahiya (the southern suburbs of Beirut), and the south.The politburo, unlike the executive council, has no administrative functions; as an advisory organ, it maintains a wide range of committees that address the organization's most important issues, from political participation to cultural relations to governance.[52] Hezbollah's three other councils, which report directly to the Majlis al-Shura, coordinate the activities of, respectively, the political, judicial, and military-strategic branches of the organization.

The addition of the subordinate executive apparatus dramatically enhanced both the size and the sophistication of the group's organizational structure. The only sector of Hezbollah not involved in these structural readjustments was its security apparatus: the military subunits, encompassing the Islamic Resistance as well as the internal and external security organs. These subunits remained under the direct supervision of the Shura Council, as they had been from the beginning, while all other parts of the group were integrated into the new complex structure. Thus, the security and military apparatus are more autonomous and more secretive in their organizational structure and composition than any other internal organ, though they are under the control of the Majlis al-Shura, which is also directly responsible for overseeing all other departments and activities.[53]

Hezbollah's highly cohesive and coordinated structure clearly shapes the relations between the group's military and political sectors, and it ensures strategic and ideological continuity between the two wings. Another key ingredient in ensuring internal unity of purpose and coordination is the figure of the secretary-general. The first to hold that position was Subhi al-Tufayli (1989–1991), followed by al-Sayyed Abbas al-Moussawi, who was elected in May 1991 but was killed less than a year later in an Israeli attack. Moussawi was the religious and political mentor of Hassan Nasrallah, who replaced him in May 1992; both men were similarly trained in the Iraqi seminar of Najaf.[54] A popular and effective leader, Nasrallah has been reelected as secretary-general ever since his initial appointment. This continuity of leadership also has enhanced the level of internal control and cohesion.

Hezbollah's organizational strength also relies on two crucial pillars: its media apparatus and its social services. First, Hezbollah operates a widespread media system, composed of newspapers and radio and television stations, overseen by the information unit of the executive council.[55] The organization's network of radio stations includes the popular al-Nour (the Light), which counts with several newspapers, including the Lebanese newspaper *al-Intiqad*, as the group's mouthpiece in both the south of Lebanon and the Beirut areas.[56] Furthermore, Hezbollah set up the Consultative Centre for Studies and Documentation, the Beirut-based think tank responsible for developing policy analysis and research on Lebanese politics, the resistance against Israel, and the Palestinian question.[57]

The group's most important media organ is undoubtedly al-Manar (the Beacon), its television station. Al-Manar, which started operating in 1991, began broadcasting by satellite in 2000;[58] it set up bureaus in Egypt, Iran, Jordan, and Dubai, as well as foreign correspondents in the greater Middle East, Europe, and the United States.[59] Al-Manar has played a crucial role in spreading Hezbollah's worldview both within Lebanon and in the Arab world, and it has similarly been vital in assisting the group's armed struggle. An especially good example of al-Manar's support is its coverage of the 2006 Hezbollah–Israeli war. The station communicated the "accomplishments of the resistance" (by showing images of dead or wounded IDF soldiers, for example) and the suffering of the civilian population in Lebanon, while at the same time minimizing Hezbollah's defeats. In this sense, as Marvin Kalb observed, "Al-Manar was to Hezbollah what *Pravda* was to the Soviet Union."[60]

Second, Hezbollah maintains an impressive network of social services that reaches out to its fighters and to the Shia community more generally. This welfare system is managed through a series of semiautonomous charities, foundations, and affiliated organizations, and it is overseen by the social, health, and educational divisions of the executive council.[61] Even those affiliated institutions that are not under the direct control of the executive council are integrated into Hezbollah's organizational structure; thus, a considerable degree of interorganizational coordination and administrative continuity is maintained. Although each institution is to some extent independent, a system of regularly rotating directors of institutions ensures considerable uniformity of action.[62] As a result of this efficiently integrated structure, Hezbollah's social network has earned a reputation for effectiveness as well as honesty, delivering basic and badly needed services where the state has been traditionally absent, including the south of Lebanon and the al-Dahiya area. For example, it created (and continues to maintain) the sewage system in the Balbeek region, installed water tanks in the southern suburbs of Beirut, and drilled water wells in the south.[63] By providing concrete benefits where the state has been unwilling or unable to do so, Hezbollah gained key political advantages over other political and sectarian movements within Lebanon.

Hezbollah's social network includes a large number of groups engaged in a range of welfare and charity activities. It maintains a system of charities to benefit its own fighters, chiefly the Iranian-funded Mua'assat al-Shahid (Martyrs' Foundation), which provides for the families of deceased Hezbollah fighters and prisoners, and the Mua'assat al-Jahra (Foundation for the Wounded).[64]

Hezbollah is heavily involved in providing health services to the Shia community, for instance, by running hospital and local health clinics. Hezbollah has also made significant investments in its educational unit, both offering scholarships to needy students and directly running a network of primary, secondary, and preparatory schools.[65]

Hezbollah manages far more organizations than are listed here. An especially important Hezbollah charity registered with the Lebanese government is Jihad al-Binna (literally effort to build, reconstruct), which provides a wide array of services in Shia areas focused on access to housing and community development. Another important example to show the wide range of activities sponsored by Hezbollah is its cross-sectarian micro-credit program, which has been active since 1995 and now has more than seventy-five thousand users.[66] Other important areas of work for Hezbollah include poverty alleviation, water delivery, agricultural cooperatives, and water sanitation, just to name a few.[67]

The *dawa* activities of the organization have contributed significantly to building its constituency, increasing its popularity, and expanding its effective control over the areas where it operates. A key element in the success of the social services department has been its adoption of a transparent and integrated business model:

The organizations are constantly evaluated, restructured, and updated to maximize their effectiveness. Hezbollah on occasion has had international consultants review its internal organizational structure and suggest needed changes, and it is constantly investing in new technology and products to take advantage of the latest innovations.[68]

The financial resources necessary to maintain this network are considerable, making Hezbollah's budget larger than that of any other political party in Lebanon. The group's need to preserve its military apparatus further adds to Hezbollah's annual expenses. The organization's financial requirements have been met through a combination of sources—Iranian contributions, donations from charities and individuals, and self-generated revenue.

The group's financial and political-strategic relations with Iran have progressed in parallel: As early as 1985, Iran was allegedly providing the group with a minimum of $30 million yearly, and the sum had already doubled by 1988.[69] Although the cash flow dropped during the 1990s, by the mid-2000s Iran was providing an estimated $100 million to $200 million a year to the organization through its official financial institutions[70] and a much greater amount through unofficial channels.[71] Following the 2006 war, Iran also declared that it had given more than $155 million to finance the reconstruction efforts within Lebanon.[72] Iranian contributions therefore continue to be essential for Hezbollah to meet its budgetary needs; though the organization's other sources of funding are increasingly more important. It draws significant portions of its revenues from donations and charitable contributions, as well as from collections of "Islamic taxes" (*Khums*) paid to the organization by members of the Shia community. Hezbollah is also generating a larger portion of its revenues from fee-based services, construction projects, investments in both local and foreign companies, and involvement in illicit trafficking.[73]

Finally, the structure of the organization relies on the support of the Shia community to recruit and maintain its membership base and to raise funds and gain political power. Hezbollah's relationship with its Shia constituency developed during the years of the civil war, when the different militias and armed groups within Lebanon became the de facto patrons of their respective communities as the political system broke down. But well beyond the end of the civil war, Hezbollah was able to maintain and even extend its governance and social welfare functions in Shia areas (from the south to Bekaa to al-Dahiya), where socioeconomic deprivation was widespread and the state generally failed to intervene. By running its social services network with efficiency and integrity, the party became enormously popular, and it was later able to capitalize further on this *dawa* work to win electoral preferences and popular support.

Hezbollah has built a strong base of followers, diverse in their levels of income, education, and level of religious observance, thereby gaining a truly mixed constituency within the Shia community.[74] Furthermore, through its women's, youth, cultural, and professional associations, the party has effectively penetrated every aspect of community life.[75]

Hezbollah's Ideology and Its Political Adaptation

The organization's core identity is Shia, and the group shares many of the values and aspirations of the Iranian Revolution, as well as those of the writings of Ayatollah Khomeini. Iran is a model state in that it embodies Hezbollah's main original political goal for Lebanon: the establishment of an Islamic state.

Hezbollah embraces Ayatollah Khomeini's call for the involvement of clerics within the government. Breaking from Shia history and the traditional role of *ulema* in Shia societies, Khomeini asserted that the only way for the clerics to safeguard the will of God was to exert direct control over society, that is, by ruling. Khomeini adopted the theory of the *Wilayat al-Faqih,* the guardianship of the (Islamic) Jurist, which emphasizes that in the absence of the Twelfth Imam,[76] the authority to oversee political and social matters falls on an Islamic cleric, who should act as supreme leader and de facto deputy of the Twelfth Imam, thereby obtaining virtually unlimited power. Hezbollah's adoption of this theory helps explain its strong relationship with and the deference it has shown to the Iranian supreme leaders, first Ayatollah Khomeini and then Ayatollah Khamenei.

Hezbollah first expressed its ideological principles and aspirations in a 1985 open letter that stated its desire to establish an Islamic state within Lebanon and rejected the possibility of participating in the existing political system, assailed as inherently corrupt.[77] In the organization's weltanschauung the creation of an Islamic state in Lebanon would be only the first step toward establishing a larger pan-Islamic state that would unite Muslims under the same government.[78] Although the 1985 manifesto clearly specified Hezbollah's final political goal, it provided few details about the means and tactics that would be used to achieve it.

Furthermore, the manifesto clearly directed Hezbollah's leaders to "call for the implementation of the Islamic system based on a direct and free choice of the people, and not through forceful imposition as may be assumed by some."[79] This assertion, together with Hezbollah's frequent emphasis on Islam's principle of noncompulsion (that is, no one should be forcibly converted to Islam),[80] has given the organization a great degree of ideological flexibility in claiming to adhere to its original manifesto while changing strategic priorities.

The organization soon began to underplay the goal of creating an Islamic state, describing it as a long-term desideratum rather than a practical political objective and noting that the political realities of Lebanon made the realization of an Islamic state impossible for now.[81] This shift in the group's rhetoric emerged at roughly the same time that the organization expanded and revised its organizational structure in conjunction with its decision to participate in the 1992 elections, thereby reversing its complete rejection of Lebanon's confessional system. Gradually, the group ceased to trumpet its aspirations publicly to build an Islamic state, began to commit itself to the existing political system, and started building bridges to other political parties and confessional groups.

Hezbollah made clear this shift in November 2009 with *The Political Document (Manifesto) of Hezbollah*, a revised ideological platform that complemented its 1985 open letter. In its second manifesto, the organization did not refer to the project of establishing an Islamic state in Lebanon and openly identified itself as part of the current Lebanese political system.

Whether this practical political move also signifies substantial changes in ideology remains to be seen. Although Hezbollah has accepted the current Lebanese political system and has invested substantial political capital in portraying itself as belonging to the mainstream, given the opportunity, a large parliamentary majority and sufficient political power, the group could likely consider to overturn the existing government and create a political system more in line with its Islamic values.[82]

At the same time, Hezbollah has not altered its original view regarding its external enemies. The group maintains that it is necessary both to repel the "corrupting influence of the West on the Islamic world" and to fight the state of Israel until that country is finally destroyed. In Hezbollah's eyes, the West has been an evil force oppressing the Muslim world; because of its dominant position in the world, the United States stands out as one of the most corrupting and omnipresent actors in the "war against the Muslim world."

For the group, one state is viewed as inherently evil: Israel. Since Hezbollah's founding in the early 1980s, Israel has been its raison d'être and primary enemy, identified with the West's attempts to take over the Muslim world. Hezbollah capitalizes on traditional Shia themes such as martyrdom and oppression in insisting that it is engaged in an existential defensive war to protect Islam. On this account, "Israel represents an eternal threat to Lebanon. . . . The role of the Resistance is a national necessity as long as Israeli threats and ambitions to seize our lands and waters continue."[83]

Resistance—confronting the enemy—becomes, in Hezbollah's worldview, a key duty and priority for every member of the Shia community. The organization's

Manichean outlook and its emphasis on the individual duty to confront directly the enemy aim at producing a widespread culture of resistance, a powerful ideological tool to unite and empower the historically marginalized and impoverished Lebanese Shia community.[84]

Complying with this duty of resistance takes precedence over obeying other value systems. Thus, a wide range of tactics can be employed to pursue this objective and to defy the Israeli enemy, including conventional and asymmetric warfare and terrorism, notably, "self-martyrdom" operations.

The Reasons behind Hezbollah's Political Participation

The 1992 Elections: Why Politics?

The brief excursus into Hezbollah's basic organizational structure and ideology shows that the group's development has been affected by its decision to create a political wing to participate in the 1992 parliamentary elections. This section examines why it decided to take part in institutional politics, while the chapter concludes by considering whether changes in the organization since 1992 are better explained by the "linear moderation paradigm" or by the "cyclical development model."

The earlier theoretical chapters asserted that the development of a political wing occurs at a strategic juncture, specifically, when the group experiences substantial shifts in its institutional priorities, as well as changes in the availability of mobilization resources, in its political opportunities, and in its internal commitment to change. Looking at the case of Hezbollah, we can see that its decision to participate in elections followed substantial changes in all of these areas.

The previous chapters formulated two hypotheses about the relation between the formation of a political wing and changes in the institution and in resource availability:

1. The choice to create a political wing is triggered by the group's institutional development and its related push to expand, which is motivated by the group's desire to acquire power and stability, while ensuring that it continues to be viewed as relevant and legitimate.

2. A political wing is created as a tool to diversify mobilization resources to enable expansion and to increase independence. A given group has the most incentive to form a political wing when its access to resources is threatened by loss of autonomy, of its claim on legitimacy, or of its reason for existence, or when the available resources fall far short of meeting the strategic need to grow.

In the case of Hezbollah, the group decided to transition toward institutional politics in the immediate aftermath of the civil war. By that time, it had been active for more than ten years and had changed from a loose umbrella organization into a highly structured, sophisticated, and tightly controlled machine.

Internally, the group was at the peak of its institutional coherence, having achieved its current institutional form. Indeed, the group has not substantially altered its organizational structure or internal division of power since the early 1990s. But when the civil war ended, Hezbollah found itself under intense pressure to reassert both its autonomy and its legitimacy.

As the country transitioned out of the civil war and the predominant state of mind shifted from confrontation to conciliation, the group needed to prove that it was still relevant in the new political climate. Moreover, it needed to change its approach to deal with its Shia political rival, Amal. During the late 1980s the level of competition and hostility between the two had progressively increased to the point that a smaller-scale internal war to control the Shia community had broken out.[85]

After Syria stepped in to broker a military cease-fire between the two parties,[86] Hezbollah's strategy to deal with this perceived threat to its "distinctiveness" and power shifted to the political realm. At this point, the group attempted to translate its military advantage over Amal into political power by creating a political wing.

Threatened by the shifting political circumstances and the increasing internal competition, the highly institutionalized organization decided to face these direct challenges to its legitimacy and relevance by expanding, and thus created a political wing. Hezbollah's leadership was realistic and pragmatic in choosing expansion in response to these challenges. The organization had become widely popular during the civil war, both by fighting the Israeli occupation and by beginning to actively provide social services for the Shia community.

Amal's so-called war of the camps against the Palestinians in southern Lebanon had been opposed by a substantial sector of the Shia community, and Hezbollah was able to capitalize on this lingering discontent to attract new supporters. This realignment was also triggered by the condemnation of Amal's attack on the Palestinians by Ayatollah Mohammad Hussein Fadlallah, Lebanon's most influential religious authority; his disapproval led part of the community to decide to openly back Hezbollah.[87] This is the case even though Fadlallah was not subordinated to Hezbollah or part of its camp.

Taking advantage of this new reality, the group chose to use this newly acquired constituency to enhance its status and its size. The creation of a political wing served as a crucial expansionary tool: It provided an easy and low-cost way to incorporate the new supporters, and it improved the organization's position with respect to Amal.

The decision to embark in institutional politics came also at a time when shifts in the internal and international political environment were putting at risk Hezbollah's access to resources. The death of Ayatollah Khomeini in 1989 and the shift in foreign policy under the early years of Ayatollah Khameini and President Hashemi Rafsanjani partially changed the political agenda of Iran, reducing the material resources available to Hezbollah and thus limiting its ability to undertake international terrorist activities and attacks on foreign targets other than Israel. Rafsanjani used Hezbollah's financial dependence on Iran to attempt to control the group's armed operations.[88] Simultaneously, Tehran chose to support Syria's claims over Lebanon, enhancing the ability of Hafez al-Assad's regime to control events there.

The civil war in Lebanon, in fact, ended with a large number of losers, starting with the civilian population, who suffered heavily as a result of the war, and one clear winner: Syria under the leadership of Hafez al-Assad. Syria had traditionally seen Lebanon through the lens of Syrian "exceptionalism," leading the country to claim "distinctive relations" (*alaqat mumayyaza*) with the Lebanese Republic.[89] In other words, since Lebanon's independence, Syria had de facto thought of Lebanese politics as a matter of both foreign and domestic policy, and thus the country had been from the outset heavily involved in the Lebanese civil war.

Through shifting alliances, assassinations, reliance on proxies, diplomatic pressure, or by direct military and political intervention, Syrian involvement in the civil war was characterized by a precise strategy: to maintain hegemony within Lebanon and to frustrate the ambitions of other foreign powers, especially Israel following its second invasion of Lebanon in 1982. While the civil war years allowed Syria to impose its military presence and political influence on Lebanon, the termination of the conflict and the national reconciliation process that followed allowed Syria to consolidate its role in the Lebanese Republic. The way Syria engineered its political role in post–civil war Lebanon represents the country's political masterpiece.

The Taif Agreement, officially known as the Document of National Accord,[90] shaped Lebanon's transition from the bloody civil war that had raged in the country from 1975 to 1990 to peace. The agreement was reached in Taif (Saudi Arabia) in the fall of 1989 by the surviving members of Parliament who had been elected in 1972—the last elections before hostilities began, and it was brokered by Saudi Arabia and the Arab League. Even if Syria did not broker the peace process, still the agreement gave Syria a legal basis to maintain a military presence in Lebanon, together with the recognition of its special relationship with Lebanon and its role as "guarantor" of Taif.[91]

The post–civil war Lebanon was very much shaped and led from the outside by Damascus and its "tutelage" of the country. As Syrian influence rose in Lebanon, Hezbollah found itself under stricter control: although Syria supported and defended Hezbollah's armed campaigns against Israel, it also sought to curtail all other military operations, whether directed against Amal or aimed at increasing the organization's control of the Shia territory.[92]

As a consequence of this diminishing external support and increasing internal control, Hezbollah felt compelled to diversify both its sources of funding and its range of activities. In turn, this situation created strong incentives to invest heavily in its social services and political activities. Because delivering more social services and achieving political power would enable the organization to increase its profile and begin generating part of its needed revenues itself, creating a political wing and joining the political system appeared to be the best way to adapt to the changing political environment.

In the early 1990s the cold war had ended, states were generally reducing their direct monetary support of terrorism and terrorist groups, and Israel and its Arab neighbors, including Syria, were actively engaged in peace negotiations; Hezbollah realized that the opposite approach—"radicalizing" and seeking new sponsors for its armed activities—was the less realistic strategy. To diversify its funding pools and activities, as well as to expand in size and strength, it began to work toward participation in parliamentary politics.

The involvement in institutional politics was triggered by the perceived threat to the organization's resources and distinctiveness caused both by changes in the regional environment and by increasing domestic competition. However, Hezbollah could not have embraced this political transformation if a series of modifications had not occurred in the political opportunity structure.

On this topic, the hypothesis of this study is that the creation of a political wing is affected by changes in the political environment.

> The political alternative is also a function of the degree of openness or lack of openness in the political system, which includes the permeability of the structures of power, the characteristics of the electoral system, the presence of mediating institutions within society, and the cultural-institutional power dynamics in place. Shifts in the electorate equally affect the calculation to join the political system.

In the case of Lebanon, significant changes in political opportunities produced external conditions that favored Hezbollah's strategic realignment. These structural modifications simultaneously improved the "openness" of the political system, providing an incentive to participate in elections and increased the costs of armed struggle.

Although the political system after Lebanon's civil war continued to present structural and normative obstacles to effective participation, the new political climate and rules dictating political participation were nonetheless dramatic improvements both from what had been present before the civil war and from the widespread chaos and violence of the war itself.

The first step in this new direction was of course the Taif Agreement. The agreement came at the height of the civil war; when, after the belligerents had failed to agree on the nomination of a president in 1988, two competing governments were created as a result of their disagreement and hostilities escalated sharply.[93] The price of that escalation was too great, for most belligerents and for the shattered Lebanese economy, and the international community, especially the Arab League, decided that, to avoid regional repercussions, the war had to be ended at all costs. After the Taif Agreement was signed, most militias were speedily demobilized; rather than integrating fighters into the new LAF, most of them returned to civilian life. In this new political context, the political and military costs to organizations of self-identifying solely as an armed militia and of continuing to fight became extremely high and thus all existing armed groups, including Hezbollah, were provided with a powerful incentive to consider joining the political system.

The ratification of the Document of National Accord led to marked improvements in the political system. First, the peace agreement allowed the return of elections, making possible real change after more than fifteen years of political deadlock. Second, it guaranteed a certain level of stability, as the massive Syrian military and political presence that it introduced into Lebanon to monitor and safeguard the peace helped reduce political volatility, thereby producing real incentives for Hezbollah to look on participation in institutional politics as a politically convenient strategy.

Furthermore, the Syrian "tutelage" that was introduced in Lebanon in the aftermath of the civil war through the Taif Agreement constituted an additional opening from Hezbollah's point of view.

In the years following the end of the civil war and the Taif Agreement, Syria worked to consolidate its military and political influence within Lebanon. This process of institutionalization of the Syrian role in Lebanese affairs took place largely undisturbed, as foreign powers generally accepted Syria's limited hegemony on Lebanon as a fait accompli, and in exchange for Syria's cooperation during the Gulf War.[94] Taking advantage of this positive laissez-faire attitude, Syria developed an intricate system to preserve its hegemony on Lebanon, grounded in military presence, intelligence infiltration of the Lebanese government, political control of key posts within the government, electoral manipulation, and silencing all political opposition.

From Hezbollah's point of view, the Syrian presence and strong grip on Lebanon was useful in at least two major ways. Syria would serve both to counterbalance the power of the Maronite Christian community and to guarantee that Hezbollah's armed wing would not be ostracized or forced to disarm. While for the Lebanese political system as a whole the Syrian interference hampered national reconciliation and the subsequent normalization of political life, for Hezbollah it ensured that the newly formed political system would allow for their political participation. This point is particularly crucial: Syria pressured the Lebanese government to endorse Hezbollah's right to fight the Israeli occupation and to abstain from interfering with its actions, thus minimizing the costs to the organization of political participation, and leaving little incentive for it to choose between to its political activities and its military operations.[95] Hezbollah was able to pull this off and to avoid the disarmament process also because during the civil war it has established for itself a reputation of commitment to fighting Israel, while for the most part refraining from turning its weapons inwards, unlike virtually all other sectarian militias during the war.

This is not to say that Hezbollah did not have to modify certain ideological or political positions to join the political system. For instance, the organization systematically downplayed its demands to create an Islamic state. It accepted the confessional system it had previously attacked. It began to engage in interfaith dialogues, and it tacitly stopped supporting the Palestinians' armed struggle by allowing the Lebanese army to disarm the PLO in southern Lebanon.[96]

A second way in which the Taif Agreement made the political system more accessible to Hezbollah, and thus directly affected its decision to create a political wing, was by restructuring the electoral system. On the one hand, although the 1989 agreement called for abolishing political sectarianism, one of Hezbollah's main prerequisites for joining the political system, in practice it preserved the confessional basis of the political system as ratified by the 1943 National Pact.[97] Under that arrangement, the main sectarian groups in Lebanon were assigned a fixed quota of seats in the Chamber of Deputies. Taif also preserved the confessional distribution of high posts, which reserved the presidency for the Maronites, the post of prime minister for the Sunnis, and the role of speaker of the chamber for the Shias.[98] Hence, the accord had the effect of further entrenching existing sectarian dynamics within the political system, dynamics left intact during the years of Syrian tutelage.

On the other hand, even if the post–civil war arrangement did not revoke the confessional system Hezbollah attacked, it significantly amended it, opening the door for the political participation of Shias. The Taif Agreement equalized the ratio of seats allocated to Muslim and Christian representatives, raised the number of deputies to 128, and distributed the Muslim seats evenly between Sunni and Shia candidates. Previously, the Parliament had been composed of 95 deputies, and the formula favored the Christians with a 6:5 ratio.[99]

These changes did not entirely guarantee the proportional and effective representation of all confessional groups. The reforms notably failed to address the formula of sectarian representation, which continues today to be based on an outdated population census carried out in 1932.[100] Obviously, Lebanon's demographic composition has changed quite substantially since then, and reliance on it produces significant anomalies within the system. For instance, under the current model, each Christian representative represents far fewer voters than does his or her Shia colleague, since the Shia population, unlike the Christian one, has been growing rapidly in recent decades, while the number of seats allocated to them has remained constant.

Nevertheless, by increasing the overall number of political seats and keeping the threshold for gaining access to the political system low, the reforms launched by the Taif Agreement provided a general impetus for the proliferation of political parties; by equalizing the ratio of seats between Christians and Muslims, they encouraged the participation of the Shia community more specifically.

These strategic shifts within Lebanon provided an incentive for Hezbollah to create a political wing and to run in the 1992 elections. Several changes at the regional level also affected Hezbollah's choice. First, as mentioned previously, the shifts in the foreign policy and political agenda of Hezbollah's main patron—Iran—affected Hezbollah's level of financial and political support and thus pushed the organization toward diversification in the form of deemphasizing its military wing and favoring the creation of alternative organizational centers of gravity.

Second, from an ideological perspective, the failure of Iran to win decisively in its war with Iraq and to export the Iranian Revolution outside its national borders had a profound influence on Hezbollah's mind-set (specifically, its view of the feasibility of imposing an Islamic state on Lebanon in the near future).

Third, the winds of peace that were sweeping the Middle East during the early 1990s were also read by the organization as a warning sign that unless it undertook a profound strategic realignment, its survival might be at stake. The organization was concerned about a possible peace agreement between Syria and Israel, which might then have led to reconciliation between the Jewish state and Lebanon. The most effective way to prevent such an outcome, which for Hezbollah amounted to a direct existential threat, was to become part of the government and to acquire enough political power to veto any future understanding with Israel.

Finally, the decision to create a political wing is a function of an organization's unity and commitment to reform:

> Political change is related to an internal commitment to reform the organization.

Hezbollah's decision to participate in the 1992 parliamentary elections was the result of a prolonged internal struggle between two different leadership cadres, which ultimately led to a split within the organization and the expulsion of the losing faction.

Hezbollah's political transition was first pushed by the man who would become Hezbollah's second secretary-general, al-Sayyed Abbas al-Moussawi.[101] Moussawi and others who supported forming a political wing began to urge the organization to embrace institutional politics immediately after the Taif Agreement was reached. At the time, their position was sharply opposed by another hard-core group of Hezbollah supporters; this one led by the first secretary-general of the organization, Subhi al-Tufayli.[102] Moussawi could count on two major sources of backing outside Hezbollah to legitimize his position: the more pragmatic post-Khomeini Iranian leadership, which supported the new political involvement of its Lebanese Shia ally, and, within Lebanon, Ayatollah Fadlallah, who had been very vocal regarding the need for the Shia community to focus on political integration. "Like all revolutions, including the French Revolution, the Islamic Revolution did not have a realistic line," Fadlallah declared, adding that the new goal should be "the normalization of relations with the rest of the world."[103] Moussawi's plan for Lebanon was therefore in line with both the new Iranian leadership in power, as well as with Fadlallah's vision of the Islamic postrevolutionary phase. Both would later prove very useful to Moussawi as he gathered the necessary internal support to back the decision to create a political wing.

The important figures within Hezbollah who argued for participation in Lebanese institutional politics failed to persuade Secretary-General Tufayli, who viewed entry into the political system as a sign that the organization was abandoning its revolutionary structure. In protest, Tufayli decided to withdraw his candidacy for reelection as secretary-general, thereby aiding the rise of Moussawi in 1991.[104] Although Tufayli, despite his prestige and seniority, could not override the will of those favoring political participation, his opposition represented a serious obstacle.

In the end, to determine whether Hezbollah would be participating in the 1992 elections, the organization decided to create a twelve-member committee of leaders, including Tufayli, Moussawi, and his pupil Nasrallah, to debate and vote on the issue. The committee's recommendation would then be submitted to Iran's supreme leader, to gain his final approval. After weighing all the advantages and drawbacks to participating in elections, the leaders concluded that taking part in the political system could be a means to strengthen the resistance: by a vote of ten to two, they overwhelmingly approved the creation of a political wing. These conclusions were subsequently submitted to Imam Khameini, who approved the committee's work and gave the green light to participating in the parliamentary elections.[105]

The organization then created a parliamentary council supervised by the Majlis al-Shura and the secretary-general, ensuring that both the military apparatus and the newly founded political wing of the organization would be under the control of the same organ.

The Israeli assassination of al-Moussawi in February 1992 was a temporary setback to establishing a political wing, as Tufayli and his supporters attempted to regain the leadership of Hezbollah and delay its involvement in institutional politics.[106] But their efforts were thwarted by the immediate election of Hassan Nasrallah, whose strategic vision for the organization appeared to conform to Moussawi's. In the months between Moussawi's assassination and the August 1992 elections, Hezbollah, under its new secretary-general, took concrete steps to ensure that its entry into the political process would be successful.

Although the decision to create a political wing had not originally been unanimous, its support by the majority of the organization (including Secretary-General Moussawi and his follower Nasrallah), backed by Iran, was sufficient to ensure Hezbollah's entry into the political system. Most important, Hezbollah's tight and hierarchical organizational structure, with its high concentration of power, made it possible to impose this decision, once made, on every internal organ. Hezbollah's organizational cohesiveness guaranteed that the political and military departments would cooperate, for they were controlled by the same leaders.

The remaining voices of dissent were first marginalized and then excluded: Tufayli ultimately lost his political power and was eventually expelled from the organization in 1998, becoming a fringe figure within Lebanese political life. Many of the military commanders who supported him in southern Lebanon were purged from the organization and replaced by militants who were loyal to the new secretary-general, Nasrallah.[107] Had these voices of dissent not been silenced at an early stage, Hezbollah's military apparatus and its political wing might have developed a relationship of competition rather than cooperation and strategic complement.

1992–2012: The Rise of Hezbollah in Domestic Politics

To understand how Hezbollah has fostered its political apparatus and how this increased political involvement has affected its other activities, it is necessary to look more closely at the political evolution of the organization: specifically, the group's political participation in the national parliamentary elections in 1996, 2000, 2005, and 2009, and in the municipal elections in 1998, 2004, and 2010. Key to this analysis is determining how the relationship between the military and the political factions has changed and whether, from 1992 to 2012, the internal balance of power between these two organizational subunits substantially shifted. In other words, have Hezbollah's political imperatives gradually become ascendant over its military objectives and can the organization's development be viewed as a linear progression toward "increased moderation"? Although the definition of that concept is extremely elusive, signs of increased moderation would be a substantial decline in the use of force, a greater interest in negotiation and compromise, and a more flexible approach toward relinquishing its armed militia and its control over part of Lebanon's territory.

According to the theoretical framework of this study, such a transition would occur only if the relationship between the military and the political wings shifted from strategic cooperation to mutual opposition and competition. Conversely, continued cooperation and mutual reinforcement of the group's military and political subunits would suggest that any change generated by the newly created political wing would merely be convergent and thus would not affect the group's strategy at its core. The high degree of integration between these two elements, which have continued to be supervised by the same group of leaders, suggests that the political wing and the armed group are extremely unlikely to experience substantial friction. And, in the absence of strategic competition between the two factions or their development of opposing institutional logics, the organization would probably not undergo any form of strategic change, including permanent "moderation."

1992: Hezbollah's First Parliamentary Elections

It is undeniable that 1992 was a watershed year for the organization. To compete in the 1992 parliamentary elections, Hezbollah underwent a series of substantial changes (not only at the structural level). First, it had to justify its participation in a political system that it had previously rejected and explicitly condemned. Specifically, the organization had attacked the Taif Agreement, which, it protested, "was transformed into the country's Constitution, and this we cannot accept, especially because it enshrines sectarianism; sectarianism was merely a custom in the past, but after Taif it became enshrined in the constitution."[108] At the root of Hezbollah's opposition to sectarianism was its belief that the confessional system was a means to preserve the Maronite Christians' political dominance, despite their shrinking demographic base—and at the expense of the Shia community.

Yet even though Hezbollah dropped its outright rejection of the political system by agreeing to participate in it, it did not abandon its ultimate objective of abolishing sectarianism.[109] As Naim Qassem explains, "Participation in parliamentary elections is an expression of sharing in an existing political structure, Parliament being one of the regime's pillars. It does not, however, represent a commitment to preserving the structure as it is, or require defence of the system's deficiencies and blemishes."[110]

Second, the group had to embark on what was in effect a massive branding strategy to polish its external image and smooth its Islamic and Iranian edges, so that it might have greater appeal to the general electorate. This public relations operation served a double purpose. First, it was intended to help transform Hezbollah from a fringe to a mainstream Lebanese movement. Second, the group wanted to capitalize on the appeal of the "resistance," making it a national cause by becoming a nationally recognized movement, with institution legitimacy.

To enable this transformation, the group had to cease publicly promoting its goal of establishing an Islamic state within Lebanon, emphasizing instead its intention not to spread Islam through coercion. In the months preceding the election, the secretary-general took precisely this line in many statements and interviews, insisting that "we never said we want to built [*sic*] an Islamic identity through oppression and compulsion at any level[;] . . . we should not built [*sic*] an Islamic government on oppression and coercion."[111] Even more important, to rebrand itself successfully Hezbollah had to convince the Lebanese population of its national and Arab identity. It therefore adopted a Lebanon-oriented posture, depicting itself as a Lebanese nationalist movement, a stark change from its pre-1992 "revolutionary phase." Hezbollah also attempted to erase the popular perception that it was an agent of Iran. An important element of this strategy was to initiate dialogue with parts of the Christian community, ranging from informal meetings of citizens to more structured contacts between leaders of Hezbollah and members of the Christian clergy.[112]

Hezbollah also invested in a large-scale issue-based electoral campaign. It advocated social welfare and social justice reforms, as well as economic and social development programs, a posture that ensured the support of the marginalized and generally underdeveloped Shia community. Hezbollah often pointed to its own achievements in providing social welfare, both to gain the allegiance and vote of the Shia communities who had benefited from such interventions and to establish its credentials with the rest of the electorate. Hezbollah's successful track record and its reputation of efficiency won the organization credibility.

Similarly, the group relied on its honest reputation to take the higher moral ground in chastising other parties already in power for the corruption, inefficiency, and wasteful management of the Lebanese government. Setting itself in opposition to these failures, the group became a leading advocate of abolishing sectarian employment at every state level and of empowering and granting more autonomy to local governments and municipalities.[113]

In approaching its first electoral contest, Hezbollah did more to win votes than rely on its legacy of fighting Israel: it focused simultaneously on recasting its identity, now presented as a national movement, and on creating an issue-based platform that could appeal to a wide, cross-sectarian constituency. To a large extent, these efforts did succeed in turning the group into an ordinary political party, especially in the context of political party formation within Lebanon.

Political parties in Lebanon had long been sectarian, based not just on ideology, as in many Western democracies, but on confession. For that reason, labels of "right" and "left" generally fail to capture the political divisions within Lebanon,[114] overlooking the fact that most party leaders are, at their core, community leaders.[115] These leaders have historically built strong power bases by running their own communities, providing services and protection, and in return securing a tight, often clientelist relationship with their constituency.

Because Hezbollah does fit this confessional model, it does not dramatically depart from "ordinary" parties within Lebanon, which had in the past relied on private militias to back their claims to political power.[116]

Nevertheless, other elements made the group unique as a political organization from the outset of its political involvement. The quality and quantity of Hezbollah's military arsenal completely shifted the internal military balance of power in its favor. Also, though all political parties depended to a certain degree on other regional and global actors for sponsorship and funding, none had an external relationship as pervasive or as crucial as Hezbollah's with Iran. Finally, no other political party resembled Hezbollah in being simultaneously a national and a regional player.[117] To this day, all these differences set Hezbollah apart from the rest of the Lebanese political parties.

While rebranding itself as an ordinary national political movement, Hezbollah also invested significant political capital and labor in developing and implementing its electoral strategy: in the period before the elections, political activism was among the organization's top priorities.

Although its official announcement of candidacy came less than two months before votes would actually be cast, planning had begun quite some time earlier, and all elements of Hezbollah had been mobilized and directly involved in preparing for the elections. During the campaign, different branches of the organization performed complementary roles, from ensuring an effective media strategy, to providing free transportation to the polls for Hezbollah voters, to guaranteeing public order during the actual elections, as handled, respectively, by al-Manar, the Islamic Health Organization, and the security organs. Hezbollah also created a central electoral committee (with a number of subcommittees) staffed with more than 600 members of the organization; placed under the direct supervision of the party leaders, it was tasked with carefully planning every stage of the electoral campaign.[118]

Research conducted by the election committees supplied data that Hezbollah used to devise a pragmatic strategy to maximize its chances of winning elections. The organization shaped its electoral lists to correspond to the sectarian-political composition of each electoral district. In Shia majority areas where the party was already highly popular, the lists contained only Hezbollah members. In other regions, where powerful political actors who might have jeopardized Hezbollah's success were already in place, the group decided to create mixed electoral lists, allying itself with independent candidates or with other political parties. Political realism certainly guided Hezbollah's decisions either to create or to enter electoral coalitions, both in 1992 and later. In 1998 they joined the "Beirut Accord List," becoming an ally of such political groups as the Lebanese Phalange Party and the Lebanese Forces, which only a few years previously had been its archenemies because of their ambivalent relation with Israel during the civil war.[119]

The party also followed Syria's "recommendation" and agreed to create mixed lists with its former foe, Amal.[120] In the end, owing to this careful logistical and strategic planning, Hezbollah gained eight out of the twenty-seven parliamentary seats allocated to the Shia community in the 1992 elections; four additional seats were won by independent sympathizers.[121]

Hezbollah subsequently joined Lebanon's parliament, but it maintained its reputation as a "resistance party": It was the only Lebanese political formation that opposed the nomination of Sunni leader Rafik Hariri to the office of prime minister, and the only party that refused to join the executive cabinet and to award Hariri's government a vote of confidence. On the contrary, Hezbollah attacked Hariri's political platform because it failed to recognize Hezbollah's "resistance rights" and was silent on the issue of political sectarianism.[122]

Despite joining the political system and depicting itself as a Lebanese and Arab social movement, two concrete examples of political accommodation undertaken by the organization so that it might participate in Lebanon's institutional politics, the party did not sacrifice its military objectives. Speaking immediately after the elections, Secretary-General Nasrallah made clear that Hezbollah's long-term goal was unchanged: "We were, and will always be, the party of the resistance that [operates] from Lebanon. . . . Our participation in the elections . . . do[es] not alter the fact that we are a resistance party; we shall, in fact, work to turn the whole of Lebanon into a country of resistance, and the state into a state of resistance (. . .)."[123]

It is crucial to keep in mind that the organization's focus on political participation did not compromise its military activities and that, more important, the election of eight Hezbollah members of parliament was accomplished not by the group's political bureau alone but by a joint effort of every branch of the organization. The Shura Council and secretary-general personally oversaw political as well as military activities, thereby avoiding strategic or tactical tensions between the military apparatus and the political wing.

That said, it is still possible to view the organization as entering a moderating organizational phase after the Taif Agreement, as it invested significantly in the political system and became open to cross-sectarian alliances and domestic accommodation. The group halted some of its most violent practices, including the kidnapping of Western hostages, and mostly refrained from dramatic escalations of violence in its war of attrition against Israel. Although its involvement in international terrorism did not cease, as the 1992 and 1994 Buenos Aires attacks show, it could be argued that following the end of the civil war and its political rise, Hezbollah was increasingly moving away from its military emphasis. To determine whether the "moderating effect" of 1992 was a temporary phenomenon or a permanent trend in Hezbollah's organizational evolution, it is important to examine the military and political activities of the group in the years following its entry into the political arena.

1992–2000: Politics and "Resistance" under Israeli and Syrian Occupation

The years between 1992 and 2000 further shed light on the post–civil war strategy and behavior of Hezbollah as a hybrid politico-military organization. On the one hand, during this period, the organization's integration into the political system increased, culminating in its decision to participate in the 1998 municipal elections. On the other hand, Hezbollah's military activities continued throughout these years independent of the group's political agenda and without consultation with or the involvement of any other national political actors.

From the early 1990s onward, the organization repeatedly declared its intention of maintaining a degree of control over the south of Lebanon so that it might carry out its armed operations more effectively, and it vehemently rejected all attempts made by the elected government to interfere with its military actions. It continues to hold this position, summarized in a statement by Nasrallah in 1996: "We believe that if the resistance depended on the political authority of the state, there would be no resistance on the ground at all, because under such conditions resistance would simply be a *pro-forma*—a resistance in name only, staged for publicity purposes, rather than genuine, serious, and effective."[124] This refusal to have any outside check on its military activities confirmed that Hezbollah was not playing by the same rules as Lebanon's other political parties. The extent and quality of Hezbollah's military apparatus, along with its domestically unconstrained use of force, set it apart from all other sectarian parties.

Hezbollah became a strong opposition party and remained a player outside normal rules. During this period, Hezbollah kept up its military attacks against Israel in conventional, guerrilla, and "martyrdom" operations and focused on engaging the enemy within the security zone, an area, constituting about 10 percent of Lebanon's territory, under the military control of both the IDF and the Southern Lebanese Army, a largely Christian militia that acted as an Israeli proxy in the occupied areas.[125] The hostilities did not remain confined solely to that battlefield, however. As early as the summer of 1993, tensions escalated after Hezbollah's attacks within the security zone were met by Israel's counterattacks in southern Lebanon targeting Hezbollah operatives. Following Hezbollah's retaliation on Israel proper with Katyusha rockets,[126] Israel launched a weeklong, full-scale military operation, Operation Accountability, which caused extensive damage within Lebanon but failed to eradicate or even substantially weaken Hezbollah.[127] This seven-day war brought Hezbollah's independent military agenda to the attention of the newly elected Lebanese government as a challenge to its political sovereignty. Not surprisingly, Prime Minister Hariri did not react enthusiastically to Hezbollah's military escalation, going so far as to deny the group the right to rally in Beirut in support of the war and against the ongoing Oslo negotiations.[128]

In the end, Israel and Hezbollah, with the help of Syrian and American mediators, agreed to a fragile unwritten understanding that committed both parties to refraining from attacks on civilian enemy areas.[129] This status quo was short-lived, as Hezbollah's repeated strikes in the security zone led the IDF to launch another large-scale attack on Lebanon in 1996. Modeled after Operation Accountability, the new military operation—Grapes of Wrath—also inflicted extensive damage and civilian suffering but failed to eradicate the Shia organization.[130]

This second military engagement between Israel and Hezbollah led to a written (albeit unsigned) agreement that, once again, committed both parties to refraining from attacks on civilians, while de facto guaranteeing their "right to self-defense" and Hezbollah's "right" to continue its wars of attrition in the security zone.[131]

Although the Lebanese civil population was largely supportive of Hezbollah during the hostilities, mostly in reaction to the IDF's extensive attacks against Lebanon,[132] friction between the government and the Shia group reemerged. Increasingly unwilling to tolerate Hezbollah's independence and power, the government began discussing how to curb its military influence while accusing the organization of monopolizing the "resistance" and failing to share the struggle with the rest of Lebanon.[133] While conducting its own battle against Israel, Hezbollah also decided to elevate the importance of its Islamic Jihad unit by appointing the subunit's central military commander, Hajj Muhsin Al-Shakar, to sit in the Shura Council and join the leaders overseeing the rest of the organization.[134]

At the same time, the group was still in the middle of its "political accommodation phase"; it continued to participate in the country's political activities, though it failed to discuss its military operations or strategy with the rest of the political actors. This ambivalent position as an "insider-outsider" set the pattern of relations between Hezbollah and its institutional milieu that remains dominant to this day. Continuing to play by normal political rules, even while conducting its military operations and acting independently of the state, the group participated in the parliamentary elections of 1996 and the municipal elections of 1998.

Hezbollah's approach to the 1996 elections was modeled after its 1992 campaign, but it did not fare as well, even though its popularity had increased in the aftermath of Grapes of Wrath. In this electoral round, Hezbollah won seven seats in Parliament and only three independent supporters were elected. This loss of two pro-Hezbollah deputies probably had multiple causes: One important factor was the creation of a powerful ad hoc coalition against it, assembled by the Shia Amal, Hariri's Sunni-based party, and the Druze Progressive Socialist Party (PSP) and supported by Syria.[135]

A similar broad anti-Hezbollah alliance rose again in 1998, in preparation for the first municipal elections to be held in more than thirty-five years—choosing 7,662 representatives to serve on 646 municipal councils, as well as 2,041 mayors.[136] Motivated in part by fears that Hezbollah's success in providing social services would attract voters, Hariri's party, backed by Amal, initially urged that no party members should run for election.[137]

Hezbollah rejected the proposal, accusing its rivals of being antidemocratic and of impeding fair electoral competition; ignoring the request, it formed independent electoral lists, fashioned new coalitions, and joined existing coalitions (such as Hariri's broad electoral alliance for Beirut) when doing so was deemed politically convenient.[138] Significantly, Hezbollah also competed directly against Amal and did not always create a joint list.[139] The 1998 electoral results enhanced its political power within Lebanon and confirmed the party's opposition status. Hezbollah performed strongly in the Shiite suburbs of Beirut, where it defeated Amal by a very large margin, and in southern Lebanon, it prevailed in a sizable number of Amal's municipalities.[140] However, Amal remained strong in the Bekaa Valley area;[141] in response, Hezbollah doubled the number of Bekaa Valley representatives in its Shura Council, a move designed to win the electorate away from Amal.[142]

By the end of 1998, Hezbollah had evolved in two different directions. Adapting its military strategy to the post–civil war environment, it focused on a limited war against Israel, while not hesitating on occasion to escalate the hostilities. At the same time, the group became more engaged in politics, both as a national opposition party and directly through governance at the municipal level.

The group's military and political wings developed in parallel, attempting to promote a public image of two separate identities, while both remained under the control of the same leaders. In stating that "in reality any escalation or reduction in the number of the resistance's operations is not contingent upon a political decision, but rather upon the situation on the ground,"[143] Nasrallah confirmed this strategy.

As the next sections will show, the line of separation began to blur as Hezbollah's political wing became more directly involved in preserving and defending its military apparatus. The seeds for this shift are related to the 2000 Israeli withdrawal, a game changer for Lebanon and for the organization.

2000–2005: The Israeli Withdrawal

Hezbollah's security environment was dramatically reshaped by the Israeli withdrawal from Lebanon. On May 24, 2000, the Israeli army completed its hasty departure from the security zone in southern Lebanon, redeploying behind an internationally recognized border, the so-called Blue Line.[144] According to the international community, Israel's unilateral withdrawal behind this demarcation established by the United Nations put the country in compliance with UN Security Council (UNSC) Resolutions 425 and 426, adopted in 1978, which called for Israel's immediate withdrawal from Lebanon.[145] The Lebanese government, however, argued that Israel was still occupying parts of Lebanon. In particular, Lebanon claimed sovereignty over the Shebaa Farms: approximately twenty-five square kilometers, consisting of fourteen farms located on the western slopes of Mount Hermon to the south of the Lebanese village of Shebaa.[146] The core question behind this ongoing dispute is whether the area falls under Lebanese or Syrian jurisdiction; poor colonial mapping and the lack of a formal binding agreement between Syria and Lebanon offer conflicting answers. Israel, together with the international community, maintains that Shebaa Farms belonged to Syria before the IDF occupation; therefore, Lebanon has no bearing on the Israel's withdrawal from Lebanon.[147] The Lebanese government claims sovereignty over the Shebaa Farms, a position backed by Hezbollah, as would be expected, and thus refuses to acknowledge the Israeli withdrawal as complete. In another ongoing border dispute, the Lebanese government also claims sovereignty over a group of seven villages south of the Lebanon–Israel border (the Hounine villages) that had been incorporated into Palestine in 1923.[148]

From Hezbollah's perspective, the Israeli withdrawal represented a two-edged sword. The organization was able to link the Israeli unconditional and unilateral withdrawal to its war of attrition against the IDF, thereby acquiring additional domestic prestige and legitimacy. But the sudden disappearance of the Israeli occupiers from the south of Lebanon threatened to remove the entire raison d'être for the group's armed wing. In response to this potential existential threat to its military apparatus, Hezbollah called on its political and military wing to address the challenge ideologically, militarily, and politically.

Ideologically, the organization embarked on a massive campaign, simultaneously claiming that the Israeli withdrawal would not have taken place without its armed struggle and affirming that the armed struggle had to continue to protect this achievement.[149] The group also argued that because the area of the Shebaa Farms belonged to Lebanon, Israel had not fully withdrawn and that it was thus necessary to continue its attacks.

To demonstrate its relevance and effectiveness, Hezbollah's military wing remained operational in the years following the withdrawal, continuing the same strategy expressed in the 1996 memo of understanding between the group and Israel. Between 2000 and 2006, the organization mostly limited its activities, with the exception of antiaircraft firing, to the Shebaa Farms area.[150]

Hostilities might temporarily escalate elsewhere in conjunction with specific events, such as the outburst of the second intifada in the fall of 2000 or Israel's Operation Defensive Shield in the West Bank in the spring of 2002.[151] In other words, the military apparatus continued its military strategy under a "business as usual" model but further restricted its geographical scope of action. At the same time, Hezbollah's "liberation" of the south resulted in a concrete boost to the group's military apparatus: the departure of Israel enabled the organization to gain better control of the territory and to devise an even more complex support network for its operations.

The Israeli withdrawal also put its reason for having a military apparatus into question, and to deal with the threat, the organization relied heavily on its political wing. In the years between 2000 and 2005, Hezbollah's critics started to show growing dissatisfaction with the armed militia, accusing it of attempting to "monopolize the resistance," of acting without considering other Lebanese political actors, and of being a "state within the state," and they argued that, in light of the Israeli withdrawal, it might be advisable for the group to disarm.[152]

In response to these mounting external challenges to the organization's military apparatus and its goals of confronting Israel, Hezbollah reversed its policy of public separation between the group's military and political wings, employing the latter more explicitly to defend the group's possession of weapons and its military goals. The political party worked to strengthen its alliance with Syria and to become even more firmly entrenched in the electoral system.

First, leadership changes within Syria following the Israeli withdrawal led to further improvements in Hezbollah's relationship with Damascus. Hafez al-Assad died in 2000, and his political and personal relations with Hezbollah were continued and intensified by his son Bashar, who thereby provided the organization with an even stronger assurance that its operations would not be constrained by the state.[153] Meanwhile, Hezbollah began to campaign more vocally in favor of the status quo, accusing those within the political system who were criticizing the Syrian presence in Lebanon of acting against the national interest.[154] Secretary-General Nasrallah declared, "Lebanon's weapons in defense of its land, people and sovereignty were, and still are, the popular resistance and a capable, unified state with all its institutions. They are also its national unity and crucial alliance with Syria, whose forces in Lebanon bear many burdens and dangers, particularly at the current stage. The availability of all these elements is very important and maintaining them is a national duty in the first place."[155]

While campaigning actively to safeguard the Syrian presence within Lebanon, Hezbollah also dedicated substantial political efforts to its participation in the 2000 parliamentary elections so that it might become a more powerful political actor. In this electoral round, the organization was able to translate the popularity and legitimacy gained from the self-proclaimed victory over the Israelis into electoral votes. At the same time, the organization chose to campaign on socioeconomic themes, in an attempt to widen its electoral constituency.[156] This focus proved successful, as it won nine seats in the Lebanese parliament and, in a joint electoral list with Amal, gained all twenty-three seats available in southern Lebanon.[157]

Once in government, Hezbollah continued its political strategy of opposition; Hezbollah delegates were among the few newly elected politicians who refused to join the executive cabinet or to affirm the vote of confidence for Rafik Hariri, serving for the second time as prime minister.[158] Hariri returned to office in 2000 (having served a first term between 1992 and 1998) after defeating the candidate more favorably disposed to Syria, Salim al-Hus.[159] Hezbollah had supported al-Hus, and during the following years it would continue to side with the pro-Syrian forces within the Lebanese Parliament, often backing Damascus-protégé President Emile Lahoud at the expense of Prime Minister Hariri. The tense relationship between Hezbollah and the prime minister was due in large part to the government's growing efforts to reestablish control over its territory and military activities, which were met by Hezbollah's refusal to be constrained by any external actor.

The group used its political wing to block attempts to thwart the group's military activities, while the military units continued to operate without regard for the government's political agenda. For instance, Prime Minister Hariri undertook an important diplomatic visit to France and assured the Europeans that "the truth is that we really want peace. . . . Up till now, following the withdrawal of Israeli troops from Lebanon, Hezbollah has behaved well."[160] At the same time, Hezbollah decided to conduct a military operation in the Shebaa Farms; the casualties included not just a dead IDF soldier but also Rafik Hariri's international credibility.[161]

This episode led to a heated internal debate over Hezbollah's "resistance" and its right to interfere with the political process. Although Hariri publicly expressed support for Nasrallah's organization, he also affirmed that Lebanon "will spare no effort towards securing Lebanon's progress and affirming its sovereignty over its entire soil, including the remaining occupied land in Shabʿa Farms,"[162] and warned that no party should try to monopolize the resistance or claim sole responsibility for achieving the final Israeli withdrawal.[163] In the end, Syrian pressure on Hariri helped defuse the crisis between the parties and restored a surface calm in their relationship.[164]

Over the following years, Hezbollah maintained its role as opposition within the government and as antagonist to the prime minister. It again engaged actively in domestic politics in 2004, basing its campaign for the January 2004 municipal elections on socioeconomic issues and an anticorruption agenda. In the voting, Hezbollah improved markedly on its achievements of 1998 and was awarded more seats than Amal by a 2:1 ratio.[165] These results showed that Hezbollah now controlled more of the Shia community than did Amal.[166]

A few months after this electoral success, Hezbollah's political wing shifted its focus to a national political campaign to defend Syria, its ally and patron. On September 2, 2004, the UN Security Council passed Resolution 1559, calling for the disarmament of all militias within Lebanon, for fair and free elections, and, above all, for the withdrawal of all foreign forces from Lebanese soil.[167] The resolution was a response to Syria's increased meddling into the Lebanese political process, resulting in both a crackdown on internal dissent, as well as in Syria's campaign to extend President Michel Lahoud's term following its official expiration in 2004.

In response, Hezbollah protested the calls for Syrian withdrawal, adding that the group stood with "sisterly Syria under the leadership of President Bashar al-Asad in the face of all the pressures that Syria is being subjected to[.]"[168] While actively campaigning for the Syrians to stay in Lebanon, Hezbollah also supported the Damascus-backed extension of President Lahoud's term in office,[169] a move that led to the resignation of Rafik Hariri as prime minister.[170]

Although the pro-Syrian forces and Hezbollah had won this round of the conflict, their opponents did not accept defeat quietly; on the contrary, an anti-Syrian, cross-sectarian political coalition began to organize actively and to prepare for the 2005 parliamentary elections, creating new political alliances and gradually seeing Hariri rise as their de facto leader.[171]

Hezbollah responded by entrenching its role as the opposition and as the pro-Syrian party. Its political strategy of indirect involvement in the government was about to become obsolete. Hezbollah would have to take a new approach to cope with the second game-changing event in less than five years: the Syrian withdrawal.

2005–2012: The Independence Intifada and Hezbollah's New Role

The series of events that led to Syria's sudden withdrawal from Lebanon in April 2005 started with the February 14, 2005, assassination Rafik Hariri. The killing was followed by massive and coordinated public rallies, where civil society and political parties joined to demand that the Syrians leave Lebanon. This new political coalition, which originally included Hariri's Future Movement and the Sunni community, the Maronite Christian community and its main parties, as well the Druzes later became known as the "March 14 alliance," named for the date of its biggest demonstration against Syria. Countering this push for withdrawal were coordinated efforts by Hezbollah, Amal, and other pro-Syrian forces (also referred to as the "March 8 forces," after the date of their mass political demonstration). But Hezbollah's efforts were not enough, and the forces of the "Independence Intifada," backed by the international community, were able to drive the Syrians out of Lebanon on April 26, 2005.

Much as the Israeli withdrawal had thrown into question Hezbollah's mission and sense of purpose, the precipitous exit of the Syrians challenged the group by invalidating the whole paradigm behind its political strategy. Until April 2005, although it had joined the political system, Hezbollah had remained an outsider by claiming the position of opposition party and antagonist of the executive branch of government. This stance was linked to the group's need to maintain autonomy and flexibility to continue its armed struggle, but it was also connected with its ideological orientation and its critical view of the confessional political system in place within Lebanon.

By remaining at the margins of the political system and engaging both to support its military apparatus and to defend Syria, the group had found an ideal balance between acting within the political system and minimizing its direct involvement with the government. However, this strategy was premised on the vigilance and constant control of the Syrians to prevent any political actor from having the power to make decisions that could negatively affect the "resistance."

When this paradigm collapsed in April 2005, Hezbollah was forced to move one step closer toward becoming an ordinary political party, fully participating in the system. It joined the executive cabinet, first in the interim government of Najib Mikati (April–July 2005) and then in government of Foaud Saniora, formed after the 2005 parliamentary elections.[172]

Many commentators read this episode as the confirmation that the group had entered its "final moderation" stage, as at last it had become integrated into the Lebanese political system at the municipal, legislative, and executive levels. However, this interpretation does not consider the reasons behind Hezbollah's increased political involvement in the political system; more important, it fails to pay close attention to Hezbollah's behavior after the Syrians left. As the security environment suddenly became more hostile, the organization increased its political engagement so that it might better defend its military apparatus. Thus, one result of the Syrian withdrawal was that the activities of the political wing became substantially more intertwined with those of the armed wing.

Following the years of Syrian tutelage, the political party has become more active, more vocal, and more aggressive in preserving the strategic interests of the "resistance," addressing what Hezbollah perceived to be a serious threat. As Secretary-General Nasrallah explained only a month after the Syrian withdrawal, "If anyone tries to disarm the resistance, we will fight him the way the martyrs fought in Karbala."[173]

Gaining a more significant role in the political system had become a priority for Hezbollah. The group chose to form political alliances of convenience to maximize its chances of victory in the 2005 elections, including an agreement with the Hariri bloc in Beirut and with the Christian Lebanese Forces in the Baabda-Aley District of Mount Lebanon.[174] The parliamentary majority was won by the March 14 alliance, which gained seventy-two seats; while the Christian Free Patriotic Movement and the March 8 forces gained twenty-one and thirty-five seats, respectively.[175] Hezbollah controlled as many as fourteen seats in the new Parliament,[176] and it subsequently awarded a vote of confidence to the new government of Prime Minister Saniora; joining the cabinet through both a sympathizer, Trad Hamada (as minister of labor), and the Hezbollah leader Muhammad Fanayish (as minister of energy).[177]

Joining the executive transformed Hezbollah's political participation in the government, which has in turn reshaped the relations between the group's political and military wings. These changes are revealed by an analysis of two major subsequent occurrences: Hezbollah's military offense against Israel in July 2006 and Lebanon's political crisis of December 2006.

Hezbollah's military apparatus had been active throughout the political turmoil following Hariri's assassination. The group had continued its attacks on the Shebaa Farms area, while occasionally shelling Israeli towns on the border with Lebanon: both types of operation were carried out as part of its war of attrition against Israel, as well as to show its effectiveness and relevance to its supporters. In addition, Hezbollah's military apparatus had been active in the south of Lebanon, building a logistical infrastructure to support its operations (for instance, by creating underground shelters and weapons depots,) and smuggling weapons through Syria to increase its military arsenal.[178]

This period of relative quiet at the Israeli-Lebanese border came to an end after Hezbollah abducted two Israeli soldiers and killed eight more on July 12, 2006, during an ambush conducted on the Israeli side of the border.[179] This operation drew a large-scale Israeli military response, which escalated into a thirty-four-day war,[180] the bloodiest military episode inside Lebanon since the end of the civil war.

Numerous news and policy commentators pointed to the July 2006 War as a symbol of Hezbollah's radical and uncompromising nature and used it to refute those who had been arguing that the group had become more moderate and gone through a process of "Lebanonization." Instead, the Second Lebanon War—as it is known in Israel—proved that Hezbollah's political integration had been only formal and that the group was still a purely military organization.

This analysis correctly assumes that Hezbollah remains, at its core, an armed group, but it underestimates the thoroughness of its process of political integration as well as the strategic vision behind the attack that sparked the war. Hezbollah's own statements and past actions suggest that the group was not attempting to trigger a conflict with Israel but was instead acting within the existing paradigm. Kidnapping Israeli soldiers was a tool already familiar to Hezbollah.

In 2000, the group captured four Israelis, and to return their bodies, it negotiated the release of more than four hundred Arab prisoners held in custody in Israel, including four hundred Palestinians and more than twenty Lebanese nationals.[181] This episode made clear that the state of Israel was willing to pay an extremely high price to regain its own soldiers, and with this lesson in mind, Hezbollah repeatedly sought to abduct IDF personnel. Between 2005 and 2006, Hezbollah attempted five kidnappings—all of which were foiled by Israel[182]—trying to replicate the prisoner exchange that had won the organization much popular support both throughout Lebanon and within its own constituency.

Hezbollah's July 2006 ambush operation thus was not a sign of a sudden shift in approach or of military escalation but was rather a strategic miscalculation. Secretary-General Nasrallah himself admitted as much: "When we moved to carry out the capture operation . . . the way they happened—something happened that we did not intend. We were preparing for a clean capture operation."[183]

Although the July 2006 War does not represent a strategic change in the behavior of Hezbollah's military wing, it confirms another crucial trend in the organization: even as it became highly integrated into the Lebanese political system, Hezbollah also upgraded from being an important armed militia to a de facto army. Whereas the armed engagements with Israel in 1993 and 1996 had shown the group's military capacities to be superior to those of the Lebanese Armed Forces, the July 2006 War proved that Hezbollah had militarily surpassed the state of Lebanon to become a regional political and military player. The July 2006 War may therefore suggest that Hezbollah's next round of fighting with Israel cannot be on the earlier model of controlled attrition but would likely be larger in both scale and impact.

The confrontations also had substantial short-term political repercussions on the group's role and strategy within Lebanon. It was able to turn the conflict to its benefit, despite its original miscalculation of the intensity of Israel's reaction and the extended damage inflicted on its military capacity during the war, by portraying this military engagement as a "divine victory."

The group's media apparatus was extremely effective in convincing its audience that Hezbollah had prevailed and defeated the Israelis. This "success" helped boost Hezbollah's popularity within its own constituency and throughout the Arab world, mostly at the grassroots level, as did the final 2008 prisoner swap between Israel and Hezbollah, when Israel returned 199 bodies of militants along with 5 Lebanese prisoners in exchange for the bodies of its abducted soldiers.[184]

The group was also able to capitalize on its postwar reconstruction efforts. Hezbollah began at once to rebuild the war-damaged areas, and it cooperated with the government in such massive undertakings as Jihad al-Binna's Waad Project.[185] This cooperation agreement allowed Hezbollah to rebuild for free what the IDF had destroyed, in exchange for the free use of unexploited terrain. For example, if a three-story building had been razed, the group could, where zoning allowed, replace it with a five-story building, rent out the added apartments, and keep the revenues.[186]

Despite Hezbollah's popularity in the aftermath of the July 2006 War, not all political actors and groups within Lebanon were equally impressed with the "divine victory." The long-standing issue of the group's independence and at times defiance of the state reemerged as a major concern, as its right to hold weapons was openly questioned. Already on August 14, Industry Minister Pierre Amine Gemayel, a March 14 member (killed in a political assassination on November 21, 2006), had declared: "Hezbollah has to deliver its weapons to the Lebanese army, and its light weapons to the police. . . . Its fighters are welcome to join the military force and the state will then quickly regain control of all Lebanese territories."[187]

At the same time, the elected government could finally attempt to increase its control over Lebanon by deploying the Lebanese army in the south of the country, under the terms of UNSC Resolution 1701, which had ended the conflict.[188] The LAF was to operate along with UNIFIL, which had been deployed since 1978 but which now—newly tasked with monitoring the cease-fire and assisting the LAF—had a larger presence and mandate.[189] Although neither force's objective was to disarm Hezbollah, the organization nevertheless perceived them as a potential threat to its freedom of operation.

In response, Hezbollah turned with greater urgency to its political wing to restore the existing balance of power and to prevent its political adversaries from continuing to apply pressure to its military apparatus. The organization stepped up its political activism, beginning with a series of political demonstrations to force the elected government to step down in favor of a "national unity government."[190]

Hezbollah's objective was to obtain veto power in the cabinet so that it might block any decision that would compromise its core interests. Because the Lebanese constitution establishes that any policy deemed of "national interest" requires cabinet approval by a two-thirds majority, Hezbollah, together with its March 8 allies, sought eleven of the thirty available seats. The objective hence was not just to obtain political participation, but also to guarantee the right to veto, a confirmation of Hezbollah's strategy of using the political party to protect the interests of its armed militia. The Amal speaker of the chamber, Nabih Berri, organized several rounds of national reconciliation talks,[191] but Prime Minister Saniora refused to accede to the opposition's demands. The frictions escalated in November 2006, when Hezbollah and Amal cabinet members announced their resignation and the opposition launched a series of political demonstrations to bring down the elected government.[192] Following the resignation from the cabinet of the Shia Ministers, the March 8 forces and its allies (including also smaller pro-Syrian parties and the Christian Free Patriotic Movement of Michel Aoun) appealed to a Lebanese constitution clause asserting that all major sects should be represented in the executive to affirm that the government was no longer legitimate.[193] In turn, this lead to eighteen months of de facto internal political paralysis.

Interestingly, the resignation from the cabinet and the boycott of the government originated not so much over the question of obtaining veto power in the cabinet, but rather as a measure to stop the government from approving a draft protocol elaborated by the United Nations to establish a hybrid Special Tribunal to investigate and prosecute those behind the killing of Prime Minister Hariri.[194] The creation of an international tribunal was in response to the requests of the elected March 14 government, but it was opposed by Hezbollah and its March 8 allies.

To back these demonstrations, Hezbollah now counted on an even wider electoral alliance, which included the Christian Free Patriotic Movement of Michel Aoun. General Aoun, a former military commander and popular anti-Syrian politician, had returned to Lebanon in 2005 to participate in the first elections after Syria's withdrawal. His party won twenty-one seats in the parliament, and Aoun became one of the key leaders of the Christian community. Despite sharing an anti-Syrian agenda with Hariri's March 14 coalition, the FPM clashed with it on several points—notably Aoun's demand (promptly rejected by the March 14 camp) for five cabinet seats for his Change and Reform Movement—and began gradually drifting toward the Hezbollah-Amal block. In February 2006, the FPM signed a memorandum of understanding with Hezbollah, marking the beginning of a highly improbable political alliance between two parties with widely different political agendas and constituencies. The memorandum of understanding contained Hezbollah's assurance that it would disarm, given a series of conditions, including the end of the Israeli "occupation" and the liberation of all prisoners, but the agreement was generally interpreted as a tactical move on the part of the organization to create a new electoral alliance and buy time.[195]

Even in the face of this solid alliance and widespread unrest, the government refused to grant the March 8 forces their demands, and it accused the Hezbollah-led opposition of attempting a coup. Saad Hariri, who had assumed leadership of the Future Movement after his father's death, stated: "It has become very clear that the alliance existing between Hezbollah, Amal, Syria and Iran wants to bring down the Saniora government. . . . They want to control the country."[196] The result was the paralysis of the Lebanese government as its decision-making process ground almost to a halt. This political crisis, which would last until May 2008, proved that Hezbollah, despite its formal and institutional integration into the political system, was far from a status quo political party. Whereas other parties view being elected and gaining access to public office as their primary strategic interest, Hezbollah seems to see these objectives as going hand in hand with its strategic interest to safeguard the "resistance." Indeed, this episode perfectly illustrates the symbiotic evolution of the group's military and political wing and the focus of organization's political strategy.

Eventually, the political crisis escalated from peaceful protests to armed confrontation. When the government attempted to remove the Hezbollah sympathizer Wafic Shkeir from his post as security chief at the Hariri International Airport and to shut down Hezbollah's parallel communication network, the organization read these acts as a declaration of war. On May 7, 2008, it activated its military apparatus and sent its gunmen to seize the Sunni areas of West Beirut, a stronghold of Hariri's Future Movement. These seizures led to a series of bloody engagements between the different sectarian groups and to one of the worst episodes of violence since the civil war.[197]

The events of May 2008 events also showed how Hezbollah's political participation, along with its acceptance of the "rules of the game," is conditioned on the preservation of its core military interests. When the group perceives a threat to its military apparatus, it does not hesitate to abandon the logic of political accommodation. These events further strengthen the thesis that one of the principal interests of Hezbollah's military and political wings is to protect the armed struggle, and not necessarily to gain power within Lebanon (an objective that might interfere with its main goals, which are, in a way, bigger than Lebanon itself). The 2008 confrontations also represented a serious milestone for the group's military wing, as Hezbollah turned its weapons against other Lebanese citizens for the first time since the end of the civil war (aside from small-scale skirmishes with Amal supporters).

The crisis ended following a round of negotiations held in Doha (Qatar) from May 16 to May 21, 2008. There, opposing parties agreed to form a unity government, granting Hezbollah and its allies the veto power they had been demanding since the fall of 2006, and to reform the electoral law, initiate a national reconciliation process, and denounce the use of force to solve internal political conflicts.[198]

The period between the Doha agreement and the June 2009 parliamentary elections was relatively uneventful in terms of Hezbollah's political and military development. On the political front, the organization retained its veto power to prevent attacks on the "resistance" but kept a relatively low profile, attempting to allay some of the criticism and anger generated by its use of force against the Lebanese people. On the military side, the group focused on strategically regrouping and rearming.

The June 2009 elections only partially rewarded Hezbollah's post-Doha strategy: the incumbent coalition, led by Saad Hariri's Future Movement, won 71 of the 128 available seats; the Hezbollah-led March 8 coalition gained just 57 seats (with 13 going to Hezbollah itself).[199] These results, albeit skewed by the nature of the electoral system did not represent a dramatic departure from the 2005 contest. After the elections, Prime Minister Hariri and his newly elected government were again confronted with the opposition's demand to be awarded a third of the cabinet posts.[200]

This time crisis was avoided after months of internal negotiations and the external involvement of Syria and Saudi Arabia, as the parties agreed to form a "unity cabinet" composed of fifteen members of the March 14 coalition, ten members from the Hezbollah-led opposition, and five independent candidates appointed by President Michel Suleiman.[201] Three seats went to Hezbollah: the Ministry of Agriculture, the Ministry of Administrative Reforms, and the Ministry of Youth and Sports.[202] This agreement was seen as favorable to Hezbollah, which counted also on "independent" candidates to prevent the elected government from implementing reforms that would hurt the organization's strategic interests.

The creation of this national unity cabinet gave Hezbollah a more active and integrated role in the political system, a point that the organization also stressed in its 2009 manifesto. In that document, meant to be a crucial ideological and political platform, the group strongly emphasized its political agenda and its interest in promoting political reforms: "The main problem in the Lebanese political system which prevents its reform, development and constant updating is political sectarianism."[203] At the same time, recognizing that eradicating sectarianism may be unrealistic as a short-term goal, Hezbollah affirmed that "the consensual democracy will remain the fundamental basis for governance in Lebanon."[204] This last statement is particularly significant, as it shows Hezbollah increasing its political involvement and asserting its rights as a major political player. In fact, by insisting that Lebanon, a parliamentary democracy, instead follow a national unity and consensual model, Hezbollah highlighted its intention to demand more power in decision making, signaling to the elected government its determination to be consulted and involved at all levels in the political process.

At the same time, the group has been completely open about its intentions to prevent the government from discussing its weapons. Hezbollah's parliamentary leader, Mohammed Raad, warned that a political crisis would explode if the government insisted on focusing on Hezbollah's weapons.[205] Naim Qassem had also stated that "these weapons are linked to the resistance and the resistance is linked to dialogue. Dialogue requires agreement among the parties. Accordingly, this issue is not linked to the results of parliamentary elections."[206]

The organization's 2009 political manifesto likewise rejected the notion of disarmament and the option of integrating the Hezbollah apparatus into the Lebanese military forces: "the continuous Israeli threats oblige Lebanon to endorse a defensive strategy that couples between a popular resistance that participates in defending the country and an army that preserves the security of the country and safeguards its security and stability."[207]

The prospects a disarmament still appear very slim, especially considering that the group's military capability is superior to that of the army. Moreover, the sectarian nature of the LAF (which is now at least 65 percent Shia)[208] suggests that the armed forces cannot confront Hezbollah and at best could collaborate with it as its auxiliary force.

This same combination of growing political influence and simultaneous rejection of playing by the "rules of the games" can be also observed by analyzing Hezbollah's political role since the November 2009 issuance of the "Manifesto." Hezbollah in fact remained part of the Saad Hariri–led cabinet for a little over a year, between its announcement in November 2009 and January 2010, when the Hezbollah-led March 8 coalition would resign from the cabinet, causing the collapse of the government. In this case, the rupture between the March 8 and the March 14 coalitions was once again caused by Hezbollah and its need to preserve its reputation and legitimacy within its constituency.

Since its founding in May 2007, following the Lebanese government's request for the UN Security Council unilateral endorsement of its constitutive protocol,[209] the UN Special Tribunal for Lebanon (STL) had been working on Hariri's assassination case, and as of the summer of 2010, rumors spread that the tribunal was preparing to issue its first indictments. More specifically, reliable leaks asserted that the investigations had revealed the implication of Hezbollah, not Syria, the initial main suspect, in the Hariri murder.[210] And indeed, when the STL issued its first set of indictments in July 2011, the earlier leaks were confirmed as the tribunal indicted known Hezbollah figures. In response to the leaks, the organization invested in an all-out campaign to control the damage of the revelations to its reputations, while discrediting and boycotting the tribunal. Hezbollah's campaign to get Lebanon to stop collaborating with the STL and to openly question its operation led to sharp tensions with the March 14 forces, the political group who had supported the creation of the STL since the beginning. In the long run, these two mutually opposite stances with respect to the tribunal led the 10 Ministers of the Hezbollah-led March 8 coalition and an independent minister who had been appointed by President Sleiman to resign from the national unity cabinet, causing its collapse.[211]

The rise of a new parliamentary majority dominated by the March 8 forces, led by Prime Minister Najib Mikati, an independent candidate with amicable ties to Damascus, followed the end of the Hariri government. The new prime minister, after five months of internal consultations and political bargaining, in typical Lebanese fashion, finally announced the creation of a new cabinet, comprising eighteen ministers from the March 8 camp, twelve independent candidates and no members of the March 14 coalition. This development has been rightly seen as the culmination of Hezbollah's political process and of its post-2005 focus on becoming a crucial power broker of Lebanese domestic politics.

In brief, the group's political development shows that its military and political wings have consistently collaborated with and strategically complemented one another, both guided by the same integrated and consensus-oriented leadership.

On the one hand, since 1992, Hezbollah's political party has been increasingly integrated into the Lebanese political system, first at the legislative and municipal levels and subsequently as part of the executive government. The party has also joined wide cross-sectarian and political alliances with other Lebanese political actors, acting in this regard like an ordinary political party. On the other hand, Hezbollah's role as opposition party has been characterized by a clear strategy: employing all existing political tools to guarantee and safeguard the group's weapons and military apparatus. It did so first by acting as an "insider-outsider" in the years preceding the Syrian withdrawal, and then by becoming increasingly more active within the government (through its campaign to garner enough cabinet seats to veto government actions) when the political environment became more hostile to its interests.

Since the group's earliest involvement in the executive government, Hezbollah has consistently privileged its resistance agenda as well as national accommodation; thus, its political participation has led not to a stable integration in the national political arena but rather to temporary power-sharing arrangements of convenience,[212] periodically interrupted by political crises.

The military wing of the organization has also grown in size and importance, transforming from a small sectarian militia to a de facto army of regional importance. Paradoxically, as Hezbollah's political wing has moved toward legitimacy as part of the national government, it has also played a more important role as the military wing's guarantor, thus making the already existing relationship of strategic complementarity even stronger. Because the two branches operate in complete harmony, the organization alternates its periods of "moderation" and political participation in institutional politics with waves of armed confrontation and protests.

To conclude, it will be particularly relevant to look at how this dual military-political symbiosis evolves as the group faces new challenges to its legitimacy and status, as posed by the evolving "Arab awakening."

Since the beginning of the Arab uprisings in late 2010, Hezbollah has reacted to shifting political reality in the Middle East by adopting a stance of unequivocal support for the protests, especially in the cases of Tunisia, Egypt, and Bahrain. The fall of the Egyptian regime was especially welcomed by Hezbollah, which saw in the demise of President Hosni Mubarak also the decline of one of the group's main regional opponents.

Defined by the organization as an Israeli and American puppet, Mubarak had been critical of the Lebanese–Shiite group during the 2006 Lebanon war, and, in the past few years, Nasrallah's group had repeatedly expressed its opposition to the Egyptian regime, criticizing its relationships with Israel, its opposition to Hamas, and its role during the 2009 Gaza War, going as far as calling for a popular uprising against the government.[213] Similarly, Hezbollah also tried to employ the political unrest in the rest of the Middle East to boost its cause and the discourse of the "resistance." In the words of Nasrallah, the protests represented "the revolution of the poor, the free, the freedom seekers and the rejecters of humiliation and disgrace which this [Egypt] nation was subject to due to giving up to the will of America and Israel. (. . .) It is the revolution (. . .) against (. . .) the regime's policy in the Arab-Israeli struggle."[214]

These attempts to reframe the uprisings became increasingly more difficult since the beginning of the political unrest in Syria in March 2010. In fact, when the Arab Awakening finally hit Hezbollah's old-time friend and ally, the Assad regime, Nasrallah's group adopted a remarkably different posture, immediately siding with the government. The unlikely alliance between the people behind the Arab Awakening and Hezbollah has been deeply challenged by the events in Syria, showing the existing rift between the discourse of the uprisings—centered on rights and freedoms—and that of Hezbollah, paying lip service to the importance of establishing a free society while strongly supporting political repression in Syria.

This has challenged Hezbollah's status both within Lebanon as well as regionally, with Sunni March 14 leader Saad Hariri asking, "Is there in history any resistance movement that supported an oppressive ruler against oppressed people or supported despotic regimes against peoples demanding freedom?" (. . .) "it is shameful that Hezbollah views the Syrian uprising from the perspective of the Iranian interest, not the will of the Arab peoples (. . .)."[215] The pro-March 14 newspaper *Now Lebanon* has similarly stated, "Any ally of a dictator is an enemy of the Arab street."[216]

Hezbollah's support for the Assad regime represents the Achilles' heel in the group's strategy to ride the wave of the Arab Awakening, threatening the group's standing and popularity across the region. What's more, the ongoing unrest in Syria also threatens Hezbollah in a number of other ways, as prolonged internal violence and regime weakness could diminish Syria's ability to stay involved in Lebanon and continue to back Hezbollah. Finally, if the Syrian regime were to fall, Hezbollah would lose a crucial ally in the region, while the regime change could provide the "Independence Intifada" and Hezbollah's political opponents within Lebanon a powerful second wind.

For all these reasons, Hezbollah may very well find itself at a crossroads, fighting to preserve internal legitimacy, support from the Shia community within Lebanon, and regional status. As this is mostly a political challenge, one should expect the group to continue with its visible and forceful presence in the public political arena.

Assessing the Political Development of Hezbollah

The first part of the chapter looked at Hezbollah's decision to create a political wing to contest the 1992 parliamentary elections and analyzed what factors led to this important organizational development. The analysis confirmed the theory that the decision of armed groups to invest in institutional politics reflects the interplay of four main factors: (1) the group's degree of institutionalization and its related push to expand, (2) a strain in the availability of mobilization resources, (3) substantial shifts within the political opportunity structure, and (4) a significant internal commitment to reform the organization.

First, by the time the Lebanese civil war ended in the late 1980s, Hezbollah had fully transitioned from a loosely organized marginal sectarian militia to a highly structured, sophisticated, and tightly controlled organization, and thus it started to experience institutional pressures both to consolidate its power and position as well as to expand and grow. The changing political circumstances within Lebanon and the rising internal competition with the other main Lebanese Shia political actor, Amal, also pushed Hezbollah to find a venue to reassert its autonomy and legitimacy. The creation of a political wing would help Hezbollah to achieve both objectives: first, it provided a means to accommodate with the shifting political environment, thus allowing the group to remain relevant and to preserve its legitimacy. The creation of a political party would also allow the group to expand and to incorporate new supporters, building on the group's increased popularity within the Shia community, largely a result of its continued armed confrontation with Israel in the previous decade.

Second, in 1992, Hezbollah was allowed to exploit the openings within the political system created by the end of the civil war, the Taif Agreement, and the progressive "normalization" of the political life within Lebanon, marked both by the resumption of the regular election cycles and by the introduction of electoral reforms that equalized the number of Muslim and Christian seats. In addition, the beginning of the Syrian "tutelage" allowed Hezbollah to enter the realm of institutional politics with a powerful ally on its side and with the guarantee that the group's right to bear arms and to continue its armed struggle against Israel would not be questioned within the newly elected parliament.

The decision to invest in institutional politics was also a by-product of a series of external factors, first the temporary change of direction in Iranian foreign policy in the immediate aftermath of Khomeini's death, resulting in a decline of material and financial support for Hezbollah, which encouraged the organization to focus on diversifying both its sources of funding and its range of activities, again resulting in an incentive to create a political wing. The interplay of these organizational, institutional, and external factors, together with the rise of a substantial internal commitment to change and to pursue institutional politics, led Hezbollah to create a political wing to take part in the 1992 parliamentary elections.

The second part of the chapter examined the relationship between the group's political and armed factions, testing the hypothesis that the internal power distribution and the type of relationship existing between the group's political group and military apparatus are a key factor in determining whether a given organization will undergo strategic change, leading eventually to relinquishing its military wing. The research affirms that an armed group's institutional development need not entail affirming its political branch at the expense of the military apparatus. On the contrary, the research predicts waves of convergence and competition, postulating that strategic change is possible only when a prolonged perceived disequilibrium between the armed and the political factions causes leaders to question the legitimacy of one faction's institutional logic.

Again, Hezbollah proves to be a useful case to test this hypothesis: the group's highly cohesive and integrated structure and the ongoing cooperation between the group's military and political wings confirms the hypothesis that no matter how well integrated the political wing becomes in a given political system and how powerful a role it plays, a group will have no concrete incentives to relinquish its armed wing and restructure its strategy if the political and military factions lack strategic competition and conflicting institutional logics.

Since its founding, Hezbollah has shown a high degree of internal coordination and integration among the group's different branches, and even after the creation of the group's political wing, Hezbollah's political and military activities have continued to be strictly supervised by the same group of leaders, led by the charismatic Secretary-General Hassan Nasrallah. This organizational arrangement ensured the internal cohesion of the group, while lowering the potential for internal disunity of competition. Even though the original decision to take part in elections in 1992 was the result of a prolonged internal struggle between two different leadership cadres, the organization ultimately reasserted internal cohesion and unity by marginalizing and expelling the losing faction.

Since then, Hezbollah has developed its military and political apparatus harmoniously. This is not to say that the group did not undergo any changes to join the political arena. First, in the time leading to the 1992 elections, Hezbollah revised its organizational structure and began to recast its identity as a Lebanese national movement, underplaying its links with Iran and its revolutionary goals within Lebanon. The organization agreed to work within the confessional system, and it began to create pragmatic cross-sectarian alliances with other Lebanese political actors to increase its degree of political power and influence.

The group highly invested in preparing and campaigning for the 1992 elections, but its focus on political participation did not compromise its military activities, nor did it generate frictions between the political and the military wing. On the contrary, the election of eight Hezbollah members of Parliament in 1992 was accomplished not only by the group's political bureau alone but also by a joint effort of every branch of the organization.

After joining the Lebanese Parliament, Hezbollah's political participation was very much that of a "resistance party": the group refused to take part in the executive government, focused its efforts and campaigns on promoting its armed attacks against Israel, and largely refused to discuss its military activities, maintaining absolute autonomy from the government. Hezbollah emerged as a strong opposition party acting as an "insider-outsider."

This role only changed in 2005 when, following the Syrian withdrawal from Lebanon, Hezbollah's paradigm of indirect involvement became obsolete. Without the Syrians to guarantee that Hezbollah's right to wage war against Israel and to bear arms would not be questioned, the group decided to step up its political involvement and finally joined the executive government, thus becoming a more active and entrenched political party.

At the same time, the political party and the military wing became even more intertwined, as Hezbollah's political wing became even more important and active in defending the group's military apparatus. This trend has been only reinforced in the past years, as Hezbollah has shifted its political strategy from marginal participation to strong involvement within the Lebanese government, culminating in its current focus on maintaining the veto power within the executive cabinet, so that the party might block any decision that would compromise its military interests.

Although Hezbollah has become a mainstream and powerful Lebanese domestic player, it has refused to play by the same rules as all the other political parties.

Whenever the core strategic interests of the "resistance" are in potential danger, the group's logic of political accommodation is placed on hold while the group resorts to other means (including the use of armed force) to reestablish the status quo. The group's armed takeover of Beirut in May 2008 substantiates this trend.

The success and influence of Hezbollah's political party are closely related to the development and prosperity of its military apparatus, and when the latter's core interests are threatened, the logic of political accommodation is temporarily replaced so that the strategic balance between the political and military factions can be restored. Accordingly, the continuous cooperation between the group's military and political wings seem to indicate that the organization has no incentive to pursue strategic change in the form of strategic reorganization. The political and the military factions have coexisted and mutually reinforced each other for the past decades, and, at the moment, nothing indicates that this relationship is bound to change.

The Palestinian Hamas

Political Participation between Internal Cohesion and Dissent

The reasons behind choosing to analyze the political evolution of the Palestinian Hamas partially coincide with those that led to the selection of Hezbollah as a case study. Hamas also exemplifies a highly institutionalized and sophisticated organization, and thus it can also be used as a "least likely" case study to test the cyclical model of political wing formation and development.

Hamas, like Hezbollah, represents a high-profile case study of an armed organization that turned to politics. Hamas's political wing holds a record of significant political achievements, culminating in the group's electoral victory in the Palestinian legislative elections in 2006. Because of the global relevance of the Arab-Israeli conflict and its affect on Middle Eastern stability and security, understanding and assessing Hamas's political role and internal development has real-world policy implications that transcend the Palestinian political arena.

Since the beginning of Hamas's involvement in institutional politics, there has been a high degree of international attention given to understanding this new phenomenon and classifying the armed-political organization. The international community's view of Hamas (and specifically Western countries' classifications) seems more cohesive than the varying perspectives adopted on Hezbollah. Countries such as the United States and Israel have consistently rejected granting recognition to Hamas's political wing, and, from the outset, have treated the organization as a terrorist entity. The US Department of State first included Hamas on its list of groups engaged in terrorist activities in the 1993 publication *Patterns of Global Terrorism.*[1] The group was later specifically labeled as a terrorist organization through a presidential executive order in 1995, and it was subsequently included in the US Department of State's 1997 list of "Foreign Terrorist Organizations." Since then, Hamas has remained on the FTO list, and the United States has not altered its posture in light of Hamas's 2006 electoral victory.[2]

The European Union maintained for a while a formal division between Hamas's political wing and its military apparatus, placing the military wing on its list of terrorist organizations while asserting the existence of a de facto separation between the group's military and political activities.[3] This posture changed in 2003, when, during the peak of the violence of the second intifada, the EU reversed its previous "two entities" policy and included Hamas, as a whole, on its terrorist watch list.[4]

The current classification has the merit of highlighting (though perhaps overestimating) the organizational cohesion between the group's military apparatus and its political party, which will be examined in-depth in the sections that follow, but it also fails to acknowledge the plurality of identities possessed by the Palestinian Hamas, which operates simultaneously as an armed organization, a sociopolitical movement and a political party.

Background

Origins and Early History

The history and development of Hamas are deeply connected to the evolution of the Palestinian political arena. The organization cannot be understood without grasping the pluralistic nature of Palestinian politics. Palestinian society has historically been dominated by a variety of different sociopolitical groups and organizations, and its political life has been affected by traditional clan leaders, socioeconomic elites, formal party leaders, and opposition movements and civil society groups.[5] Because of this complexity, it is important to relate the creation and development of Hamas to the broader Palestinian political context.

Hamas is the acronym of Islamic Resistance Movement (*Harakat al Muqawama al-Islamiyya*) and means "courage" or "zeal."[6] Hamas was officially founded in 1987–1988, shortly after the outbreak of the first intifada, although its roots can be traced to the late 1930s and the development of the Egyptian-based Muslim Brotherhood in Palestine.[7]

Founded in Egypt in 1928 by Hasan al-Banna, the Sunni revivalist Muslim Brotherhood rapidly spread through the Arab world, attempting to establish a society based on Islam and calling for the creation of a political system and state modeled after the values and aspirations of Islam.

As early as 1936, after the first Arab general strike in Palestine, the Muslim Brotherhood began actively to support local protests through the Central Committee for Aid to Palestine, headed by al-Banna.[8] The group's presence in Palestine expanded in the following years, and, by 1945, the first local branch of the Brotherhood had begun to operate in Jerusalem.[9] The group further increased its presence and boosted its constituency in the years preceding the 1948 war, when it played an important role in mobilizing and rallying different Palestinian groups together in preparation for the outbreak of hostilities. The organization later split because of the 1948 war and the creation of the state of Israel, and two additional permanent branches of the Brotherhood were later established in the West Bank and in the Gaza Strip.[10]

The West Bank branch lost its autonomy and was incorporated into the Jordanian chapter of the Brotherhood immediately after the 1948 split. Within Jordan, the group focused its activities on implementing a social, rather than a political, agenda, and it invested in maintaining a positive relation with the Hashemite Kingdom.[11]

After the 1948 war and the 1952 fall of the Egyptian monarchy, the Muslim Brotherhood was allowed to prosper in Egyptian-controlled Gaza, where it maintained its independence and gained both political strength and popular legitimacy through social and educational programs aimed at the Islamization of society. The relationship between the Brotherhood and the Egyptian regime then sharply deteriorated after 1954, with the rise in power of Gamal Abdel Nasser: At that time, the organization was banned in Egypt and in Gaza, forcing the group to become clandestine.[12] The Brotherhood's popularity and influence became negligible in the decades that followed. This situation was reversed with the beginning of the Israeli occupation of Gaza after the 1967 war, when the ban on the Muslim Brotherhood was finally lifted and the group was allowed to reorganize.[13]

After the 1967 war, the Muslim Brotherhood grew exponentially within Gaza, as it reasserted its role as a revivalist and socioreligious movement aimed at reshaping and revitalizing Muslim identity in Palestine. The Brotherhood also avoided direct political confrontation with respect to Israel and the Palestine Liberation Organization (PLO).[14]

Instead, it focused on creating a *dawa*[15] infrastructure and network, on maintaining an active presence in mosques, and on controlling the main religious organizations and institutions in Gaza. For instance, Sheikh Ahmed Yassin, one of the leaders of the Muslim Brotherhood and later founder of Hamas, created the Al-Mujamma Al-Islami (Islamic Center) in 1973, through which the Brotherhood directly controlled a large part of the religious establishment within Gaza, including a significant portion of Gaza's *waqfs* (religious endowments).[16]

The Brotherhood's popularity increased during the 1970s, although the group's lack of direct involvement in opposing the Israeli occupation started to create internal problems and frictions that, eventually, led to a first internal split in the early 1980s and to the creation of the Palestinian Islamic Jihad group.[17]

Sheikh Yassin, Muslim Brotherhood leader and head of the Islamic Center—

albeit he did not endorse a change of strategy for the organization—reacted to the rise of armed Islamic movements in Gaza by attempting to form two paramilitary units in early 1983. He was later arrested by the Israeli authorities and held in custody for more than ten months, stalling the military evolution of the group.[18] This increased activism in the early 1980s also came as a reaction to the PLO's military defeat in Lebanon in 1982, an important event that gradually started to shift the center of gravity of Palestinian politics and military activism against Israel from the Diaspora to the Occupied Palestinian Territories, both in the West Bank and in Gaza.

With the eruption of the December 1987 intifada and the increased armed operations and activism of the Islamic Jihad, the Muslim Brotherhood found itself under growing pressure to become more actively involved against the Israeli occupation. The organization first reacted to the beginning of the confrontations between Israel and the Palestinian population by issuing a leaflet that openly endorsed the uprising and urged people to join the protests.[19] Moreover, the Muslim Brotherhood leadership decided to create a separate armed wing to join the intifada directly: Hamas was born.

The creation of Hamas was important to the Brotherhood as it allowed the group to maintain a certain degree of doctrinal consistency. The Brotherhood had openly stated that the time for jihad had not come for Palestine, asserting that jihad should only be implemented after completing the internal process of Islamization of the Palestinian society. The creation of Hamas allowed the group to create and maintain a separate branch to join the armed confrontations without rejecting its earlier doctrine, thus preserving a certain degree of internal consistency.[20] At the same time, the Brotherhood needed Hamas to stay politically relevant in the new political environment created by the intifada, and to deal with the growing competition arising from new armed factions, like the Palestinian Islamic Jihad. The combination of these two opposing needs led to the establishment of Hamas as a separate armed wing of the Brotherhood.

Hamas: Military, Political, and Social Evolution

The intifada marked the beginning of Hamas's direct involvement in the armed struggle against the Israeli occupation, as well as its increased role in internal Palestinian politics. After the outbreak of the intifada, Hamas launched its first violent campaign, known as the "knives war," which involved stabbing individual Israelis.[21] At this stage, the group's role was not as significant as the one played by its secular-nationalist counterpart, Fatah, through its control of the PLO.

Hamas's direct participation in the 1987 protests slowly allowed the group to increase its political power and status, as the intifada was both a rebellion directed outward—against the Israeli occupation—and inward, to challenge traditional authority within Gaza and the West Bank and to redefine the Palestinian polity.

From the outset, Hamas could count on two main advantages when challenging Fatah and its monopoly over Palestinian politics: (1) its Islamic identity and (2) its local orientation. Unlike Arafat's Diaspora-based movement, Hamas was a truly local organization, rooted in Gaza and integrated in the Palestinian reality on the ground.[22]

Hamas early on established a political niche for itself by questioning Fatah and its policies in a process that would eventually lead the group to emerge as the Islamist-nationalist alternative to Fatah. As early as 1988, after the Palestinian National Council met in Algiers in November of the same year and declared its de facto agreement to a two-state solution in the context of the Arab-Israeli conflict, Hamas was able to first assume the role of political opponent to both Fatah and the PLO by condemning what the group interpreted as the PLO's "moderate drive."[23]

The competition and tension that characterized the relations between Fatah and Hamas during the first intifada built on the historic opposition that already existed between the Muslim Brotherhood—and the Islamic movement in general—and Fatah, which was a deeply nationalist and secular organization. The rift between Hamas and Fatah was ideological, along secular-religious lines, but also political, as both camps were interested in monopolizing political power and force within the occupied Palestinian territories.

Hamas's political and armed campaign to establish itself as a main Palestinian political actor received a temporary setback in 1989, when Israel arrested the group's leader, Sheikh Yassin, along with several important leaders and cadres. The organization was later able to regroup under the leadership of Musa Abu Marzouq.[24] Moreover, around the same time, two events marked Hamas's transition from a marginal player to a central armed group and an increasingly powerful political actor: the Gulf War and the creation of a structured military wing.

First, during the Gulf War, Hamas opposed both the American intervention and the Iraqi invasion of Kuwait, unlike the PLO, which had initially sided with Iraq. This showed that Hamas had a pretty solid understanding of regional and global dynamics, and it allowed the organization to gain international credibility and political leverage and to receive financial benefits from the rest of the Arab world.[25] Criticizing Iraq allowed Hamas to distance itself further from the PLO, to erode part of the latter's supporting base, and to strengthen its ties and form a temporary alliance with Saudi Arabia.

In the same year, Ziccaria Walid Akhel established the Izz al-Din al-Qassam Battalions, Hamas's military wing.[26] The new suborganizational apparatus was focused solely on carrying out military operations against the Israeli Defense Forces and Israeli citizens, and this compartmentalization of tasks led to a better implementation of the jihad strategy in Palestine. While boosting its international and domestic credibility and its military apparatus, Hamas also became involved in grassroots-political activities, by participating, for instance, in elections of professional associations, unions, and students and youth organizations.

Israel reacted to Hamas's increasing power by attempting to downsize and weaken the movement. Specifically, in December 1992, Prime Minister Yitzhak Rabin signed an executive order authorizing the expulsion of 418 Hamas and Islamic Jihad members from the Occupied Territories. Most of the expellees went to southern Lebanon, although by 1993, they were allowed to return to Gaza and the West Bank. By the time the "exiled" Hamas leadership returned to the West Bank and Gaza, the group had learned from the Lebanese Hezbollah's tactics, and it was able to resume its military campaigns against Israel with increasing lethality and sophistication.[27]

In the Gaza Strip, Hamas became increasingly more active in the years preceding and following the 1993 Oslo Declaration of Principles between Israel and the PLO , which the group vehemently opposed. Even in the years preceding the Oslo Accords Hamas had consistently protested the PLO's discussions regarding Israel, criticizing the 1991–1993 Madrid process, a series of bilateral talks between Israel, Jordan, Syria, and the PLO.[28]

Although the group protested the agreement mostly on ideological grounds, Hamas also saw the "peace process" as a direct challenge to its political power and status and as a worrisome boost to its historical rival, Fatah. To strengthen its position, Hamas created a broader anti-Oslo political coalition, the Ten Resistance Organization (TRO).

This loose umbrella group included both Islamist Hamas as well as secular, leftist Palestinian organizations. It was created ad hoc during the October 1991 World Conference in Support of the Islamic Revolution in Palestine, organized by Iran.[29] The TRO allowed these disparate organizations to coordinate their protests and rejection of the Oslo Accords and of the subsequent creation of the Palestinian Authority (PA), and it simultaneously consolidated Hamas's role as the leading opposition movement to Fatah.

Political confrontation increased between Hamas and the PLO in the early 1990s. Hamas accused the PLO of losing its status as "sole representative of the Palestinian people" because of its "moderate drive" and its endorsement of a peace process with Israel. Hamas also intensified its attacks against Israel both to express its opposition to the ongoing negotiations and to affirm its role as the leading Palestinian armed organization. Hamas adopted violence and terrorism as its main tactics when confronting its Israeli enemy.

The February 1994 attack against Palestinian civilians at the Cave of the Patriarchs in Hebron by a Jewish settler was the precipitant of this transformation and facilitated Hamas's escalation of violence from individual killings and kidnappings to large-scale terrorist attacks. The first car bomb attack occurred on April 6, 1994, when a bomb was detonated on a bus in the center of Afula, killing eight civilians.[30] These terrorist operations carried out by Hamas in the aftermath of Oslo and the creation of the PA also contributed to escalating further the preexisting tensions between Hamas and Fatah, which was now in charge of the newly created PA.

Hamas's strategy was to criticize the PA openly while avoiding direct armed confrontation with Fatah. Despite the general absence of armed hostilities between the two groups, Hamas and Fatah periodically clashed throughout the 1990s, especially when the PA attempted to crack down on or regulate Hamas's military activities.

The creation of the PA in 1994 and the subsequent 1996 legislative elections had a profound effect on Hamas's overall strategy. These events first pushed the group toward discussing the creation of a political wing to compete in the upcoming elections. On that occasion, Hamas decided against taking part in the 1996 elections directly and openly, preferring to avoid any direct involvement with a process created by the Oslo Accords. Still by the mid-1990s the group began to discuss its role within the Palestinian political arena, a fundamental step toward creating a political party.

Hamas's increased interest in institutional politics also reflected the organization's attention toward the inclination and preferences of its constituency. From the beginning, Hamas was highly sensitive toward the shifts in the Palestinian public opinion. It always sought to boost its popularity and number of supporters, which represented a highly heterogeneous constituency and came from virtually all different sectors and strata of society.

In the years following the creation of the PA, Hamas found itself in a challenging position. Most Palestinians supported the peace process and the PA, while the number of supporters of Hamas diminished.[31] Hamas's legitimacy crisis abruptly ended concurrently with the repeated failure of the negotiations between Israel and the PLO during the latter part of the 1990s.

The outbreak of the second intifada in 2000 allowed Hamas to increase its political power and strengthen its role as the second-most powerful group after Fatah, allowing it to challenge the supremacy and hegemony of its secular counterpart. In the years following the beginning of the second intifada, Hamas became the most active Palestinian armed group fighting Israel. Terror was the main tactic employed, mostly through bombings, kidnappings, and assassinations, with the aim of both projecting Hamas's strength and disrupting the functioning of the government and civil society. By the end of 2001, in addition to carrying out suicide and car bombings, Hamas began to employ Qassam rockets to attack the Israeli population from within the Gaza Strip. Rocket attacks, although capable of causing only limited injuries, were capable of disrupting the Israeli society, while asserting control over territory, projecting power, and inspiring other terrorist organizations.[32]

Hamas also continued its internal discussion regarding the creation of a formal political wing and the possibility of directly participating in institutional politics. While the organization began to set the stage for its formal entry into institutional politics as early as 1994, the group did not actually join the political system until after the death of historical Fatah leader and PA President Yasser Arafat in November 2004. Following Arafat's death and the gradual opening of the Palestinian political system, Hamas took an active role in domestic political life, first, by running in the 2004–5 municipal elections, and then by taking part in the 2006 legislative elections. Since Hamas's victory in the 2006 elections and its subsequent takeover of the Gaza Strip in 2007, the armed-political movement has become deeply entrenched in institutional politics through direct governance. Assessing the institutional development of the Palestinian Hamas has led the international community to adopt two substantially diverging narratives about the group's evolution, similar to the dichotomous framework employed by many scholars and policy makers when examining Hezbollah.

On the one hand, the "moderation" school of thought on Hamas asserts that the organization has a fundamentally pragmatic nature and affirms that, through its development, it has pursued an increasingly accommodation-seeking agenda. To highlight this trend, scholars point out the cost–benefit analysis basis of Hamas's decision-making process, stressing that the group's ultimate objective—the establishment of an Islamic state in "Palestine"—has been pursued through a policy of "controlled violence, calculated participation, and negotiated existence."[33]

Hamas has constantly balanced its need to show its military strength to its enemy with the desire to maintain a strong internal legitimacy. All the tactics and strategies adopted by the organization have to be understood as an attempt to balance between these two concrete priorities. While at times violence against Israel has been used to boost domestic support and recruit for the group, there have also been occasions when terrorism against Hamas's main enemy has been a liability for the group.

Hamas has relied on very pragmatic considerations when deciding to conduct its military operations: Political and popular support systematically influence Hamas's decision-making process. For instance, when the Palestinians at large seemed to reject the armed struggle alternative and to prefer the option of negotiations, Hamas both focused its internal discussions on joining the political system and substantially diminished its external attacks against Israel (for example, in the 1998–2000 pre-intifada period).[34] As Hamas increased its political status and internal power, the group has also showed the capacity to accompany its uncompromising ideological premises with a more pragmatic political discourse.

Hamas's nature has always been pluralistic, and the group has always been active politically and socially. More specifically, its activities have been focused outward as much as inward—within Palestinian society—with the objective of enhancing its legitimacy and attracting new recruits and supporters. Examples of such "inward-looking policies" include the creation of a broad welfare system, the development of continuous media campaigns, and the maintenance of a massive presence on the ground to strengthen social ties with the population.

On the other hand, the second main school of thought on Hamas dismisses the notion of Hamas as an accommodation-seeking entity and refers to the increasing political involvement of the group as a tactical maneuver that fails to alter the radical agenda of the organization. Supporters of this school may refer to Hamas's unmodified 1988 charter—calling for the destruction of Israel—as well as to its consistent role as spoiler in the context of the Israeli–Palestinian peace process. To highlight Hamas's failed political integration and moderation, backers of this school also refer to the consistent employment of violence and terrorism to emphasize the military core of Hamas's organizational structure, as well as the increasing use of armed force against other Palestinian groups in the aftermath of the 2006 electoral victory.

These perspectives can provide an important starting point for a more in-depth inquiry into the political evolution of the Palestinian Hamas if they are brought together into a more "holistic" framework. This can be accomplished by looking at the organization's alternate stages of armed struggle and political accommodation, as well as at the consistent internal divisions within Hamas.

Organization and Ideology

Internal Organization and Leadership Structure

Hamas's organizational structure has undergone a series of changes since its founding in the late 1980s. It has become more complex and bureaucratic and encompasses a larger number of internal subunits, committees, and affiliate organizations. This transformation was a response to the group's institutionalization and its growing size and power, which demanded a more formalized organizational structure, and to the need to adapt and restructure itself according to the external situation, in terms of responding to Israeli countermeasures and gathering Palestinian support. Currently, Hamas is formally organized as a bureaucratic hierarchy[35] and has an internal vertical chain of command topped by the Shura Council, followed by the Political Bureau, a number of smaller regional Shura councils, and local cells.[36]

The Shura Council (Majlis al-Shura) is in charge of overseeing and formulating Hamas's policies and grand strategy. It is composed of Hamas representatives from Gaza, the West Bank, the leadership in exile, and the Israeli prisons.[37] The composition of this body—including the number and identity of its members—has traditionally been kept secret, although some estimates assert that the Shura Council has at least thirty-two members.[38] The Shura Council, whose members are elected by members of the regional councils, has the power to issue binding decisions, and it is the final organizational decision maker. Among its key responsibilities, the council also elects the group's Political Bureau.[39]

Until early 2012, the bureau was headed by Khaled Mashal and located in Damascus.[40] Following the rising level of violence and instability within Syria, and in light of the deteriorating relations between Hamas and the Syrian regime led by Bashar al-Assad as a by-product of the protests, the bureau vacated its headquarters in Damascus. Hamas's lack of strong support for Assad and his regime strained the relations between Hamas and Damascus, leading the Political Bureau to seek to relocate its premises.

Similarly, the ongoing relocation of the bureau may also result in a change in leadership, as Khaled Mashal announced his intention to step down from its leadership position in early 2012.

The bureau is dominated by Hamas's "external" leadership and is in charge of the group's day-to-day operations, as well as the implementation of the Shura Council's policy directives. In practice, these activities include foreign policy, Diaspora relations and funding, propaganda, military affairs, and internal security.[41] The bureau directly oversees all these activities, and it operates by a number of smaller district committees (seven in the Gaza Strip and five in the West Bank), subcommittees, and affiliated groups, such as Hamas's social services organizations.[42]

Also connected with the Political Bureau, albeit with a great degree of autonomy, are the Izz al-Din al-Qassam Battalions, founded in 1991 to be Hamas's armed wing and named after Izz al-Din al-Qassam, Palestine's first leader who conducted guerrilla operations against the British in the 1930s.[43] Hamas's armed wing is funded by and technically subordinate to the Political Bureau, but the organization maintains a separate, decentralized, and secretive cellular structure, encompassing both the district and regional operational units, as well the internal security apparatus (the Majd).[44]

At a formal level, Hamas's decision-making process relies on internal deliberation and consultation to reach internal strategic decisions, and it is not uncommon for the Shura Council to consult with other subordinated bodies as well as with Hamas members and activists before deliberating on a specific matter. The process somewhat adopts the "democratic centralism" principle of early Communist parties: allowing internal debate and consultation in formulating policies while mandating compliance once such policies have been adopted by the executive body of the organization.[45]

Within the Shura Council, decisions are adopted by consensus, although the highly secretive nature of the body (to the point where members are not always informed of the identity of all the other members) prevents knowing how the organization deals with cases in which the Shura members sharply disagree over a given question.[46] Hamas's de jure formal and vertical internal chain of command is matched, however, by a de facto high degree of local autonomy and decentralization in the daily operations of the group, and by the existence of a parallel horizontal and informal organizational structure based on personal relations and preexisting bonds and loyalties.

This informal and horizontal power structure operates side by side with the formal structure both at the local and grassroots level.[47] The actual implementation of the Shura Council's decisions is at times slowed down or even hindered by local autonomy. Even the formal hierarchy of power can at times be blurry, and the internal compartmentalization and division of power can be extremely fluid. As a result of this decentralization and organizational fluidity, and despite the strong organizational emphasis on cohesion and conformity, intraorganizational conflicts are not uncommon.

First, as already mentioned, the Izz al-Din al-Qassam Battalions have shown a consistent degree of autonomy, at times openly contradicting both the Political Bureau and the Shura Council's directives,[48] and producing organizational tensions along the armed–political wing divide. Second, the Political Bureau has also repeatedly transcended its role as the Shura Council's executive arm to formulating and implementing its own policies, while Hamas's individual leaders also at times have been at odds with one another, and they have shown this internal disagreement by publicly issuing mutually contradictory declarations.

Although generally cohesive, internal divisions along the armed wing and political leadership line, and at times between external versus local leaders, have periodically occurred within Hamas. Hamas's cohesion problem is also attributable to its multipolar leadership, geographically dispersed between "exile," the Gaza Strip, and Israeli prisons. Also the group has been characterized by frequent internal turnovers and reorganizations, mostly as a result of Israel's military campaigns against the group. For instance, the "external" leadership first shifted from an auxiliary organ to a central role in the organization's decision-making structure as a result of the 1989 incarceration of the group's founder, Sheikh Ahmed Yassin.[49] Later on, the group had to reorganize after Israel killed two of its main leaders, founder Yassin and Abd al-Aziz Rantisi, in March 2004, which also forced the group to cease to disclose its leadership structure publicly.[50] In the aftermath of Yassin's death, the group does seem to lack the figure of a central leader and decision maker, as no one has been able to replace Yassin and to acquire the same level of personal decision-making power. Still, Hamas can rely on a number of prominent figures that definitely contribute to shaping Hamas's direction and guide its development. In addition to the already mentioned Political Bureau chief Khaled Mashal, the main organizational leaders include deputy head Musa Abu Marzouq;[51] Mahmoud Zahhar, historic Gaza-based leader and foreign minister; Ismail Haniyeh, senior leader and prime minister in the Hamas-led government; and, until his assassination by Israel in November 2012, the leader of the military wing Ahmad Ja'abari.

Although it is undeniable that the "external" leadership does have a high degree of influence on the rest of the organization, it would be reductive to assert that the Diaspora is in charge of Hamas's strategy and is able to impose it on the local leadership. The group is simultaneously influenced, through the Shura Council, by five centers of power: (1) the Political Bureau leadership, (2) the Diaspora, (3) the prisoners, (4) the local political leaders in Gaza (and, to a much lesser degree, in the West Bank), and (5) the Qassam brigades and its leadership.

Through its organizational structure, Hamas oversees a plurality of activities that complement its politico-military agenda and contribute to increasing the group's legitimacy and popularity among its Palestinian constituency. First, under the supervision of the Political Bureau, Hamas maintains a media and communication department, which is responsible for media coverage and press releases. In the context of the media's overexposure of the Arab-Israeli conflict, the organization developed a strategic interest in communicating through mainstream media and through media owned by sympathetic groups, and through its own media channels.

Starting in the mid-1990s, Hamas established a number of publications, while also counting on a number of sympathetic media, such as *Al-Risalah,* which was first published in 1997 and has since become the group's biweekly newspaper.[52]

Hamas has been also actively broadcasting through its radio station, al-Aqsa Voice, and its new satellite television channel, al-Aqsa TV, a replica of Hezbollah's more established al-Manar.[53] It is active on the Internet, through web pages created by sympathizers, and through directly affiliated websites and web-based publications.

Second, building on the legacy and work of the Muslim Brotherhood in Gaza, Hamas continues to maintain an effective and extensive welfare system, providing education, health care, and food distribution and financial support for indigents through its local network. Hamas has maintained the Muslim Brotherhood's focus on social issues, as well as the group's objective to Islamize Palestinian society through grassroots and social work, and thus, while evolving into a more bureaucratic political and military organization, it never ceased to operate as a social movement organization.

Hamas's dawa infrastructure, an appendix of the Political Bureau, is centered on mosques and affiliated charities in the West Bank and the Gaza Strip, and it benefits Hamas members and their families, as well as the Palestinian population at large. The Islamic Center (al-Mujamma' al-Islami), founded by Sheikh Yassin in the 1970s, traditionally played a crucial role in coordinating this extensive welfare apparatus through its seven committees: preaching and guidance, welfare, education, charity, health, sport, and reconciliation. Through these institutions, Hamas continued the Brotherhood's traditional work in religious education and proselytism, and today, the group is still heavily involved in religious institutions, including mosques and *zakat* committees, as well as in Palestinian basic and higher education.

Even before 2000, Hamas controlled more than 65 percent of all primary education in the Gaza Strip; and to this date, it is in charge of the majority of the kindergartens in the Gaza Strip.[54] Hamas also holds considerable influence over Gaza's second-largest university (after the Fatah-affiliated Al-Azhar), the Islamic University of Gaza, an Islamic higher education institution created in 1978 that boasts a student body of about eleven thousand five hundred pupils.[55]

Hamas has expanded its realm of activities beyond the classic boundaries of the Brotherhood's social work, and the group is today involved in poverty alleviation and community development.[56] For instance, the group's Islamic social institutions directly support and provide relief to a large number of Palestinians, while the group also directly supports hospitals and health clinics in Gaza.[57]

Hamas's welfare system and its social activities are crucial to maintaining a wide base of supporters and followers within Palestinian society, and this infrastructure has also been vital in allowing the organization to distance itself radically from the image of corruption and inefficiency associated with the Palestinian Authority and the Fatah party.

To maintain this costly apparatus, Hamas developed an independent funding system that effectively integrates revenues from local activities with funds from external donors and sponsors. Throughout its sociopolitical and military development, this self-financing model has been effective at achieving organizational sustainability.

Hamas's financial needs and responsibilities increased dramatically after its rise to power and the subsequent international boycott against its government. To meet these financial demands, Hamas relies on various sources of wealth, including affiliated international charities and donations from individuals, either sympathizers or from Diaspora groups. In the past decade, the international community and Israel have conducted an extensive counterterrorism campaign to identify and freeze these external sources of support, though a number of affiliated organizations have managed to survive. Hamas also finances its activities through a wide range of business enterprises—legitimate business, illegal revenues, and criminal activities. In the aftermath of the group's electoral victory in Gaza in 2006, Hamas has been able to collect revenues and taxes from within Gaza and run an extensive smuggling network of weapons and contraband goods through a system of underground tunnels between Gaza and Egypt.[58] Historically, Hamas has also been able to count on a certain level of state support, for example, from Iran and Saudi Arabia. While Saudi Arabia's support diminished dramatically after Hamas's electoral victory in 2006, Iran's financial support increased in the past decade. Through this complex combination of self-generation of revenues, sponsors, and supporters, Hamas has created an economic base that allows the group to implement its strategy effectively, despite the substantial financial challenges that it faced following its electoral victory in 2006.

Hamas's Ideology and Its Political Adaptation

Hamas's main ideological document is the 1988 Charter of the Islamic Resistance Movement[59]—the constitutive *manifesto* of the organization—although the group's ideological framework has, over time, been substantially developed and adapted. Some scholars claim that the charter is no longer a central reference point of the organization.[60] In the charter, Hamas identifies itself as the local branch of the Muslim Brotherhood and stresses its role as an Islamic Palestinian movement, combining its religious identity with a local nationalist agenda and an ethos of *wataniyya* (nationalism) and patriotism. Unlike other Islamist movements, Hamas never rejected nationalism in favor of a broader Pan-Islamic agenda; on the contrary, it formulated the Palestinian national struggle in Islamic terms, thus subordinating nationalism to Islam and contributing to Islamize Palestinian identity. The organization constructs its social identity on the basis of the Brotherhood's call to Islamize and revive Muslim societies, thus emphasizing the importance of social work, while merging these principles with Sayyid Qutb's revolutionary appeals for jihad.[61] The charter is deeply infused with religious references, in line with Hamas's mission to bring Islam into the Palestinian struggle and to redefine it as an essentially Islamic issue, in contrast with the PLO's secular charter. The charter also introduces a series of non-Islamic themes borrowed from the Western tradition—from classic Christian anti-Semitism, to the notion of democracy—thus producing an original ideological mix.[62]

The charter expresses Hamas's ultimate objective in unmistakable terms: the liberation of Palestine through jihad. By referring to Palestine as a religious trust (a *waqf*), Hamas underlines both its inherent sanctity and its status as belonging to the entire Muslim *Umma*. A corollary of this statement is that no party would ever be entitled to forfeit the *Umma*'s rights on Palestine and that attempts to conquer or occupy such land are seen as both an attack against the Palestinian people and against Islam. Hamas stresses jihad as the individual duty of every Muslim, albeit restricting it to the purpose of "liberating Palestine," and it similarly rejects the principle of a negotiated settlement of the Arab-Israeli conflict, as "in contradiction to the principles of the Islamic Resistance Movement."[63]

In the past two decades, Hamas has articulated a parallel political discourse that has allowed the group to combine the ideological beliefs expressed in the charter with the shifting political and security circumstances on the ground. Although Hamas has never formally renounced its ultimate goal to liberate mandatory Palestine and to reject the state of Israel, it has developed a series of political concepts that have provided the group with additional political and practical flexibility.

As early as 1993, Sheikh Yassin expressed his acceptance of a ten- or twenty-year temporary *hudna* (truce) with Israel, provided a series of conditions were met that included an Israeli withdrawal to its pre-1967 borders and the creation of a free Palestinian state.[64] Similar offers, along with proposals for short-term lull (or *tahdi'ah*), have since been reiterated by the group on several occasions.[65] By incorporating the hudna discourse into its political analysis, Hamas recognized the de facto existence of the state of Israel without having to forfeit its ideological premises and its "non-recognition" dogma.[66]

The hudna discourse also allowed the group to support and agree to participate in a Palestinian state in the pre-1967 borders without having to compromise its ultimate objective, as a long-term hudna would not be the equivalent of a "final status agreement" but merely a "pause" in the struggle to liberate Palestine.

Hamas's charter not only focuses on the group's agenda with respect to the Arab-Israeli conflict but also describes the group's domestic goals for Palestinian society. According to its charter, Hamas's plan involves both the Islamization of society through social work and the ultimate establishment of an Islamic state. Such a state would be governed according to the principles of Sharia law, would include participatory elections of its citizens, and would be created in the final stage of a large Islamization process instead of as a product of top-down coercion.[67]

Over the past two decades, to accommodate this ideological and political objective with the reality of Palestinian society, Hamas's political discourse started to downplay the centrality of the Islamic state project and to emphasize other aspects of the group's Islamic political agenda, such as its interests in fighting corruption or providing relief for indigents within society. In its 2004 electoral platform, for instance, Hamas's mentions of the Islamic state project were minimized in favor of a rhetoric that endorsed "political freedoms, the freedom to form parties, to hold elections, and on the peaceful rotation of power," while praising the importance of "dialogue and reason to resolve internal disputes."[68] Without relinquishing its ideological premises, Hamas's political discourse and its rhetoric have evolved and grown more sophisticated and politically savvy when compared with the views first expressed in the charter.

Hamas now maintains simultaneous discourses that emphasize different aspects of the organization to appeal to different audiences. The group focuses on the "resistance ethos" when addressing the Palestinian population at large, it underlines its political and pragmatic agenda while downplaying its jihadist and religious orientation when dealing with external actors, and it still heavily resorts to Islamic values when talking to its own members.[69]

Another important topic analyzed in the charter is the group's view of the Western world in general and of Israel in particular. Hamas has not altered its Manichean description of Israel as the ultimate source of evil, nor has it completely abolished its anti-Semitic rhetoric. Still, the group has somewhat distanced itself from the language of the charter, which proposes an unsophisticated racial account of Jews conspiring to control the world and blames them for disparate plots, such as starting the French Revolution or creating the League of Nations to rule over humanity.[70]

Instead, while maintaining an anti-Semitic rhetoric, the group has placed increased emphasis on promoting an anti-Zionist discourse, and it has, at the same time, developed a more nuanced view of its external enemies besides Israel. While sharply criticizing the West and the states that support Israel, the group has been equally careful not to expand its pool of direct enemies beyond Israel.[71] Hamas has also increasingly refrained from repeating its early accusations of "treason" with respect to "moderate" Arab regimes, generally relying on more ambiguous language to avoid alienating regional players.[72]

Hamas: Explaining the "Phased Political Participation"

Understanding the fragmented nature of Hamas's organizational structure and the group's reliance on a dogmatic ideology coupled with a pragmatic political discourse provides the basis for analyzing the group's political strategy and its progressive "politicization." By applying the "four-factor model" of political participation (institutional pressure, shifts in the availability of mobilization resources, changes in the political opportunity structure, and rise of an internal commitment to change), this section accounts for Hamas's political strategies in key years of 1994 and 2004/2006, explaining the process that led the group to take part directly in institutional politics.

The 1994 Elections: A Failed Transformation

Hamas's first serious internal discussions about forming a political party occurred in the post-Oslo environment, concurrently with the creation of the Palestinian Authority and in the period preceding the first 1996 Palestinian legislative elections. Following a long and heated internal debate, as well as an extensive round of consultations among Hamas members, the group decided not to take part in the legislative elections.[73] This refusal did not constitute a complete rejection of the idea of entering the sphere of institutional politics, as—in the same time period—the group also remained in favor of participating in future municipal elections, and agreed to comply with the terms of an unofficial cease-fire in the latter part of 1995 to allow the legislative elections to take place.[74] Hamas failed to enter the political system directly because, despite the existence of substantial institutional and internal pressures that were pushing the organization in that direction, the political opportunity system itself was not yet "ripe" for direct political participation.

First, by looking at Hamas's *degree of institutionalization* in the early 1990s, it is possible to see how the organization had grown, both quantitatively and qualitatively, from its creation at the outset of the first intifada, acquiring both organizational complexity and political relevance. The group was under institutional pressures to upgrade its position within the existing political system and to maximize its power and stability. Even more important, Hamas in the early 1990s was also facing a substantial challenge to its relevance and legitimacy within Palestinian society, which in turn was challenging the group's *availability of mobilization sources.*

The winding down of the intifada and the ongoing peace negotiations between the PLO and Israel represented a direct challenge to the group's legitimacy, as they eroded part of the political power gained by Hamas during the intifada and restored the preexisting internal balance of power in Fatah's favor. The signing of the Oslo agreements and the creation of the PA enhanced this process, and both events diminished Hamas's relevance and threatened to place the group on the margins of Palestinian politics.

As a result of the changing political environment, the group's legitimacy and appeal started to wane. At the time, Palestinian society was divided among three main political blocks: (1) the pro-Oslo, mainstream Fatah-aligned supporters; (2) the leftist and secular opposition represented chiefly by the Popular Front for the Liberation of Palestine (PFLP) and the Democratic Front for the Liberation of Palestine (DFLP); and (3) the Islamist forces. With the creation of the PA, Palestinian public opinion strongly converged around the mainstream Fatah forces, and support for the opposition declined rapidly: While approximately 23 percent of Palestinians supported Islamist groups before the creation of the PA, that number had dropped to only 15 percent by mid-1998.[75]

Concurrently, Palestinian support for Hamas's reliance on force and terrorism against Israeli targets also diminished, as they tended to be interpreted as attempts to stall the creation of an interim and self-governing administration in parts of the West Bank. For instance, while general support for attacks against Israeli targets was 57 percent in late 1994, this had dropped to 21 percent in March 1996, in the immediate aftermath of the Palestinian elections.[76] This diminishing support, in turn, also affected the group's ability to mobilize its supporters, putting a strain on the available human and financial resources.

The repeated crackdowns on Hamas's armed wing and financial revenues by Israel and by the newly formed PA eroded the group's military strength and further threatened the group's access to human and financial resources.[77] In other words, on the eve of the 1996 elections, Hamas faced a paradox: Institutional pressures, a growing threat to the group's legitimacy and relevance, and a drain on its mobilization sources all pushed the group toward creating a political wing and participating in the new Palestinian political system. This would have served as an accommodation tool and reasserted the group's relevance in the shifting political environment, while allowing Hamas to diversify the group's activities and find alternative sources as a supplement to the shrinking pool of supporters and founders. However, to expand and create an effective political wing, Hamas needed (and lacked) a strong constituency of supporters; otherwise, it would risk performing poorly at the ballot boxes, further losing ground to its main political opponent, Fatah.

The second, most significant, obstacle against the creation of a political wing and the direct participation in institutional politics was definitely the lack of a substantial "opening" within the *political opportunity structure.* The post-Oslo years offered an improvement in the Palestinian political system by establishing limited self-government and by creating a legislative framework to regulate access to power through elections. Oslo partially changed the cultural-institutional dynamics in place and encouraged both Hamas and Fatah to engage in a reciprocal dialogue.

In the post-Oslo years, IDF forces were redeployed and the degree of control and effective presence of the Israelis softened, thus partially opening Palestinian society to self-administration. From Hamas's perspective, this partial improvement of the system did not substantially alter the degree of permeability of the political system and the concrete possibility of accessing power.

The Palestinian political system, as established in the Israeli-Palestinian Interim Agreement of 1995, was set up around two main institutional branches: the Palestinian Legislative Council (PLC) and its executive arm, the presidency. From the outset, it appeared evident that center of executive and legislative power resided in the president, Yasser Arafat, and that the lines between the role and tasks of the PLC and of Arafat would blur.[78] Therefore, the degree of permeability of the system was low because of the high centralization and low separation of powers within the Palestinian system, a by-product of the de facto control of the system by Fatah's historic leader.

The established electoral laws used to elect the PLC also contributed to enhancing Fatah's grip on Palestinian politics, thus discouraging political participation. The representatives of the PLC were to be elected by a majoritarian "winner-takes-all" system, which, unlike a proportional system, penalized smaller and emerging parties and rewarded consolidated and mainstream political formations (such as Fatah). The sixteen electoral districts devised to elect the PLC tended to favor traditional families and clans, which Fatah had previously worked to co-opt under its wing.[79]

From Hamas's perspective, the low degree of permeability of the political system, the majoritarian electoral laws, and the political monopoly of Fatah all constituted insurmountable obstacles to the group's effective participation in institutional politics, and they provided a strong deterrent to the creation of a directly associated political party. Still the decision to abstain from joining the political system was not self-evident to everyone within the organization, and it generated a heated internal debate, splitting the group between those who advocated for participating in the elections and those who opposed the political path.

Discussions started as early as 1992 when Hamas's senior leaders received an internal document evaluating the possible political responses to an Israeli-Palestinian agreement and to the subsequent creation of a Palestinian self-rule system. The document pragmatically assessed the pros and cons of four possible courses of actions with respect to the anticipated political developments: (1) full participation in the elections, (2) indirect participation through a proxy political party, (3) peaceful political boycott, and (4) armed action to foil the self-rule political process.[80] From the outset, the core of the Gaza leadership, which could count on substantially more popular support than could Hamas in the Fatah-controlled West Bank, supported the creation of a political party, arguing that it would boost the group's power without compromising its armed struggle agenda.[81] Historic leader Sheikh Yassin also supported this view, arguing that Hamas could use the PLC to conduct serious political opposition while further spreading Islam, and his position was backed by official spokesmen in the Occupied Territories, such as Mahmoud Zahhar, and by such Gaza leaders, such as Ismail Haniyeh.[82]

The main opposition to the notion of creating a political party seemed to come from Hamas in the West Bank and more substantially from the group's "external" leaders, who denounced the move as a possible weakening of the "resistance" agenda. This position was justified on ideological grounds, as participation in the PLC elections was seen as tantamount to recognizing the Oslo process, as well as on political grounds, as the external leadership questioned the desirability of blurring the lines between Hamas and the PA. In addition, the creation of a local political wing was seen as a potential threat to the Political Bureau's control of the organization.[83] In the end, following the failure of several rounds of negotiations between the PA and Hamas in Khartoum and Cairo in the fall of 1995 (both organized by a group of Gaza leaders and aimed at reaching an agreement with Fatah, convincing the external leadership to support the electoral option), the organization settled for a passive boycott of the elections.[84] Around the same time, a loose group of Islamist leaders, including a few former Hamas members, were co-opted by Arafat in the hopes of establishing a political alternative to Hamas. This effort led to the creation of the National Islamic Salvation Party (Hizb al-Khalas), which would then also abstain from participating in the PLC elections and which would rapidly become a marginal local political party.[85]

Despite the internal disagreements regarding this decision, the Shura Council was able to impose it on the Gaza leadership and several leaders who had previously announced their intention to run in the elections, including Ismail Haniyeh, withdrew their candidacy.[86] Hamas therefore abstained from direct participation in the elections, but it did not ostracize independent Islamists who chose to run, nor did it actively discourage Palestinians from voting.

Because the registration lists for the PLC elections were to be used to create the electoral lists in any upcoming municipal election, where Hamas was open to participation, by dissuading Hamas supporters to register for the PLC elections, the group would have done itself a disservice for the future.[87] While Hamas abstained from developing a political wing, it attempted to respond to its legitimacy and relevancy crisis by emphasizing and expanding its social movement dimension, trying to build consensus and popularity, and to increase its constituency by employing a bottom-up, grassroots approach.[88]

2004: The Political Transformation

To understand why the group officially joined the Palestinian political arena in 2004, it is important to recognize the factors that prevented Hamas from creating a political wing and participating in the Palestinian general elections of 1996. In 2004, Hamas first chose to take part in the local municipal elections, a decision that paved the way for the group's participation in the 2006 legislative elections. The decision to become integrated in the formal political system followed shifts in internal commitment, political opportunities, resource availability, and institutional directions.

In terms of the *degree of institutionalization* and *the availability of mobilization sources,* there are several important commonalities between the challenges Hamas faced in the early 1990s, when it first started to explore the option of creating a political wing, and those that the group had to confront in the period preceding the 2004 decision to join the political system.

Hamas had continued to institutionalize and develop in the decade following the Oslo Accords, boosting its social services structure as well as its politico-military apparatus. As the group had become more complex and bureaucratic, the institutional pressures to seek stability and accommodation had increased with time. Hamas also faced a challenge to its institutional legitimacy and relevance in the mid-2000s. After the peak of the second intifada in the early 2000s, the initial enthusiasm for the armed struggle had started to wane as early as fall 2002, while the general approval of political negotiations started to rise steadily during 2003, a trend that took place even among traditional Hamas supporters.[89] This shift in public opinion represented a potential threat to Hamas's relevance in the event of renewed political negotiations, which tend to marginalize and exclude noninstitutional players such as Hamas. By creating a political wing, Hamas could reassert its ability to adjust to the shifting political environment and to stay relevant by competing with its adversaries in the newly revitalized political arena.

The group's level of available resources was at that time compromised by the changing internal and international political and security environment. These changes affected in particular the effectiveness of the group's military apparatus. As a result of the intense and prolonged military confrontation with Israel and of numerous direct attacks, arrests, and targeted assassinations, Hamas's military capacity was affected and the group found itself weakened, which also pushed the organization into accepting a Fatah-brokered cease-fire in June 2003.[90] This affected both the resource mobilization potential of the group and its claims for relevance and legitimacy.

Together with this progressive drain on its military resources, the group's financial structure was also under considerable pressure because of the international community's post-9/11 increasingly more aggressive efforts to crack down on its founding sources. In the aftermath of 9/11 and in the period preceding and immediately after the beginning of the US military operations in Iraq, Hamas's state sponsors within the Arab and Muslim world, including Iran, took a more cautious approach in supporting and funding the group and its military operations.[91]

Political participation in the elections and the creation of a political wing not only allowed Hamas to compensate for the temporary weakness of its military apparatus but also allowed the group to further diversify its activities and funding pool. Even if the organizational challenges, including the legitimacy and relevance threat and the ongoing strain in mobilization sources, faced by Hamas in the early 1990s, were fundamentally similar to those confronted in the early 2000s, Hamas in 2003 was differently positioned and thus able to tackle these challenges by expanding and creating a political wing. At this time, in contrast with the group's position in the post-Oslo environment, Hamas could count on a larger and more established constituency, as well as on the declining popularity of its main political rival, Fatah.

Since the late 1990s—in parallel with the deterioration of the Israeli-Palestinian peace process—the level of credibility and popularity enjoyed by Hamas had started to grow. The Palestinian society at large gradually started to become more religious during the 1990s, with the overall number of mosques built increasing exponentially along with the number of regular worshippers and the percentage of the population self-identifying as religious and advocating for Islam to have a greater role in Palestinian politics.[92]

During the first two years of the intifada, the group acquired an unprecedented level of popularity due to its successful operations against Israel. Although in the long run Palestinian enthusiasm for the intifada and the suicide operations had started to wind down, Hamas could still rely on its past "achievements" to build a political constituency.

The group's investment in developing and maintaining a more extensive social services network in the mid-1990s also contributed to building popular support that could be translated into political legitimacy. Still, the key factor that provided Hamas with the political strength to pursue the political wing option did not come only from the organization's direct successes but rather from the failures of its opponent and from the state of disarray of both Fatah and the PA.

Palestinian society had in fact become increasingly disillusioned with the PLO-led peace process, which in turn had a negative effect on the level of support for the organization. The PA government was increasingly perceived as inefficient and corrupt, and the high levels of unaccountability and centralization of power had further alienated part of the Fatah electorate. Fatah's power and control was further compromised because the group was plagued by internal divisions between the traditional PLO leadership, who had largely returned from exile in 1994, and the local "young guard," a process that was only enhanced by the parallel weakening of the PA.[93] Therefore, unlike in the early 1990s, Hamas was able to capitalize on its political strength and on the simultaneous crisis of the group's main political opponent to gather a significant electoral constituency and reaffirm its relevance and legitimacy through institutional expansion. This development would probably not have taken place without one additional new development: a concrete opening of the political arena.

The most striking difference between the sociopolitical context in the early 1990s and preceding the 2004 decision to run in the municipal elections is a substantial *shift within the political opportunity structure*. First, the single element that had most deterred Hamas from taking part in the political system, namely, Arafat's solid centralization of power and the low degree of permeability of the political system, started to crack under internal and international pressure.

Within Fatah, a growing number of leaders started to demand internal reforms of the PA, including the approval of a Basic Law to regulate the internal functioning of the PA, as early as spring 2002. This followed an escalation of violence between Israel and the Palestinians and Israel's Operation Defensive Shield in the West Bank in spring 2002. Even if this internal pressure for reform and accountability began to wind down after Arafat finally ratified the Basic Law in May 2002, international pressure started to constrain the president's power, and this eventually forced Arafat to amend the law and create the position of the prime minister, first appointed in March 2003.[94]

The appointment of Mahmoud Abbas as prime minister and his actions between March and September 2003 (when he resigned from his post) did not radically alter the balance of power or weaken Arafat's centralized leadership of the PA. They constituted the first crack in the system; signaling to opposition groups that the political reality on the ground was slowly shifting and that the internal divisions within Fatah were there to stay.

This gradual opening up of the political system continued in 2004, and it progressed dramatically following the sudden death of Arafat in November 2004. This single event swiftly altered the preexisting power equilibrium and increased the system's permeability, thus providing a strong incentive for Hamas to pursue political participation through institutional politics. Other preexisting obstacles to political participation had also gradually started to weaken in the mid-2000s; for example, the lack of accountability had lessened after the approval of a Basic Law that would make the entire political system more accountable. These changes helped to convince Hamas to join the municipal race in 2004, and to initiate a "phased participation strategy" that would eventually lead them to run in the second national legislative elections in 2006.

In formulating this decision, the group also relied on a 2005 reform of the electoral law, which had increased the number of seats in the PLC from 88 to 132, and which had determined that 66 of these seats were to be elected through a proportional system.[95] Proportional electoral quotas, a larger number of seats, and a low threshold for gaining political office all constitute important incentives for the participation of smaller parties, and they certainly facilitated Hamas's entry into the political system.

Another important change in the political opportunity framework stemmed from the already discussed erosion of the political consensus and the popularity of Fatah and the rise of internal divisions with that organization. This not only expanded Hamas's potential constituency, it also generated a temporary and partial opening within certain sectors of Fatah with respect to Hamas. Notably, the June 2003 cease-fire was partially a by-product of a more conciliatory and inclusive approach with respect to Hamas from "young" Fatah leaders such as Marwan Barghouti.[96] Because of these substantial changes in the political opportunity structure, the decision to create a political wing and to join the political system was not as debated or controversial as the one the organization faced in the early 1990s, resulting in a *high internal commitment to change.*

A main ideological objection to political participation in 1996, namely, the link between the elections and the Oslo process, was now much less relevant. The group argued that the Oslo process had been effectively killed by the second intifada, and thus the preexisting link between the PA and the peace process was tenuous.[97] Although participating in the elections meant that Hamas de facto accepted the political and organizational infrastructure created by Oslo, the organization was still able to justify this shift by arguing that the Oslo-driven peace process and its political legacy were essentially dead.

The political dynamics in place in 2004 allowed the group to apply a "trial-and-error" approach to elections; first, by participating in the 2004 municipal race (which the group had never opposed and always wanted to be a part of), and then by using this first electoral experience to build a larger internal constituency to support Hamas's candidacy in the PLC elections. The decision to join institutional politics in 2004 was, as in the previous decade, strongly supported by Hamas's local leaders in Gaza, and this group's pro-electoral stand increased even further following Israel's assassination of Sheikh Yassin and Rantisi (even though they also supported electoral participation) with the rise of traditional supporters of political participation such as Ismail Haniyeh. These assassinations also further pushed Hamas's organizational control into the hands of the Bureau and the external leadership.[98] With increased organizational power and control, it is likely that the external leadership felt less threatened by local political participation than it did in the 1990s, when the internal balance of power was more equally split among local and Diaspora leaders. Hamas's decision to join institutional politics in 2004–5 was reached without intense internal strife and dissent, generating a certain degree of organizational unity and consensus.

One important element that has to be considered when assessing the group's overall internal commitment toward elections is the relative lack of involvement of the Qassam Battalions—Hamas's armed wing—in the process leading to political participation. Although the armed wing's leaders had then and continue to have the opportunity to express their position with respect to institutional politics through their role in the Shura Council, the development and creation of a political wing did not substantially involve armed wing leaders. To this day, political candidates are, for the most part, not part of the military apparatus, creating a de facto separation between armed leaders and political ones.

It is interesting to analyze how this de facto separation between the armed and the political wing, together with the already discussed internal divisions along armed-political and external-local lines, have influenced Hamas's organizational development since the group's official involvement in institutional politics. This is particularly relevant in light of the study's main hypothesis: that core strategic organizational change, including permanent moderation, is in fact encouraged by protracted internal competition among a given armed group's political and military leadership cadres. To test this claim, the next section describes Hamas's political development in the past two decades, emphasizing the shifting relations between the armed and the political wings.

Has the group developed in a linear fashion, thus becoming progressively more "moderate" and politically integrated? Have Hamas's military and political wings grown in a cohesive and integrated manner without experiencing internal strategic change, as in the Hezbollah case study? Or has Hamas followed a cyclical pattern where phases of political integration have been followed by stages of open internal and external confrontation, producing repeated internal clashes and increasing the potential for strategic change?

1987–2012: Political Development and Organizational Divisions

1987–2000: Early Political Strategy and Organization-Building

Since the rise in popularity and influence of the Muslim Brotherhood in the Gaza Strip during the early 1980s, and especially following the 1982 expulsion of the PLO from Lebanon, the Hamas's leadership started to consider ways to increase its political status and relevance.[99] Originally conceived as the Brotherhood's armed wing, Hamas from its outset was a hybrid armed and political organization. Since its inception it has been considered a political alternative to the more established Fatah. Already in the early 1990s Hamas had published a booklet (*Between Pains of the Present and Hopes for the Future*), asserting that the movement represented the political future of Palestine and that they would eventually become the main leaders within Palestinian politics, replacing Fatah.[100]

Hamas's interest in elections and in the Palestinian political system dates back to the organization's formative years, and its first direct involvement with the question of elections occurred in April 1989, following Israeli Prime Minister Yitzhak Shamir's call for elections in the Palestinian Territories to mitigate the tensions caused by the intifada. Hamas conducted a public campaign—"Let our slogan be 'No!' "—to reject the idea of elections until the end of the occupation.[101]

Hamas was always politically involved at the grassroots level. Hamas's Mahmoud Zahhar explains this posture: "For us there are three types of elections. The first ones are nonpolitical popular elections (…). These include elections for chambers of commerce, municipalities, trade unions, professional associations, and so on. We have always participated in this type and will continue to do so."[102] Hamas had consistently and directly taken part in elections in universities, workplaces, and trade unions. Given the highly politicized nature of Palestinian society, these elections are generally highly participatory, and thus they are to a certain degree representative of larger trends in Palestinian politics. It is therefore highly significant that Hamas's electoral record in these "grassroots elections" throughout the 1990s reflects a solid degree of support for the group.[103] This both laid the basis for the group's later involvement in institutional politics and allowed Hamas to increase its presence and status within Palestinian society by controlling labor unions and students' councils in Gaza and in the West Bank.

Hamas competed in these elections with pragmatic electoral programs and campaigns, and it did so by respecting both the electoral procedures and results of the elections, and generally attempting to avoid clashes with its main political opponent, Fatah. While taking part in politics at the grassroots level, Hamas's political involvement in the pre-PA era attempted to shape Palestinian institutional politics from the bottom-up, while rejecting the PLO and Fatah's attempts to co-opt the group.

An example of these two trends can be seen as early as 1991. Hamas first questioned the PLO's claim to be the sole representative of the Palestinian people. It also declared that the group would indeed be willing to become part of the PLO, provided the allocation to Hamas of 40 percent of the seats in the PLO's quasi-parliamentary Palestinian National Council, the end of all negotiations with Israel, and the repeal of UN Resolution 242, which set the basis for a two-state solution.[104] To Fatah, these terms were deliberately unrealistic, but Hamas held they were based on the group's level of support among the Palestinian population, and by presenting them, Hamas was able to reassert its autonomy from the PLO and question the group's structure and role. Also in 1991, Hamas showed its interest in establishing a separate and relevant political identity from the PLO when it promoted the already described anti-Oslo TRO. These actions demonstrated the political will to challenge the PLO and Fatah but also revealed the group's reliance on the tactics of a social movement and other extra-institutional political tools to do so. While consolidating its political agenda and strategy, in the early 1990s Hamas also boosted and reorganized its military wing, especially in the aftermath of the 1992–93 expulsion of some of its leadership to Lebanon, an event that shifted the internal balance of power from within Gaza to the external leadership and the Political Bureau.

The development of the group's military and political strategy coincided with and developed harmoniously in the early 1990s, as the Qassam Battalions' attacks only reinforced the main political objective of derailing the Oslo process and self-asserting the group's identity as a political alternative to Fatah. The creation of the PA in 1994 and the subsequent countdown to the 1996 legislative elections divided the organization along military-political as well as external-internal lines for the first time, with the local Gaza leadership supporting the formal entry into institutional politics and the externally led bureau insisting that the time was not ripe for official political involvement.

Although Hamas's Shura Council was ultimately able to prevent internal divisions to rally the organization behind Hamas's final decision not to run in the 1996 elections, the organization still clearly showed the existence of two opposing leadership subunits with a certain degree of autonomy. For example, even before Hamas had reached a final decision on the issues of political participation, several members of the Gaza leadership, including Ismail Haniyeh, had proceeded to register to compete in the PLC elections (a move that they would later have to retract). Sheik Yassin had asserted on numerous occasions the potential interest of the organization in joining the political system.[105]

It is interesting to compare Hamas's organizational response to this internal dissent with Hezbollah's policy when deciding to join institutional politics in 1992. Although both groups experienced internal divisions over the initial question of whether to take part in elections, Hezbollah's decision-making process was cohesive, and the organization ultimately chose to marginalize those members who had objected to the parliamentary path. Hamas, however, showed less unity in reaching the final decision to reject institutional politics in 1996, and both "internal" Gaza leaders who had favored the political course as well as "external" and military leaders who had imposed their view on political participation remained an integral part of Hamas.

Hamas's choice to remain on the margins of the Palestinian political system was in effect a victory for the group's bureau and an affirmation of the Qassam Battalions' strategic agenda, but it still reflected some input from the leaders who had supported the idea of running in the 1996 elections: The group limited itself to a passive boycott of the electoral consultations, it still endorsed local candidates, and it abstained from discouraging its supporters from voting. The group chose not to reject the political track permanently, and it invested substantial political capital in discrediting the official results of the elections, both claiming that the PA had coerced part of the Palestinian population to vote, thus obtaining the high electoral turnout of 86 percent, and that Fatah had been involved in electoral fraud.[106]

In the years between the 1996 elections and the beginning of the second intifada in 2000, Hamas also focused heavily on its grassroots political presence and on its social network, thus preserving a strong political identity outside the institutional system, while also continuing to declare its intention to participate in future municipal elections. While Hamas's political leadership within both Gaza and the West Bank was leading these efforts to boost the group's domestic legitimacy through social work and grassroots politics, Hamas found itself once again divided along political-military lines in January 1996.

Despite the December 1995 agreement with the PA to observe a period of cease-fire to allow the smooth running of the elections, members of the Qassam Brigades unilaterally broke the cease-fire to avenge Israel's killing of one of its leaders and chief bomb maker, Yahya Ayyash. The attacks were perpetrated by a subunit within Hamas's armed wing, and they enraged the organization's political leaders in Gaza, who reacted by urging the armed wing to cease its military operations. The decision to strike at Israel despite the ongoing cease-fire was supported by Hamas's external leadership—which oversees the Qassam Brigades. The political bureau publicly denounced the local political leadership's calls to halt the attacks.[107] In the end, the group's military and political leaders were able to prevent the broader escalation of this internal fight, mostly thanks to the return in 1997 (respectively, from Israeli prisons and extradition) of prominent political leaders such as Rantisi and Yassin to the Gaza Strip and Abu Marzouq to Jordan.

These leaders held a more "centrist" view of Hamas's direction, and they also enjoyed strong internal credibility. They were thus able to prevent the escalation of this internal rift while asserting a nonconfrontational line with respect to the PA and a "retaliatory" military approach concerning Israel.[108] Although this helped patch up Hamas at the time, the tensions with the organization's military wing, which was in extreme distress because of Israeli military operations and PA-led crackdowns, did not completely cease in the years preceding the 2000 intifada. The year 2000 would prove to be a watershed for the organization, boosting its internal legitimacy and political status and reestablishing the balance of power between the armed and political wings.

2000–2004: The Second Intifada and the Political Rise

Since its founding in 1987 Hamas went through an initial stage during which it experienced the harmonious development of its military and sociopolitical wings. This was followed by a period of increasing intraorganizational unrest, often along a political versus military line, in the aftermath of the Oslo Agreement and the creation of the PA. By the late 1990s, Hamas found itself with an ever stronger social movement and an increased interest in grassroots activism, while the group's military wing was showing signs of distress and weakness. Overall, since the establishment of the PA, the group had been partially struggling to assert its political relevance in the context of Palestinian society's growing support for the ongoing negotiations with Israel. As the PA government proved to be incompetent and corrupt, and as the political process between Israel and the PLO started to crumble, Hamas's popularity began to rise again, while the group's military activities started to regain approval and credibility.

The event that "relaunched" Hamas and boosted the organization's military wing was the outbreak of the al-Aqsa Intifada in late September 2000. Regardless of the event that precipitated the outbreak of the second intifada and whether it was deliberately planned by either party, this event has to be read in the context of the growing disillusionment of Palestinian society with respect to the peace process, along with rising internal competition within Fatah. The second intifada represented the attempt of Fatah's new guard to gain prominence with respect to the party's traditional leaders and to change the political course of the Palestinians in the aftermath of the failed Camp David negotiations by reaffirming the armed struggle option. At the beginning of the intifada, Arafat and his "old guard" refrained from controlling or coercing the uprising, thus implementing a "noninterference" policy in the hope that the intifada would generate leverage to be later used at the negotiating table.[109]

Their hopes, however, conflicted with the new guards' interest in shifting the Palestinian arena back to a phase of active armed struggle, which resulted in the creation of the National and Islamic Higher Committee for the Follow-Up of the Intifada (NIHC), a loose coalition of fourteen secular, leftist, and Islamist groups and factions.[110]

Hamas saw its golden opportunity to reaffirm its power and domestic status: the group thus joined and became politically influential within the NIHC, balancing Fatah's power in the organization. It stepped up its armed operations to meet its increased competition from Fatah-associated and secular brigades, such as the Al-Aqsa Martyrs Brigades and the Popular Resistance Committees, but also from the Palestinian Islamic Jihad. Hamas was thus able to improve its credibility and popularity considerably as a result of the intifada, while its numerous suicide missions put it at the forefront of the armed struggle, boosting the Qassam Battalions.

The intifada and the collapse of the political process between Israel and the PLO also contributed to factionalize and weaken Fatah further, leading a growing number of Palestinians not only to become disaffected with Fatah but also to redirect their political loyalty toward Hamas and the Islamist camp. From 1996 to 2001, Islamists registered an 80 percent increase in their popularity, ranging from 15 percent to 27 percent of popular support.[111]

Between 2000 and 2003, a strategic rapprochement between Hamas's military and political leaderships occurred, as the actions of the Qassam Brigades became a central tool in the group's political strategy to assert its prominence and undermine Fatah. Suicide attacks within Israel became Hamas's prime tool to discredit the PA, blamed for failing to halt such operations, sidetrack the diplomatic and negotiation process, and improve its political influence. Hamas would often carry out suicide operations that openly contravened Fatah's commitments to temporary cease-fires or, more generally, that undermined the PA's strategy with respect to Israel. As expected, this policy also contributed to heightening interorganizational tensions between Fatah and Hamas.

Hamas's violation of the period of quietness urged by Arafat in the aftermath of the 9/11 attacks generated anger and condemnation from the PA, while Hamas-backed protests against US military operations in Afghanistan were met by harsh police repression, resulting in the death of Hamas supporters.[112] In the fall of 2001, Hamas's repeated attacks against Israel added pressure on the PA and on Arafat's leadership, as the international community started to call on the president to dismantle the Palestinian "terror networks" and to agree to a cease-fire, while Israel declared the PA "an entity that supports terrorism." The PA was too weak and discredited at home and abroad to be effective, and Hamas was too militarily and politically relevant to be forcibly coerced by the PA to halt its attacks. The group was eventually politically persuaded by political leaders such as Barghouti to agree to a cease-fire in December 2001, a commitment that would be honored for the following three weeks.[113]

Hamas's strategy in 2002 and 2003 remained substantially similar, relying on its military activities to achieve political power and influence within Palestinian affairs, and to affect the course of the conflict. On March 27, 2002, the same day when the Arab League endorsed the "Saudi Initiative," which promised the normalization of relations with Israel in return for a full withdrawal to the pre-1967 borders and the implementation of a solution to the refugee question based on UNSC Resolution 194, Hamas, which strongly opposed the plan, launched a massive suicide operation in Netanya, killing thirty Israelis and silencing any debate over resuming political negotiations. This operation also triggered Israel's almost total reoccupation of the West Bank with the massive military operation Defensive Shield. The main victim of Defensive Shield, other than the Palestinian civilian population at large, was certainly Fatah's credibility and power, a decline that even the push for reforms in the spring of 2002, culminating with Arafat's appointment of Mahmoud Abbas as Prime Minister in March 2003, was not able to completely reverse.

As for Hamas, the Israeli reoccupation of the West Bank resulted in a net gain: It allowed the group to assert additional independence from Fatah (especially in the reoccupied villages of the West Bank and Gaza), to continue its defiance of Fatah-brokered cease-fires, and to gain political parity with Fatah in numerous reoccupied areas.[114]

Even if the Palestinian support for armed attacks gradually began to wane at the end of 2002, in parallel with rising internal decentralization of power, factionalism, and civilian distress, Hamas had already built a strong constituency for itself and had asserted its prime relevance in Palestinian politics.

But the increasing lethality of Israeli operations against Hamas's Qassam Battalions, combined with the shifting political mood and political opportunity environment and with the growing pressure from Fatah—led Hamas to regroup strategically and to agree to a cease-fire, officially referred to as *hudna* in June 2003.[115] This short-lived lull lasted only six weeks and failed to achieve national unity or to diminish the rivalry that had characterized Fatah-Hamas relations throughout the second intifada.

Between the beginning of the second intifada and the death of Palestinian president Yasser Arafat in November 2004, Hamas upgraded its military and political status in the Palestinian area. With its reliance on its military wing, Hamas was able to gain support through its armed operations and to influence the course of the political process with Israel by acting as a "spoiler" whenever it deemed it convenient to do so. With its military and social activities, the group was also able to derive benefit from the widespread chaos within the Occupied Palestinian Territories and to fill partially the civic and security vacuum left by the partial collapse of the PA and its security forces, especially in Gaza.[116]

Even when the armed wing started to weaken in 2003, Hamas could still rely on this accumulated political leverage, and it could start to think seriously about how to convert it into concrete power. The death of Arafat and the "opening" of the Palestinian political system gave the group the opportunity to achieve this objective. In starting this new organizational chapter, old divisions between the armed and the political, and the local and the external leaderships, would reemerge, following the relative organizational cohesion of the intifada, which had been dominated by the military wing and external leaders.

2004–2006: The Post-Arafat Era and the Entry in Institutional Politics

Until 2004, Hamas's organizational development had been characterized by an initial linear and simultaneous development between its military and political activities (1987–1993). This was followed by a stage of occasional internal divisions (1993–2000) when there was much debate over the logic of armed struggle and political participation, which occasionally flared up into antagonism. A later period of relative organizational cohesion during the second intifada was characterized by the primacy of the group's military activities (2000–2004).

The progressive wearing down of the group's military wing after 2002, together with a significant shift in Palestinian society's alignment with respect to the conflict with Israel, and with a gradual "opening" of the political arena led to significant internal changes within Hamas and to its transition toward institutional politics.

Following Yasser Arafat's death in November 2004, the Palestinian political system went through a strategic change, inaugurated by internal discussions over holding a new round of presidential elections for the first time since 1996. Hamas decided to stay at the margins of the post-Arafat presidential debate, which would quickly end with the election of Mahmoud Abbas in January 2005,[117] because of the identification of the presidency with the much-criticized Oslo process, and because it made little pragmatic sense to attempt to overtake an institution that was so profoundly dominated by Fatah.

Hamas also started to push toward holding new municipal elections, a position consistent with the organization's early rejection in 1994 of the PA practice to appoint, instead of elect, municipal representatives.[118] In 2004, Hamas objected to those within Fatah, who, fearing that the death of Arafat would allow opposition forces to gain the upper hand over Fatah, suggested postponing both presidential and municipal elections. In the end, municipal elections were held in the West Bank and Gaza over four electoral rounds from December 2004 to December 2005.[119] The electoral results were significant because they showed that Hamas was willing and able to transition toward institutional politics and to challenge Fatah's previously undisputed domain.

The first round of local elections, held between December 2004 and January 2005, took place in thirty-six municipalities (twenty-two in the West Bank and fourteen in the Gaza Strip), and Hamas obtained roughly 36 percent of the total seats in the West Bank (against the 45% won by Fatah), and 65 percent of the seats in the Gaza Strip (compared with the 24% gained by Fatah).[120] These results were particularly impressive given that Fatah had decided to start the elections in some of its traditional strongholds in the West Bank, and they were given additional credibility by the extremely high voter turnout, estimated between 80 percent and 90 percent.[121]

The second and third rounds of elections, respectively, in May and September 2005, seemed partially to erode Hamas's first electoral gains by awarding Fatah between 54 percent and 56 percent of the available seats;[122] the group still confirmed its electoral strength by maintaining a record of victories in major urban centers and by performing strongly in the West Bank in the last electoral round in December 2005, gaining the majority in local councils of major centers such as Nablus, Jenin, and El Bireh.[123] Hamas's electoral victories were often concentrated in densely populated urban areas.[124]

The elections were conducted in a generally orderly fashion, although the old rivalry between Hamas and Fatah reemerged as early as the second electoral round. Following Fatah's accusation that Hamas was committing electoral fraud and the Central Election Commission's demand to recount the ballots in the contested electoral districts, tensions between the two parties escalated and risked jeopardizing continuing the political process.[125]

In the municipal elections, Hamas ran through a number of independent but affiliated candidates, as well as through the Change and Reform list, and it invested substantial energies in devising a political program focused on social change, anti-corruption and transparency, progress, and development and poverty eradication.[126]

During the political campaign, Hamas also explained pragmatically the reasons behind its entry into mainstream politics: "Resistance is Hamas' main focus, and we call for its continuation, but we also hope to become more involved in Palestinian society and provide services to the Palestinian people, hence our participation in these elections. . . . It is our duty to progress, to move forward, to invest in infrastructure, and to invest in change and face challenges."[127]

While investing in the Palestinian political system through its participation in the municipal elections, the group also placed increased focus on political integration: in the aftermath of Arafat's death, the group began discussions with newly elected president Abbas, agreeing first to an official cease-fire in February 2005, and then engaging Fatah at the political level.[128]

With these objectives in mind, Hamas, Fatah, and other main Palestinian factions, met in Cairo in March 2005 to begin a process of national reconciliation.[129] First, the Cairo talks obtained the renewal of the cease-fire with Israel, generating a period of relative calm that lasted from March 2005 to June 2006.[130] The cease-fire allowed Hamas and the other Palestinian factions to focus on the ongoing municipal and legislative elections. This decline in emphasis on military activities corresponded with the relative weakness of the group's military wing, which had been strongly hit both by Israel's assassination campaigns, and by the construction of the "security fence," which impaired perpetrating and implementing armed attacks within Israel from the West Bank.

Second, the Cairo Declaration, which was issued as a result of the talks, constituted a double victory for Hamas, as well as a sign of its increased interest in political integration. The document ratified the Palestinian people's right to resist, thus leading Egypt and Fatah to accept de facto the legitimacy of Hamas's "resistance" agenda, strengthening its claims as a legitimate and mainstream organization within Palestine. Even more important, the document also laid the basis for future PLO reforms, recognizing the need to expand organization membership to make it "truly representative."[131] When implemented, such reforms would mostly favor Hamas, by ending Fatah's monopoly of the PLO and by awarding additional recognition to and facilitating the political integration of the group.

The Cairo talks were a practical demonstration of Hamas's increased political weight and status, as well of its ability to play a strong role in dictating the political agenda for the Palestinian people. Not surprisingly, during this period of unprecedented political strength, Hamas also started to disclose its plan to take part in the upcoming legislative elections. On March 12, West Bank leader Sheikh Mohamed Ghazal disclosed the group's intention to join the electoral race for the PLC, after the group had been urging Abbas to set a date for the electoral contest since November 2004.[132] Fatah's reaction was one of support for Hamas's decision; as Abbas stated: "Democracy would be meaningless once we start banning any faction from taking part in the democratic process."[133] At the same time, Fatah tried to manage the "Hamas threat" by attempting both to co-opt the group and delay the electoral process.

After the Cairo talks, Abbas first offered Hamas participation in his cabinet in exchange for accepting a postponement of the legislative elections, originally scheduled to be held in July 2005 and later postponed to January 2006.[134] Abbas was surely influenced to delay elections ahead of Israel's unilateral "disengagement" from Gaza in July 2005 to avoid a massive rise in Hamas's approval rates, penalizing Fatah. Another reason for the delay was the need to follow through on the Cairo Declaration's commitments to reform and modify the electoral law by raising the number of council seats to 132 (from the initial 88) and by introducing a proportional-based system with a 2 percent threshold to elect 66 of the total representatives in the PLC.[135]

These changes allowed the parties to agree in August 2005 to hold elections on January 25, 2006, although the tensions between Fatah and Hamas did not cease. In the period preceding the actual voting, Fatah threatened to postpone the electoral process; first, by attempting to modify the electoral law and questioning the mixed proportional system (which was largely seen as an improvement for Hamas, as explained in the previous section),[136] and then by conditioning the elections to Israel's allowing the voting of East Jerusalem residents. Hamas largely interpreted both moves as attempts to derail the political process. So the group used its political leverage and refused to agree to further delays. Elections were finally held on January 25, 2006, and they concluded with Hamas's list winning 74 of the 132 available seats in the PLC , gaining the majority of the Legislative Council and becoming the majority party in Palestinian politics.[137] To achieve this impressive political result, Hamas showed a high degree of political will, reflected in its well-structured political platform and in its electoral campaigning strategy.

Hamas's political program and statements, while underlining the resistance character of the movement, its unaltered goals to "liberate Palestine" and its commitment to Islam as a way of life were also aimed at smoothing the movement's edges, emphasizing domestic issues and practical themes over ideological ones, and assuring voters that the Islamic character of the movement "does not mean fanaticism and isolation or harming anyone else." Hamas's political platform also focused on social justice and development, together with an emphasis on transparency and on promoting democracy. The group openly questioned Fatah's governance record, and it responded to the party's attempts to delay the elections by asserting that Fatah's conduct was "raising our worry and deepening our fear for the fate of the democratic process."[138]

These themes were further developed in the Change and Reform electoral platform, which laid out, in fourteen pages, the group's social, political, and economic agenda.[139] This is not to say that Hamas did not rely on the achievements of its military struggle to gather support, but still the bulk of the political program was focused inward, directed at Palestinian daily life and internal governance. This decision was a rather pragmatic one, as Hamas heavily relied on polls, including some conducted by an in-house polling unit, to map out the concerns and interests of the Palestinian electorate.[140]

Hamas also invested significant political capital in running a full-fledged electoral campaign, mobilizing the group's entire social and charitable network to showcase its record of effectiveness in delivering social welfare, and relying on its electoral victories in the municipal elections to demonstrate that, if elected, the group would be able to achieve those same impressive results through mainstream politics. The group also relied on electoral alliances, often trying to recruit independent candidates from affluent clans and powerful local families, and thus trying to break into Fatah's historical practice of co-opting local and traditional authority figures to boost its political party.[141]

Hamas showed the same degree of pragmatism and political awareness of its real strength by nominating only as many candidates as its expected electoral support, thus avoiding Fatah's practice of nominating too many candidates for any given electoral district, thereby dispersing its electoral support. Finally, Hamas relied on its grassroots supporters to be massively present and visible during the electoral campaign; for instance, the Change and Reform block sent observers to assist the electorate in virtually every polling station.[142]

The electoral victory was therefore preceded by an intense campaigning period, where the bulk of organizational activities focused on political participation: first by taking part in the municipal elections, then by discussing inclusion in the PLO, and finally by competing in the PLC electoral race. If the phase of the second intifada was characterized by general organizational cohesion and prominence of the armed wing, then a definite resurgence of the group's political agenda characterized the 2004–5 period. To assess the impact of this "political moderation" stage, it is important to analyze the postelectoral phase, observing both the developing relations between Hamas's armed and military wings and the interaction between the logic of military struggle and that of political accommodation.

2006–2012: Hamas in Power

Hamas's victory shocked the international community, which was largely unaware of internal Palestinian politics, as well as Fatah's leadership, which, failing to grasp the political reality on the ground, had anticipated being able to integrate Hamas into a Fatah-led government. Hamas's political success was likely the result of a combination of a number of factors. These included Fatah's ongoing decay and internal divisions, coupled with a record of corrupt and ineffective administration; Hamas's successful record as a social movement and its honest reputation; the overall failure of the Fatah-led peace process; and the appeal of the group's "resistance" and Islamic ideology.

Hamas was able to portray the Israeli unilateral disengagement from Gaza in the summer of 2005 as a direct result of its armed struggle, and this also contributed to enhancing its political appeal (the Palestinian Center for Policy and Survey Research reported that as many as 84 percent of Palestinians were convinced that Hamas was directly responsible for Israeli withdrawal).[143]

Hamas's Islamic identity also played a role in attracting electoral consensus, in line with a domestic, as well as regional, process of increased personal religiosity and support for Islamist politics, and with the parallel gradual decay of "secularism" as a viable political model.[144] Although most political observers affirmed that the victory also came as a surprise to Hamas, an in-depth analysis of the organization's behavior and statements during the pre-electoral phase leads one to believe that the group was anticipating a very strong performance at the ballot boxes.

They were expecting to gather at least 40 percent of the total electoral preferences, in line with their previous performances in the municipal elections, as well as in grassroots elections (including trade unions and student councils) where they had successfully competed since the early 1990s. But, while Hamas was confident in achieving a strong electoral result, it is also likely that the group had failed to predict its electoral victory and was at least to some degree overwhelmed by it. It is not surprising that one of Hamas's first moves in the postelectoral phase was to reach out to Fatah and attempt to form a national unity government, an opening promptly rejected by the Abbas-led party.[145] This refusal led the Hamas-elected representatives in the PLC to elect Gaza leader Ismail Haniyeh as Prime Minister.[146] The new PM then proceeded to form a Hamas-only cabinet in March 2006, awarding important positions such as foreign minister and interior minister to prominent Hamas members, such as Mahmoud al-Zahar and Said Siam.[147]

The decisions to participate in the PLC elections and in the electoral campaign were conducted under conditions of substantial internal unity, although the group's increased political activism put the local political leaders at the organization's front, while the group's military wing largely stood at the margins of the political process, as very few military leaders directly joined it. The period immediately following Hamas's electoral victory further increased the status of the local political leaders and generated a momentum for this group to push forward a political agenda that would enhance its status, often by adopting a more accommodation-prone attitude with respect to external and internal foes. This was permitted by Hamas's internal reorganization to allow the political leaders involved in the government to have more freedom of action: it is believed that elected officials tended to, at least officially, discontinue their internal roles of members of the bureau or the Shura Council, thus granting a level of separation between the Hamas government's view and the movement's position.[148]

For instance, in the proposed (and rejected) national unity government program, the group's political leaders attempted to smooth Hamas's rejection of preexisting agreements between the PLO and Israel and international accords, and it affirmed that it would cooperate with the international community and consider respecting signed agreements insofar as they preserved the "ultimate interests of our people." The document also stressed Hamas's focus on ending occupation and achieving a Palestinian state within the 1967 borders, largely staying clear of divisive language and omitting references to more controversial concepts such as the "destruction of Israel," albeit clarifying that the achievement of this Palestinian state would only be a step toward the achievement of the "final liberation."[149]

Dr. Nasser a-Din Shaar, Prime Minister Haniyeh's deputy premier and Minister of Education and Culture, asserted the possibility of coordinating with Israel over governance matters, without however linking this idea with the recognition Israel's right to exist.[150] These were references to a de facto recognition. Although these statements clearly fell short of the international community's request to recognize Israel, renounce violence, and accept all preexisting agreements as preconditions for them to recognize and deal with the Hamas government, they were still highly significant. They expressed the political leaders' attempt to adopt a more pragmatic and accommodation-seeking tone in the hopes of boosting the newly elected government.

This trend was further confirmed by the early conciliatory tone that the political leadership had assumed within Palestinian politics, in the hopes of achieving a unity government. This position was held by Hamas leaders in government, as well as by Hamas prisoner Abdul Khaliq al-Natche, who signed (but later retracted) the Prisoners' Document in the spring of 2006.[151] This document, later renamed National Conciliation Document and used as the basis of the February 2007 Mecca Accord, was pushed by Fatah "young guard" leaders such as Barghouti, and it urged both Hamas and Fatah to create a unity government based on the January 2006 electoral result, while recognizing the common goal of creating a Palestinian state in the pre-1967 borders.[152]

These efforts were matched by attempts, at the international level, to improve Hamas's position with respect to the international community, hoping to avoid the cut of direct aid for the newly elected government, a measure which was nevertheless implemented both by the United States and the EU, starting in April 2006.[153] Examples of this trend include a public relations campaign launched in Western newspapers and media, as exemplified by the opinion article published by Haniyeh in the *Washington Post* in June 2006, in which he tried to appeal to the Western audience by adopting the discourse of human rights, self-determination, and democracy.[154]

These openings were, however, not always seconded by Hamas's military and external leaders, who often adopted a less nuanced and more bellicose tone, a signal of the multifaceted dimensions of the organization. In the aftermath of the elections and in parallel to the local political leadership's openings, Mashal's discourse sought to reiterate the Charter's language: "Our mission is to liberate Jerusalem and purify the al-Aqsa Mosque (...). This victory [in the PA elections] is a message from the Palestinian nation that it is united behind the *Jihad* option."[155] More important, the "hard core" military and external leadership seemed at times to contradict the local calls for national unity and reconciliation, showing less restraint in confronting Fatah.

The first political clash between Hamas and Fatah took place at the parliament's first meeting, when Hamas's elected representative decided to abrogate a number of preexisting laws passed by Fatah to enhance Abu Mazen's power, leading to Fatah's boycott of the parliament.[156] The early rift paved the way for the development of two opposing centers of political power: the presidency—led by Abbas and Fatah—and the Hamas-led government. This division was not just political but also geographical, with the presidency based in the West Bank and the Hamas leadership largely residing in Gaza.

While the local political leaders had initially attempted to co-opt Abbas's party and bring it into the elected government, the more militant sector of the organization did not follow the same course of action: As early as April 2006, Khaled Mashal publicly stated: "Very soon we will uncover the true face of these criminals who are sacrificing the national interest for their personal interests [Abbas and Fatah]. The criminals have left the coffers empty and have even stolen the furniture from the ministries before they transferred them to us."[157]

The local political leadership maintained a level of distance from Mashal's declaration; for instance, on April 23, 2006, Nasser a-Din Shaar tried to restore internal peace by assuring the Palestinian public that Mashal's declarations "do not necessarily reflect the position of the Hamas government but rather only of the Hamas organization," a clear attempt to draw lines within Hamas.[158] However, in the months following the January 2006 elections the relation between Hamas and Fatah deteriorated sharply, eventually leading to violent clashes and to widespread internal unrest. By the summer of 2006, increasing pressure stemming from the international boycott against the Hamas government combined with increasingly tense relations with Fatah, gradually started to reverse the initial openings of the local political leadership.

First, Hamas leaders in government were put under pressure due to the international boycott against Hamas, and their effective power and status was further undermined in the summer of 2006, when—following an armed attack against Israel and the kidnapping of IDF corporal Gilad Shalit by a loose coalition of armed groups within Gaza, including Hamas's Qassam Brigades, the Salah al-Din Brigades, and the Gaza-based Salafist-jihadist Army of Islam (Jaish al-Islam)—hostilities between the Israel and Hamas exploded again in the Gaza Strip, putting an end to the ceasefire that had been in place since March 2005. The armed attack, which ended sixteen months of cease-fire with Israel and which formally lasted until November 2006,[159] resulted in a mass-scale military response against Hamas in Gaza and in the arrest of sixty-four Hamas officials in government, including members of the PLC and ministers.[160] This series of events sidetracked the trend of the rising political and organizational power of Hamas's local political leaders, while they also contributed to ease preexisting internal tensions within Hamas.

Contrary to the widespread interpretation of the Western media that Shalit's kidnapping underlined deep divisions between the group's armed wing and the political leaders in government, the political wing's reactions to the armed operations reflected organizational cohesion and support for the Qassam Brigades. Because of Hamas's compartmentalization of responsibilities and the relative freedom of operations enjoyed by the group's armed wing, which, however, still coordinated its attack with the Political Bureau in Damascus, the political leadership in the Palestinian government was not involved in the preparation and execution of the attack, though it supported it ex post facto.[161]

Second, another source of strain on the rise of the local political leadership and of the accommodation-prone discourse was the progressive deterioration of the relationship with Fatah. Hamas and Fatah became involved in repeated armed clashes, and, from April 2006 to June 2007, the two groups alternated phases of open armed confrontation within Gaza and the West Bank, with temporary cease-fires and attempts to reach an internal agreement and maintain a functioning unity government.

Hamas did not always present a united front when dealing with the Fatah crisis, as the group's "hard core" leaders at times attempted to derail the internal reconciliation process. For instance, on November 25, 2006, after Israel accepted the terms of a cease-fire proposed by Abu Mazen and Hamas to boost a new round of "unity talks,"[162] Mashal publicly threatened a third intifada within the next six months.[163] Although these statements reflected internal tensions regarding how to resolve the Fatah crisis, they did not lead escalate and lead to more widespread organizational tensions. No serious reconciliation step was taken unilaterally by the Hamas leaders within the government without the direct involvement of the bureau; for example, no real progress was made in the course of the February 2007 Mecca Negotiations until both Haniyeh and Mashal were brought to the negotiating table with Abbas.[164]

Involving all levels of the Hamas leadership eventually led to the "Mecca Agreement," based on the National Conciliation Document between Fatah and Hamas, and to the subsequent creation of a national unity government.[165] The reasons that led Hamas to agree to a national unity government were extremely pragmatic. The Hamas political leaders were mindful that at the time they were experiencing a steady decline in popular support, with 54 percent of Palestinians highly disapproved of their actions and favored creating a national unity government. In addition Hamas also viewed the national unity option as a chance to cease the movement's international isolation and to ease the burden of sanctions.[166] The temporary reconciliation was, however, extremely short-lived, as following yet another round of armed clashes between Hamas and Fatah in June 2007, the Islamist group assumed control of the Gaza Strip, leading President Abbas to dismiss Prime Minister Haniyeh and the unity government and to create a parallel government under the leadership of Salam Fayyad as prime minister in the West Bank.[167] Hamas's armed takeover of June 2007 had a profound organizational effect on the group, which found itself in the position of ruling over Gaza. The group's main priority in the aftermath of its takeover of the local institutions was to establish control over the Gaza Strip, especially ensuring the group's monopoly of force. A first move in that direction was certainly its open challenge to traditional families and clans over their right to employ armed force in Gaza, while another early move was to implement massive internal security operations to crack down on local criminal organizations to establish public order.[168] Hamas's anti-crime campaign was largely successful, as they managed to establish law and order within Gaza, but it was also matched by a concomitant crackdown on civil, social, and political opposition, including media, local nongovernmental organizations, and civil society groups.

The main target of the campaign was initially Fatah. A massive repression against Fatah leaders and activists alike followed the June 2007 takeover, further exacerbating the tensions between the two parties. Within a year of taking power, Fatah presence in Gaza had basically been wiped out.[169] Hamas also targeted any other political and military opposition to the group. It did so in many cases by relying on extralegal tools and by engaging in human rights violations, ranging from abductions, to arbitrary detentions, and unlawful killings.[170]

To secure control of Gaza, Hamas also boosted its military apparatus: It reformed the internal security system by reorganizing the Executive Force (Tanfithya) it had created in April 2006 as a response to Fatah's complete domination over the PA security sector. The Executive Force was then dissolved in October 2007 and integrated in the Gaza security sector (comprising the civil police, the National Security Forces, the Internal Security Apparatus, and the Security and Protection Apparatus) and turned it into an efficient law-enforcement and military apparatus to act as a substitute for the PA security forces.[171] Despite integrating some non-Hamas personnel into the new security sector, Hamas maintained a solid grip on Gaza's security forces, often employing them to gain control of Gaza's centers of power and governance and to liquidate internal dissent.[172] The chance for Hamas to develop this parallel security sector had been provided, inadvertently, by president Abbas when—following the June 2007 takeover of the Strip—he had ordered PA police and security forces active in Gaza report for duty.[173]

While building a parallel security system, the status and power of Hamas's military wing, the Qassam Brigades, also shifted from underground organization to mainstream armed militia within Gaza. At the same time, Hamas's military wing also upgraded its military arsenal and boosted its finances, also by gaining control of Gaza's underground tunnel–smuggling business.[174]

The Hamas political leadership made increased efforts to ensure its total control of the government and bureaucratic structure and to deal better with the huge challenge of administering Gaza. This was daunting because of the long-standing freeze of direct aid implemented by the EU and the United States, and because of Israel's June 2007 tightening of the cross-border traffic of people and goods to and from Gaza, which amounted to a blockade. From an organizational perspective, the June 2007 armed takeover had a mixed effect: On the one hand, the group's military wing was empowered by upgrading its status in Gaza, by gaining increased influence within Hamas, and by boosting its military capabilities. On the other hand, the local political leadership found itself in an increasingly more complicated position, confronted with a popular backlash in response to the group's armed takeover, an unfavorable set of circumstances that impaired its political performance and undermined its domestic legitimacy, and the loss of influence within the West Bank.[175] The takeover also escalated the tensions between Fatah and Hamas, lowering the chances of future reconciliation and amounting to the division of Palestine into two separate entities, a political nightmare for all the parties involved and a historic setback to Palestinian aspirations for statehood.

By being in charge of Gaza, the political leadership also found itself juggling between conflicting organizational imperatives; if, on the one hand, the group had to promote the internal process of Islamization and external jihad, these priorities had to be accommodated with the need to govern and provide for the people in Gaza, as well as with the necessity of staying in power, and with improving the movement's international status.

Interorganizational tensions along the political-military line have been far from uncommon in the aftermath of the takeover, and there has been a process of growing internal dissent and defection from the military ranks of Hamas.[176] Disenchanted Hamas militants have been joining new Salafist-jihadist groups, which have been mushrooming in Gaza ever since the armed takeover of Gaza. These groups are challenging Hamas's leadership and criticizing its "moderation" in applying Sharia law and in conducting its jihad against Israel. Some of these groups, like Swords of Righteousness (Suyuf al-Haq) or the Jaljalat, have allegedly been directly founded by former Hamas members.[177]

The "window of opportunity" that had opened in the immediate aftermath of the January 2006 victory, when part of the Hamas government leadership attempted to become increasingly integrated in the political system and to gain legitimacy and recognition, closed with the armed takeover and the imposition of a unilateral governance model. The Hamas political leadership became increasingly more entrenched in Gaza and more preoccupied with preserving its control of the Gaza Strip.

Reconciliation between Hamas and Fatah remained unsuccessful between 2007 and 2011, as the parties repeatedly failed to agree on the creation of a new national unity government, on the procedures and times to hold new presidential and parliamentary elections, and on the mechanisms to reform the PLO. Despite the repeated rounds of intragroup negotiations, no substantial progress was achieved, with both groups maintaining a hostile stance with respect to the other group's supporters and leaders. In the years between the takeover of Gaza in 2007 and the May 2011 Hamas-Fatah reconciliation agreement, the bulk of the organization maintained a "hard-bargaining posture" with regard to Fatah, with the exception of certain Hamas leaders within the West Bank, who displayed a more accommodation-prone tone with respect to engaging Fatah and restoring the pre-June 2007 status quo.[178]

There have not been substantial shifts in the group's relations with Israel in the aftermath of the June 2007 takeover, with the group maintaining the same level of controlled violence that marked the post–January 2006 elections, with temporary escalations, such as in the summer of 2006, 2007, and in January 2008, when the two sides engaged in open armed conflict, resulting in both Israeli operations in the Strip and in the launching of rockets from Gaza. Hamas then entered into an official Egyptian-brokered cease-fire with Israel in June 2008. Among the key conditions to implementing the cease-fire, Israel asked for the halt of armed attacks from the Gaza Strip into Israel and the end of weapons smuggling through Egypt.

On June 17, 2008, Hamas announced its acceptance of the cease-fire, demanding the end of Israeli military operations within Gaza, as well as the end of the economic blockade. This cease-fire lasted more than six months, despite both parties' repeated violations of its terms, and it terminated in December 2008 with the beginning of the December 2008–January 2009 Operation Cast Lead in Gaza. Following the end of this round of hostilities in January 2009, Hamas and Israel maintained an unofficial "calm."

The rules of the game between Hamas and Israel in the aftermath of Cast Lead have revolved around a precarious policy of "mutual restraint." Accordingly, Hamas for the most part refrained from both participating or allowing other groups to wage massive attacks against Israel, while permitting (and at times perpetrating) smaller-scale and more sporadic rocket attacks. Israel, for the most part, restrained its military reactions against the rocket attacks, while continuing military operations against militants in Gaza and without fundamentally reversing its policy of non-recognition and isolation with respect to Hamas. The "mutual restraint" has been built on a shaky basis and periodic flares between Hamas and Israel have been far from uncommon. Between 2008 and 2012, the most serious escalation of hostilities took place in November 2012, in the days preceding and (especially) following Israel's targeted assassination of Hamas's military wing leader Ahmad Ja'abari. In response to the assassination, rocket attacks increased exponentially, with Gaza militants showcasing their improved arsenal and, for the first time, shooting rockets that could reach as far as Tel Aviv and Jerusalem. This escalation brought both Hamas and Israel again on the brink of yet another round of fully fledged armed confrontations. In the end—also thanks to third-party mediations led by Egypt—Hamas and Israel agreed to yet another shaky cease-fire.

In this context of stalled progress in both the relations with Israel as well as with the historical political opponent Fatah, an important new chapter in Hamas's internal development has begun since the Arab Awakening.

The beginning of the massive wave of social protests across the Middle East took Hamas and Fatah by storm, and the groups reacted to it by partially changing their strategies to adjust to the new political environment in the Middle East. Concretely, this not only resulted in Hamas's offering political support and praise for the revolutions in Tunisia and Egypt but also led the group to give more weight to Palestinian public opinion demands to end the political rift with Fatah. Hamas agreed to a reconciliation deal brokered by the post-Mubarak Egyptian leadership at the end of April 2011.

The terms of the agreement, which included creating a unity government of technocrats and foresaw holding new presidential and Legislative Council elections within a year from the signed accord, had been on the table since at least October 2010. (Fatah had accepted this Egyptian plan while Hamas had rejected it.) Hamas was only able to accept it in spring 2011, following the change in leadership within Egypt, the stall of the political process with Israel, and the overall change in the political climate caused by the Arab Awakening.

The 2011 reconciliation agreement created another momentum for Hamas to boost its political strategy and test its capacity to pursue political accommodation. Since May 2011, there have indeed been a few examples of this renewed political opening. For instance, according to a much-quoted Jane's intelligence report, in November 2011, the group officially signed an agreement with its historical political opponent, Fatah, accepting to shift gears and suspend its violent activities.[179]

Even leaving aside the (unconfirmed) report, in the months following the reconciliation deal, Hamas leaders repeatedly stated that, although the organization refuses to renounce its right to resort to violence, they were still willing to give "peaceful activism" a chance.[180] Some leaders of the group, like Political Bureau leader Mashal, even asserted that unarmed politics would now represent the preferred strategic tool to confront Israel, without however denying the organizational right to resorting to armed struggle.

On the one hand, Hamas's recent emphasis on the nonviolent struggle discourse can indeed be seen as part of the group's long-standing strategy to create parallel political frameworks to get beyond its own inflexibilities. On the other hand, the opening reflects Hamas's pragmatism and capacity to adapt to the shifting circumstances of the Middle East. First, the effect of the Arab Awakening, with its new discourse centered on sociopolitical rights and freedoms, has led Hamas to rethink its branding strategy.

The new regional developments seem to point out to a new, albeit not yet fully developed, model exemplified by the rise of nonviolent groups such as the Muslim Brotherhood in Egypt. It is unsurprising that Hamas wants to be associated more with the new rising stars of Middle Eastern politics, than with "old" despots like Assad and his crumbling regime.

The Arab Awakening has represented an ideological challenge to Hamas as well as a rather pragmatic one: With the ongoing turmoil raging in Syria and the potential demise of the Assad regime, the group has become concerned with finding new strategic allies. Hamas's refusal to back Assad in the course of the protests weakened the group's relations with Syria and Iran, in turn opening a window of opportunity for Hamas to redefine its regional alliances by moving away from the "Axis of Resistance" and its discourse, and repositioning itself more closely with "moderate" regional actors, such as Egypt or Qatar.

From this perspective, the potential shift in the regional balance of power and the growing popularity of the "Muslim Brotherhood brand" of Islamism in the region helps with understanding why Hamas has been focusing on inter-Palestinian reconciliation and on marketing its nonviolent strategy to stay popular and relevant. Since Hamas has been in charge of the Gaza Strip in 2007, the realities of power had already substantially degraded the number and magnitude of armed attacks perpetrated by the group against Israel, thus reaffirming the need to focus on alternative strategies to confront its enemy. Although this organizational development is significant, it is far from clear whether this partial opening will result in progressive accommodation and in the affirmation of the political accommodation strategy over the armed one. On the contrary, this opening may very well be temporary and reversible like the ones analyzed all throughout the group's history. In this sense, the flares of violence between Hamas and Israel in 2012 offer a cautionary tale on the subject.

Going forward, it seems that the political development and accommodation of Hamas continues to depend on three main issues: (1) the attractiveness and feasibility of the political accommodation path, (2) the rise of political accommodation and armed struggle as mutually exclusive alternatives, and (3) the ability of the group to manage internal dissent. First, for the accommodation option to have internal traction, the political path needs to be perceived as promising. If the inter-Palestinian reconciliation leads to the normalization of Palestinian political life (and of Gaza) and to the creation of a united political coalition, then Hamas will have a higher interest in investing in nonviolent politics, provided the group is allowed to have a significant share of political power in "postreconciliation" Palestine. Similarly, if the group perceives the security environment as nonthreatening, it may have an interest in deemphasizing its military apparatus. A resolute international and Israeli refusal to deal with any Palestinian government that includes Hamas may lead to a renewed marginalization of the group, which could in turn backfire, empowering Hamas's more radical leaders and minimizing the unarmed strategy.

Second, for Hamas to follow the "moderation" path, the group needs to perceive a need to choose between accommodation and armed struggle; otherwise, the organization may very well choose to preserve its hybrid nature. Until now, the "accommodation" process and reconciliation has been stirring up internal divisions along the political-military line, as well as highlighting the different concerns of the "external" and the local leadership. A case in point is the February 2012 diatribe between bureau chief Khaled Mashal and Gaza-based leader Mahmoud Zahhar over Mashal's agreeing to Abbas leading the national unity government to be established by Hamas and Fatah. Mashal accepted Abbas's leadership by signing an agreement in Doha (Qatar) at the beginning of February, leading to a sharp protest of Zahhar and other prominent Gaza leaders, who accused Mashal of going behind the Shura Council and hurting the organization's interests. The conflict did not escalate further, also because the reconciliation with Fatah remained de facto frozen, but it did reveal an important internal dynamic. The Mashal-Zahhar controversy highlighted the growing disparity between the Gaza leadership, interested in preserving its power over Gaza, and the external leadership—looking at the broader organizational picture. This trend is extremely important because it demonstrates the important effects that gaining control of Gaza has had on the organization. First, ruling Gaza has contributed to shifting the organizational center of power away from the external leadership and back to the leaders in Gaza. Second, historically, Gaza leadership was considered the most accommodation-prone organizational subunit within Hamas, with the Political Bureau and the Diaspora-based leaders seen as the most ideologically rigid and inflexible group. However, in the past months, these assumptions have been deeply questioned, with Diaspora-based leader Mashal embarking in compromise deals with Fatah and with the Gaza-based leaders denouncing them on the basis of their post-2007 interest in preserving their power and status within Gaza.

Third, Hamas needs to continue in its transition while avoid splintering or imploding. Since 2006, the group has invested in boosting its military apparatus, thus indicating that any attempt to sideline the military leadership could result in dire internal conflicts. It is unclear whether Hamas's "hard core" constituency would allow a nonviolent strategic shift, or whether this would lead to additional internal conflict, deeply threatening the internal cohesion of the group. When looking at the political trajectory of Hamas following its electoral victory in 2006, it appears evident that the group has undergone important internal shifts, albeit still falling short of transitioning toward becoming a fully politically integrated actor.

In the aftermath of the elections, the local political leadership seemed to be adopting a gradually more accommodation-seeking tone and to value pursuing further political integration, at times openly clashing with both the external and the military leaders. However, the international and domestic isolation of the Hamas government quickly led to the closing of the "window of opportunity," while the subsequent armed takeover of the Gaza Strip shifted the political leadership's agenda from seeking political integration into Palestinian politics to focusing on political survival and staying in power in Gaza. More recently, the Arab Awakening and changes in the regional political arena have pushed Hamas again toward adapting its strategy and rebranding itself, resulting in renewed internal conflicts.

Assessing the Political Development of Hamas

Hamas, simultaneously an armed group, a social movement, and a political party, is an important case study to assess the reasons behind armed groups' decision to participate in institutional politics and to analyze this organizational development. As with Hezbollah, Hamas provides an example of a highly institutionalized and sophisticated organization, and thus it can be used as a "least likely" case study to test the cyclical model of political wing formation and development.

The chapter first examined the political development of the Palestinian Hamas, highlighting the reasons behind the group's formal entry into institutional politics. Hamas's decision to take part in elections appeared related to the interplay of four factors: (1) the group's degree of institutionalization and its related push to expand,

(2) a strain in the availability of mobilization resources, (3) substantial shifts within the political opportunity structure, and (4) a significant internal commitment to reform the organization.

Hamas first considered taking part in the Palestinian elections in the mid-1990s, at the same time as the creation of the PA in 1994 and the subsequent 1996 legislative elections. However, Hamas decided against competing in the upcoming elections, mostly because there had not been any substantial opening within the domestic political system that would have allowed the group to compete successfully against its main political adversary, Fatah.

The newly created PA was characterized by a high centralization and low separation of powers, by-products of the de facto control of the system by Fatah's historic leader, Yasser Arafat. The lack of an opening in the political opportunity system deterred Hamas from creating its own political wing to participate in institutional politics, even though the group was facing institutional pressures to expand, along with a strain in its popularity and mobilization resources. This finding confirms the original hypothesis that the creation of a political wing equally depends on organizational (the internal commitment to change and the group's degree of institutionalization) and external factors (the availability of mobilization resources and the existence of a favorable political opportunity structure).

Only a decade later, following the death of PA president Yasser Arafat and the substantial opening of the domestic political system in 2004, Hamas changed its posture with respect to institutional politics and chose to compete in the municipal and legislative Palestinian elections in 2005 and 2006, respectively. This decision was again related to a major change in the group's political opportunity system.

In the mid-2000s, Hamas was also facing relative weakness of its military wing together with a decline in popularity of the armed struggle option, accompanied by a substantial strain in its financial resources. These factors resulted in the organization's experiencing an important decline in its mobilization resources, thus pushing it to further diversify its activities and funding sources by forming a political wing.

The group was also under pressure to expand, and it wanted to seize the opportunity to increase its political constituency by attracting that sector of the Palestinian population that over the years had become highly critical of Fatah. Hamas then took advantage of the new favorable political opportunity structure to create a political wing, which allowed the group to accommodate itself to the changing political environment, to strengthen its legitimacy and relevance, and to expand its supporting base. Hamas is also a useful case study to inquire into the organizational development of an armed group once it has chosen to pursue political participation.

The theory focuses on the relation between a given group's political front and its military wing as an important factor in determining the group's organizational dynamics. The hypothesis affirms that commitment to strategic change (resulting in the group's "moderation" and eventual disarmament) is the result of a prolonged internal conflict between the armed and the political leaders within a given organization. Conversely, in the absence of internal frictions, armed groups will have little incentive to choose between their armed struggle and their political activism, and thus they will continue to operate as hybrid politico-military organizations.

Hamas is an interesting case to test this hypothesis as, unlike Hezbollah, the group's organizational structure is less cohesive and integrated, and, at time, intraorganizational conflict arises between "local" and "external" leaders, and with respect to the political and military leadership. Because of the higher level of internal disunity and competition, the research would expect Hamas's potential for strategic change to be higher than Hezbollah's. The analysis of the group's political development confirmed this trend, showing that Hamas's political evolution follows a cyclical pattern where phases of solid collaboration between the group's military and political wings are followed by stages of internal and external confrontation, producing repeated internal clashes and thus increasing the potential for strategic change.

Since its founding in 1987, Hamas has gone through cycles of internal cooperation and competition. Before the creation of the PA (1987–1994), Hamas's evolution was characterized by the harmonious development of its military and sociopolitical wings, as the Qassam Battalions' attacks were crucial tools in promoting the organization's main political objectives of derailing the peace process with Israel, self-asserting the group's identity as the Islamist alternative to Fatah, and discrediting Arafat's group.

The creation of the PA in 1994 and the progressive decline in Palestinian support for Hamas and its armed struggle both led to increased intraorganizational unrest along political versus military lines, dominated by the internal debate on whether to take part in the Palestinian legislative elections of 1996. This phase of competition would then end with the beginning of the second intifada in the year 2000, which resulted in a strategic rapprochement between Hamas's military and political objectives, as again the actions of the Qassam Brigades became the main tool in the group's political strategy to assert its prominence and undermine Fatah. The progressive winding down of the second intifada and the death of Yasser Arafat in 2004 made Hamas shift gears again and invest substantially in creating a political party to compete in the Palestinian municipal and legislative elections, resulting in the group's electoral victory of January 2006.

This led to new stage of intraorganizational competition. The period following the group's rise to power, between January 2006 and April 2007, was characterized by the political leadership's attempts to increase its status and power, often by adopting a more accommodation-prone attitude. This attitude led to increased internal conflict with the "hard core" military and external leaders. In the end, however, this "opening" did not result in a more prolonged and deep internal friction between the two wings, as the ongoing international boycott against the Hamas government and the deteriorating relationship with Fatah quickly marginalized and discredited the political leadership's "moderation" agenda.

More important, in the aftermath of the June 2007 armed takeover of Gaza, the political leadership's main objective swiftly shifted away from pursuing political integration to ensuring its political survival and perpetuating its staying in power in the Gaza Strip, a task that requires backing and support from the military wing. Since the beginning of the Arab Awakening, Hamas has increasingly sought to reverse the previous isolation and to seek to redraw regional alliances and boost its credibility and legitimacy. This has also spurred a political opening within the group, which now seems to be increasingly interested in political accommodation. This process has not been cost free, as the reconciliation has increased the level of internal divisions within the group. Similarly, political openings have been also accompanied by renewed chapters of violence, signaling that the organization is still pursuing a hybrid politico-military agenda. In the long term, the way Hamas handles the internal dissent will be crucial in both preserving internal cohesion and progressing in the "political accommodation" path.

The future of Hamas's unarmed strategy is uncertain, hanging by the thread of the Palestinian reconciliation process, the internal tensions along the political-military line, the evolution of the Arab Awakening, and the international and Israeli responses to these developments.

The Irish Republican Army and Sinn Féin in Northern Ireland

A Model of Political Transition?

The Provisional Irish Republican Army (IRA or PIRA) is an Irish republican paramilitary organization and one of the most popular armed groups of the last century.[1] The IRA is known as the oldest-operating terrorist organization active within Western Europe and is responsible for some of the most infamous operations of the past decades. The IRA has generated a high level of scholarly and political interest.[2]

The IRA was chosen as a case study for this book because it is most often cited in the literature as a group that illustrates the linear "armed-to-political" development model, offering a prime example of an armed group that permanently gave up violence to join the political process. A significant amount of scholarship on the IRA asserts that its involvement in institutional politics was the key factor that eased the group into relinquishing its military apparatus.[3] It is particularly useful to test the cyclical development model and to generate hypotheses that address the question of policy responses to terrorist groups' activism.

Despite committing to a nonviolent strategy and accepting the decommissioning of its military apparatus, the IRA is still listed as a proscribed terrorist organization by the British Home Office.[4] Although the IRA was publicly condemned by US authorities when it was still operational, the group was never inserted into the US State Department's list of Foreign Terrorist Organizations (FTOs).[5] However, the US State Department has decided to add two splinter groups of the IRA, the Real IRA (RIRA) and the Continuity IRA to its list of terrorist organizations, in agreement with the current European Union and UK policy.[6]

The republican party historically affiliated with the IRA—Sinn Féin—although widely regarded as the political arm of the IRA, was not defined as an illegal organization by the United Kingdom or the international community and since 1974 has been recognized as a legitimate political party, eligible to take part in local and national elections.[7] As this chapter will analyze, the relationship between the IRA and Sinn Féin is more complex and fluid than the traditional perception of Sinn

Féin as a subordinate political front of the IRA. Despite the proximity between the two Republican groups, they have been de facto treated since the beginning as two separate entities. Contrary to previous case studies, the United Kingdom was able to differentiate its policy responses when dealing with the IRA and Sinn Féin. Before examining how politics and elections contributed to the organizational development and shaped the relationship between the IRA and Sinn Féin, the next section analyzes the context that led to the rise of both groups.

Background

Origins of the Conflict: Early History of the Irish Republican Movement

Scholarship on the origins of the modern Northern Irish conflict is diverse, lacking consensus on the existence of the conflict and its longevity. Key theories on the roots of the violence (the Troubles) in Northern Ireland from the 1960s to 2005 focus on different dimensions of the conflict: political, ethnic religious, economic, and psychological.[8]

At its core, the Northern Ireland conflict can be seen as political. Modern ethnic strife in Northern Ireland is linked to the historical legacy of colonialism and to the English conquest and settlement of Ireland, dating back to the twelfth century.[9] Permanent colonization and settlement of Northern Ireland began in the seventeenth century, known as the "plantation of Ulster,"[10] and culminated with the British partition of Ireland and Northern Ireland in 1921. This ad hoc measure by the Crown was also in response to pleas by the Protestant majority who, as approximately 60 percent of the total population in the sixth countries,[11] worried that they would become an ethnic-religious minority in a united and predominantly Catholic Ireland. As a result, two separate, nonintegrated communities—Protestant and Catholic—developed radically different and mutually exclusive political ideals: (1) a permanent integration with the United Kingdom and (2) the reunification with the rest of Ireland. It follows that the conflict is "not just about how Northern Ireland should be governed, but as to whether it should continue to exist at all."[12]

The second "constitutional" aspect of the political struggle in Northern Ireland is more modern and rooted in the Catholic minority's demands, which began in the 1960s, to end the systematic discrimination perpetrated by the Protestant-dominated Ulster government and to gain substantial access and influence in the existing system of government.[13] According to this framework, the political strife between the two communities is a by-product of the preexisting ethnic and religious cleavages.

The conflict in Northern Ireland is not necessarily about freedom of worship. Yet religion still represents the primary factor in describing one's identity within Northern Ireland, and it also represents a highly accurate indicator of the political, social, and economic conditions of the two communities.[14] The political conflict then is deepened by the nonintegration and reciprocal distrust between two separate ethnic-religious communities, which subsequently produced political disagreements on the nature of the state, as well as its legitimacy.[15]

Economic theories on the origins and continuation of the Northern Irish conflict are limited and mostly grounded in Marxist analysis that portrays the violence as a by-product of class divisions within Northern Ireland.[16] The explanatory power of the economic theories seems limited; nonetheless, this set of theories highlights the socioeconomic dimension of the conflict. Aside from ethnic and religious cleavages, Protestant and the Catholic communities were historically divided socioeconomically. The Catholic community was politically underrepresented, economically disadvantaged, and marginalized and excluded from the centers of political and economic power.[17]

Finally, analyzing the psychological aspect of the conflict aids the assessment of determining why the preexisting political struggle and ethnic-religious divide produced such a prolonged and bitter confrontation. The Catholic and the Protestant communities developed without real integration or widespread intergroup contacts. Reciprocal avoidance and segregation, including residential, social, educational, and economic, became the main characteristics that regulated relations between the two groups. A by-product of this segregation was the reinforcement of negative perceptions of the other ethnic group, which fostered a high level of mutual distrust. The Protestant community developed a "siege mentality," while Catholics perceived themselves as underprivileged and systematically discriminated against.[18]

Understanding the psychological, economic, religious, and ethnic dimension of the Northern Irish conflict is crucial when analyzing the history of the Troubles. Yet all of these aspects can be seen as the by-product of the political struggle that originated in the 1921 partition of Ireland. Similarly, the history of the contemporary Irish republican movement is linked to events that led to the 1921 division of the island, as well as to the partition.

The Sinn Féin ("ourselves," also translated "we, ourselves") party was formed in Dublin in November 1905, based on the slogan and political program of Dublin-based journalist and intellectual Arthur Griffith.[19] Since its foundation, the party became involved with institutional politics and competed for the first time in the 1908 Westminster elections, despite having adopted a strategy of abstentionism.

Accordingly, Sinn Féin competed in the elections but refused to take office in the

UK governmental system.[20] At this early stage, Sinn Féin was not a mass-based or a revolutionary party. The party became more prominent after the Easter Rising of 1916, an anti-British rebellion led by the Irish Republican Brotherhood (IRB), and mostly fought through the Irish Volunteers and the Irish Citizen Army.[21] Sinn Féin per se did not directly lead the revolt, although some of its members did join the anti-British fight. After 1916, Sinn Féin gradually transformed from an elitist into a mass-based republican party as the surviving groups and leaders of the uprising, including Irish Volunteers's surviving member Eamon de Valera—gradually became integrated and acquired power within Sinn Féin.[22] In the 1918 Westminster elections, the "new" Sinn Féin won a landslide victory and gained seventy-three seats (out of 105).

Committed to abstentionism, the party refused to take office in the British system. Instead, it formed a secessionist parliament, known as the Dáil Éireann, headed by de Valera. The Irish Volunteers, now trained and reorganized with the help of leaders like Michael Collins, pledged allegiance to the Dáil and renamed themselves the Irish Republican Army (IRA), while they continued their armed operations against the British presence on the island.[23] The Dáil's declaration of Independence also marked the beginning of the Anglo-Irish war (the Irish war of independence) which saw the IRA confronting the British Army between 1919 and 1921.

Meanwhile, during 1920, the UK government passed the Government of Ireland Act, which de facto partitioned Ireland into two areas: twenty-six counties in the south and six counties in the north and granted the northern Protestant population a separate parliament from the south.[24] This act later constituted the basis of the negotiations between the Crown and the Irish nationalists that eventually produced the Anglo-Irish Treaty of 1921.

The treaty laid the foundation for the future independent Republic of Ireland by setting up the Irish Free State in the twenty-six counties; but it also ratified the partition of the island by granting Northern Ireland the right to opt out of the newly independent Ireland and to rejoin the United Kingdom.[25] In January 1922, the Dáil ratified the treaty by a 64–57 margin, which led to a split between the antitreaty faction of Sinn Féin, led by De Valera, and the protreaty forces, which reorganized themselves into the Free State Parliament, leading the country into a brief civil war.[26]

The parallel and symbolic government established by De Valera after the 1922 split would soon lose legitimacy, and he would himself leave Sinn Féin in 1926, after failing to convince the party to abandon the policy of abstentionism to join the Free State Parliament. De Valera exited Sinn Féin and formed the Fianna Fail party, while Sinn Féin grew closer and more subordinate to the IRA, as they both withdrew support from the existing political institutions and granted sole legitimacy to the Army Council.[27] In the following years, the IRA would switch its focus mostly to Northern Ireland, although without granting legitimacy to the government in the south.

Following the partition, the situation in the six counties had taken a dramatic turn for the Catholic community: London left virtual autonomy and exercised very little oversight on the local Ulster government,[28] which was completely monopolized by the Protestant community, adamant in creating a Protestant Ulster, a goal achieved through systematic discrimination and marginalization of the Catholics.

For example, the Stormont-based Northern Ireland parliament manipulated the electoral system to minimize the political power of the Catholic minority, while relying on the "Protestant" police (the Royal Ulster Constabulary, or RUC) as well as on "informal" volunteer-based paramilitary organizations to crack down on IRA and republican supporters.[29] Furthermore, the parliament introduced draconian measures such as internment without trial, first used in 1922. In these days, however, the IRA hardly presented a threat to the Stormont government: after the 1926 split and after numerous unsuccessful armed campaigns, the IRA and Sinn Féin were in a state of decay north and south of the partition border. By the mid-1960s, they were both relegated to marginal, rural-based organizations.[30] However, as will be discussed in the upcoming section, this trend would be dramatically reversed during the 1970s with the beginning of the Troubles.

The decade preceding the outbreak of the Troubles in 1969 led to the breakdown of social order that would later characterize Northern Ireland during the 1970s and was marked by the growing impatience of the Catholic community, who refused to live under conditions of structural discrimination.[31] These widespread feelings led to the decline of traditional "moderate" parties, including the Nationalist Party, which had previously dominated politically in the Catholic community, as well as to the parallel rise of a broad civil rights movement.[32]

The Northern Ireland civil rights movement was a heterogeneous force that included civil society organizations, trade unions, and citizens who took off in the streets of Belfast and Derry by the mid-1960s, demanding equal civil and political rights. In response to this peaceful protest movement, the Stormont government grew nervous, wary that its entire system was under threat and reacted with violent crackdowns on protesters by official and paramilitary "security" or "defense" forces.[33]

By the end of the 1960s, the Ulster government started to take measures, encouraged by London, to reform partially the Stormont system and to address the Catholic community's grievances.[34] But it was too little and too late. Also the intent to reform did not stop the violence and the attacks against Catholics, which peaked in August 1969. This violent escalation led the British army to intervene directly in Northern Ireland, officially with the objective of guaranteeing order and security.[35] Amid this turmoil, the IRA's absence was conspicuous. Since the early 1960s, the group had been in a state of internal disorder, with little funding, supporters, or legitimacy.[36]

The IRA had taken a communist angle and was internally torn between those who advocated for it to end its policy of abstentionism, recognizing existing power structures and beginning to operate through Sinn Féin like a communist vanguard organization, and those who vehemently rejected this approach.[37] By 1967, the communist-inspired faction had grown powerful, and it had downgraded the role of the army and amended the IRA's constitution to create a "Socialist Republic."[38] More important, by December 1969, the Army Council of the IRA had publicly endorsed an end to abstentionism, a move that led to the creation of a breakaway group that rejected the recommendations of the Army Council and set up a Provisional Army Council.[39] The organizational turmoil peaked in January 1970 during the Sinn Féin annual convention. Echoing the frictions within the IRA, the party also split between the majority anti-abstentionists and the pro-abstentionists, which exited Sinn Féin and pledged allegiance to the Provisional Army Council.[40]

The Provisional IRA (PIRA) and Provisional Sinn Féin were born. The Official IRA (OIRA) and Official Sinn Féin, as they came to be known after the 1970 split, quickly lost importance and were permanently relegated to marginal players, with Sinn Féin transforming into the Workers Party and the OIRA ceasing all military activities in 1972. The 1972 cessation of military activities led to the partition of the OIRA and the creation of the Irish National Liberation Army (INLA), along with its political wing, the Irish Republican Socialist Party. During the 1970s, the OIRA and the INLA engaged in a bloody internal feud, which further contributed to the decline of their power and strength. The INLA split in 1986 to create the Irish People's Liberation Organization (IPLO) and to engage in another internal war between the new militia and the INLA.[41] While these other splinter groups remained marginal in the context of the Northern Ireland conflict, the Provisional IRA (the Provos) would gradually assume a crucial role in the following decades, becoming the most important armed and political group in Northern Ireland.

The Troubles and the Rise of the PIRA: From Armed to Political Organization

To understand the rise of the PIRA from marginal group to central player in the early 1970s it is important to understand the dynamics of the Troubles. The Catholic community initially welcomed the British army's arrival in Northern Ireland and hoped the army would be able to reduce the violence and protect all citizens from violent attacks. The initial positive feeling was soon replaced by disillusionment and anger. The army not only failed repeatedly to protect the Catholic community from loyalist attacks but also introduced measures specifically against the Catholics such as the curfews in Catholic areas during the spring of 1970. Eventually, British troops became involved in the violence, a trend that peaked following the army's killing of thirteen Catholics during a peaceful civil rights demonstration in Derry on January 30, 1972 (Bloody Sunday).[42]

By the summer of 1969, the Catholic community increasingly felt under attack and it felt the need to organize to defend itself. In this context, the Provos were able to gradually emerge and claim the role of defender of the community.[43] The United Kingdom's aggressive military and political campaign to target and dismantle the Provos, which included reauthorizing internments without trial,[44] caused a tremendous backlash, which led to the rapid growth in members and in supporters of the IRA.

Armed activities also rose dramatically. By the early 1970s, the IRA had launched a massive bombing campaign, first within Northern Ireland and then in the United Kingdom. In 1972, the IRA organized and planted more than 1,300 bombs.[45] Following the escalation of violence in Northern Ireland, the United Kingdom suspended the Stormont parliament and introduced direct rule in March 1972, while attempting to find a political solution for the Troubles.[46] The result was the Sunningdale Agreement of December 1973 supported by the "moderate" unionist forces of the Ulster Unionist Party (UUP) and the nationalist Social Democratic and Labour Party (SDLP).

This agreement established a new Northern Ireland assembly and executive based on power sharing and proportional representation between the two ethnic communities, as well as envisioning the creation of a Council of Ireland as an Irish and Northern Ireland consultative body.[47] However, all attempts to control the conflict failed, as the new government was brought down by a prolonged strike of the anti-power-sharing unionist forces. This led to the collapse of the executive, the return of direct rule, and another rapid escalation of the conflict.[48]

The IRA had opposed the Sunningdale process as it failed to deal with the organization's main objective: the reunification of Ireland. The IRA used its armed wing to voice its dissent, for example, by plotting bombing attacks in parallel to the development of the negotiation process and by escalating the level of violence within the United Kingdom, also resorting to a no-warning policy.[49]

The group attempted to delay the political process by urging the population of Northern Ireland to boycott the elections for the new assembly. However, the early

IRA failed to gain popular support, and by the end of 1973, a combination of the temporary successes of the political process and an increasingly effective counterterrorism campaign had seriously weakened the organization.[50]

The announcement of a short cease-fire in December 1974 to be followed by a longer one in February 1975 was a relief for the Provos, giving them time to regroup, to reorganize, and to allow them to resume their struggle in August 1975, in the period after the collapse of the Sunningdale system and the rise of local intergroup violence.[51]

The peak of Republican violence was between 1976 and 1989. The IRA continued its bombing campaigns within Northern Ireland and the United Kingdom, which grew in sophistication and lethality.

In the 1980s, the group began to strike highly prestigious targets, including Hyde Park and Regents Park (July 1982), the Brighton Grand Hotel during the Conservative Party Convention (October 1984), and the Royal Marines barracks in Deal, Kent (September 1989).[52] Attacks did not cease in the following two decades—as proved by the February 1996 Canary Wharf bombing—yet the level and intensity of the IRA's armed campaign failed to reach those of the previous decade—until the end of all armed activities and final decommissioning in 2005.[53] From the 1980s, Sinn Féin's role and status grew as did the level of interest in institutional politics, which led to the group's partial abrogation of its policy of abstention in 1986.

The remainder of the chapter deals with an in-depth analysis of the political and military evolution of the IRA and Sinn Féin from the early 1980s, focusing on the interactions between these two units of the republican movement and the process of transition from armed to unarmed politics.

Organizational Structure and Ideology

Internal Organization and Leadership Structure

The ideological and organizational origins of the Irish Republican Army and the Sinn Féin party can be found in the broader Irish republican movement born at the beginning of the twentieth century. Both organizations developed and changed quite substantially from their original structure following the 1969 internal partition and the birth of the Provisional IRA and Sinn Féin.

In the years preceding the 1969 split, the IRA was modeled after a traditional army. This organizational structure became increasingly outdated and ineffective during the 1970s, following a lack of concrete victories and a profound internal crisis, which resulted in the emergence of a new leadership and organizational structure.[54]

After the 1975 cease-fire and in response to the increasing infiltration of the IRA from British intelligence, the IRA chose to downsize its armed wing and shift from a mass-based movement to a more secretive cell system. Under the new system, each cell, at times composed of only two or three members, would maintain a functionally distinct task and would coordinate with the larger movement by reporting through a vertical chain of command, headed by the Army Council.[55]

This seven-man council was elected by an executive body appointed during the General Army Convention, composed of representatives from local units. The Army Council was the highest authority within the IRA; its decisions were considered binding. The council was in charge of the main policy and strategic decisions, as well as with selecting the organization's chief of staff and highest army officers. Along with this organizational restructuring, the IRA enhanced its technical skills, boosting its bomb-making capacities and acquiring a sophisticated arsenal.[56]

These changes were possible due to the rise of a new group of leaders, which first emerged in the mid-1970s following the creation of the IRA Northern Command.[57] In the following decade, the internal balance of power shifted, moving from the traditional southern elite to a younger generation of northern leaders. The new IRA leaders, born and raised in Northern Ireland, would be responsible for the internal restructuring of the IRA.

In parallel with these changes at the military level, the republican political organization, Sinn Féin, also rose and became more prominent. The growth of the party began in the early 1980s, as the next section will examine in detail, in parallel with the rise of Gerry Adams as its leader. Furthermore, this growth reflected the development of the "Armalite and ballot box" strategy that claimed that the republican movement would be best served by conducting simultaneously a political and a military campaign.[58] Sinn Féin's structure was diametrically opposite to the IRA's. Sinn Féin favored grassroots participation through local associations (the *cumman*), entered alliances with trade unions and civil society organizations, and attempted to draw broad mass support from the population in Southern and Northern Ireland, in contrast with the IRA's underground activism.[59]

Although the groups were formally separated, with the Army Council ruling the IRA and the Ard Comhairle (National Executive) overseeing Sinn Féin's activities, still there was an overlap in the membership of the two organizations regarding the bases, leadership, and political candidates chosen by the party to run for office. The council's decisions were reportedly also equally upheld by the IRA and by Sinn Féin.[60] Since its early days, the relationship between the IRA and Sinn Féin was blurry and complex. Although Sinn Féin publicly denied influencing the IRA and its decisions, it still periodically accepted to be the intermediary between the British government and the Army Council, showing the organization was a lot closer than what Sinn Féin was comfortable admitting.[61] Conversely, the IRA, at times, held a cease-fire to facilitate the electoral campaign of Sinn Féin. This further cast doubts on the party's assertion that the two organizations were totally distinct and that Sinn Féin had no influence over the military operations conducted by the army.[62] Even though Sinn Féin's political struggle and the IRA's military campaigns were seen as ideologically compatible, based on the Armalite and ballot box paradigm, their relationship was complicated by the fact that, in the long term, the IRA's actions damaged the legitimacy and popularity of Sinn Féin.[63]

As the next sections will analyze, the armed operations of the IRA often undermined the political support and electoral performance of Sinn Féin, especially in Ireland. Furthermore, these operations also eroded the group's international support, legitimacy, and impact on its credibility. The rest of the chapter will examine how, along with the political rise of Sinn Féin, the logic of military confrontation began to clash with the logic of political accommodation and how the organization responded to this challenge while avoiding major internal fractures.

The internal tensions that would develop along the political-military line within the IRA are interesting, especially given the organization's own propensity to internally split over involvement in institutional politics. Even after the 1969 rift and the creation of the PIRA, the organization further split, first in 1986—with Sinn Féin marking the end of abstentionism—a decision that led a group of Republicans to leave the IRA and create the Republican Sinn Féin and the Continuity IRA.[64]

Later, in 1997, the participation of Sinn Féin in the peace process and the beginning of political talks at Stormont led to an additional split, resulting in the creation of the Real IRA. Like in the previous splits, the rise of the military RIRA was reportedly accompanied by the creation of an affiliated political wing, which many identify in the 32-Counties Sovereignty Movement (32CSM).[65] In light of the IRA's history of internal divisions, it is therefore relevant to analyze how the movement managed to forgo its military agenda and transition to politics without losing its core constituency and supporting base. In contrast to Hamas and Hezbollah, the IRA did not rely on a massive social movement to gather and maintain support. The group never became a large-scale provider of social and political goods.

As with the other groups, the IRA still had to invest and prioritize in fund-raising to cover its annual costs, estimated in the early 2000s at about US$2.5 million.[66] Over the years, the organization was able to effectively fund-raise, and its annual income averaged at US$9 million. The group obtained the necessary funds to finance its activities and armed operations through direct involvement in illicit and semi-licit activities, as well as through community-based and foreign donations. The group's involvement in criminal enterprises included armed robberies; extortions; smuggling and sale of counterfeit goods, gasoline, tobacco, and alcohol; and drug trafficking, tax evasion, and active frauds. The IRA was also involved in running legitimate and semi-licit businesses, including drinking clubs, gaming machines, black cabs, and security companies and delivery services.[67] The IRA was able to raise most of its voluntary contributions within Northern Ireland, and, especially before 9/11, it was also able to fund-raise in the United States, drawing support from the large Irish Diaspora.[68]

Since the birth of the republican movement in the early twentieth century, the US Diaspora had supported the republican cause, and following the rise of the PIRA in the late 1960s, a number of Irish-American organizations were founded to help the Irish Republican struggle. One of the most important organizations in terms of relations and proximity with the Provos is believed to be the Irish Northern Aid (NORAID), even though the group always denied being an IRA front.[69] Especially in the years before the end of the cold war, the IRA was also able to count on financial support from states such as East Germany or Libya, which equipped and armed the IRA with arms and explosives. Finally, the IRA maintained contacts with a broad range of insurgents and terrorist organizations worldwide, including the Basque ETA, the PLO in the Middle East, and a number of armed groups in Central and Latin America.[70]

Tracking the Political Evolution and Organizational Strategy

The IRA and Sinn Féin's political ideology are rooted in the Irish leftist republican movement and in its nationalist struggle for Irish self-determination.[71] Within the context of Northern Ireland, this acquires a secessionist value with the clear goal of establishing an Irish Republic in the thirty-two counties, reversing the effects of the partition. Under this framework, the main enemy of the republican movement in its early stages was the British government and its institutions. In classic Republican ideology, the British government became the main foe because of its presence in Northern Ireland but also because of its historic legacy of colonialism over Ireland, culminating in its partition.[72]

The IRA maintained control of the armed struggle against the "British occupier," and it rejected all the political institutions established in the context of such "occupation." While the IRA carried out the military struggle, Sinn Féin's campaigns were focused on the political arena, without however accepting the legitimacy of the political institutions created by the partition. Initially, the group refused to participate actively in institutional politics not only in Westminster and Stormont but also in Dublin.[73] This principle of political abstentionism, first developed by Arthur Griffith in the early twentieth century, became the pillar of Sinn Féin's ideology and political strategy until the mid-1980s.

When the Provisional IRA and Sinn Féin were created following the 1969 split, they built on these ideological notions to develop their political and military programs and ideology. From a military stance, the Provos in the 1970s started to develop the "long war" strategy. Failing to envision a quick defeat against the British army through direct engagements on the battlefield, the IRA shifted to fighting a war of attrition against the United Kingdom.[74]

The objective was to inflict a sufficient level of damage to demoralize the British army and people and to deflate the country's will to continue its involvement with Northern Ireland. This would be achieved by targeting the army personnel and the economic and financial interests of the United Kingdom, with the aim of making Northern Ireland ungovernable. Triggering violent repression was also seen as a useful military tactic, as the British response to the IRA violence and its repression of the Catholic community in Northern Ireland further alienated the population and drew them closer to the Provos.[75]

As stated in the 1977 version of the IRA training manual (*The Green Book*), the IRA had the right to wage war against the United Kingdom based on "the right to resist foreign aggression; the right to revolt against tyranny and oppression; the direct lineal succession with the Provisional Government of 1916, the first Dáil of 1919 and the second Dáil of 1921."[76]

Along with the IRA reformulation of its military strategy in the early 1970s, which showed remarkable continuity with classic goals and views of the early republican movement, Sinn Féin's also reformed the organization's political program. A new political program was introduced through Eire Nua (New Ireland), a political platform written in 1971 and adopted the following year by Sinn Féin's Ard Fheis, the annual party assembly.[77]

The document wanted to identify the ideological differences between the Official IRA and the Provos, as well as the OIRA's Marxist and communist agenda. Eire Nua also presented the IRA's political project of establishing a federalist and socialist Republic in the thirty-two counties, while highlighting its renewed commitment to political abstentionism. Despite the adoption of a political program, at this early stage, Sinn Féin was fairly marginal, as overall the republican movement relied most on the Provos and on military activities, at the expense of political activism and electoral participation.[78]

Sinn Féin began a transition toward institutional politics in the 1980s, following the adoption of the Armalite and ballot box strategy of 1981,[79] which led Sinn Féin to increase its efforts to widen its support bases domestically, forge new alliances, establish contacts with other insurgent organizations and protest movements internationally, and expand the party's political program.[80] The strategy was centered on the notion that the republican movement had to focus on waging simultaneously a political and a military battle, and that these two campaigns would be mutually reinforcing and contribute to strengthen the movement.

An example of this shift would be the party's gradual amendment of its political program to remove references referring to the establishment of a "federalist Republic," and the increased involvement in electoral politics.[81] This culminated with the 1986 decision to end the policy of abstentionism in Ireland. Similarly, in the following decade, Sinn Féin adopted the strategy of fostering relations with other nationalist parties in Northern Ireland, namely, the SDLP, as well as with the Irish government, to end its previous isolation.[82]

The strategy behind this transition was to increasingly employ the political wing of the movement to draw support for the group's military struggle. It aimed at complementing the military war of attrition with a political one, also aimed at undermining the British government's decision to stay in Northern Ireland.[83] By the late 1980s, the republican movement held ideological continuity with its previous ideals of armed struggle toward the establishment of a united Irish Socialist Republic, but it had partially reversed its political principle of abstentionism. Also in the same period, the IRA also readjusted its military strategy by openly referring to armed struggle as an "option" available to the group, as opposed to its sole raison d'être.[84]

The peace process of the 1990s gradually brought Sinn Féin to the negotiating table. By then, the IRA increasingly relied on force as a hard-bargaining tool to influence the outcome of negotiations and to increase the political weight and status of Sinn Féin, indicating again a shift in the group's strategic outlook.[85] The engagement in the peace process and the 1998 signing of the Good Friday Agreement (GFA) revealed the transition of the republican movement from its initial refusal of all political settlements that did not contemplate a united thirty-two county Ireland, to the acceptance of an agreement that de facto recognized the reality of the partition.

Ideologically, Sinn Féin did not amend its political platform, and the group presently advocates for the creation of a thirty-two counties Ireland.[86] However, Sinn Féin de facto accepted to take part in the Northern Ireland government, although on an interim basis. According to Sinn Féin leader Martin McGuinness, the group "would like to see a 32-county republic in Ireland, but what we're trying to bring about is a situation where all the people of Ireland get a right to national self-determination."[87] This substantial shift in the group's political strategy and outlook is parallel to the group's change of perception of its traditional enemies, the British government, and the unionist forces.

By the mid-1990s, the republican movement stopped conditioning its direct political involvement with the United Kingdom following its unilateral withdrawal declaration, showing a more pragmatic attitude. In addition, it began to describe the conflict in terms of internal struggle between two distinct communities. Traditionally, the republican ideology saw unionism as a by-product of the British presence in Northern Ireland and argued that, following the United Kingdom's withdrawal, the "problem" represented by unionism would disappear on its own.[88] However, during the 1990s, the outlook shifted. Sinn Féin's political discourse in the 1990s recognized that unionist forces were a permanent feature of the Northern Ireland political arena and that a future settlement would have to include them as much as the British "occupiers." Under this new paradigm, the group, recognized the more complex dimensions of the conflict. This included asking the United Kingdom to act as a "persuader" to convince the unionist community to agree to a united Ireland.[89] This shift in the group's political discourse was indeed crucial and allowed it to take a more direct role in the peace process of the 1990s.

Toward the End of Abstentionism

Unlike previous case studies, the republican movement in Northern Ireland was composed of two separate, yet interrelated, armed and political units, respectively, known as Sinn Féin and the IRA. According to the definition of political wing adopted by this research, the (Provisional) Sinn Féin only became a functioning political wing in the 1980s, despite its active involvement in institutional politics since its creation in the 1969 split. By the 1980s, the group started not only to compete in elections but also to accept the idea of assuming office once elected. Accordingly, the study refers to political wings as special subunits within an armed group that engages in aboveground institutional political activities through contending elections and assuming office once elected. Increased political involvement and entering institutional politics are commonly referred as the "end of abstentionism" and are associated with the decision to take office if elected in the Irish Dáil. This change of policy was first adopted and ratified by the Sinn Féin annual convention are November 1986. The previous month, the IRA—through a meeting of the General Army Convention—had endorsed discussing the issue of abstentionism while allowing IRA members, for the first time, to support elected republican politicians who decided to take seat in the Dáil.[90]

The "official" end of abstentionism can be rightfully seen as the culmination of a process of increased political activism that started a few years earlier. In parallel with the rise of the Armalite and ballot box strategy, during the 1981 Sinn Féin annual convention, the group decided to start participating and taking office in local elections in Northern Ireland, which first took place in 1983.[91] The following section analyzes the factors that accounted for Sinn Féin's initial decision to run and take office in local elections in 1981 and what led the group to carry through with its initial decision, first in 1983 and then in 1985, when fifty-nine elected Sinn Féin candidates took office as local councilors in Northern Ireland.[92] This strategic shift is counted for by applying the "four-factor model" of political participation: (1) institutional pressure, (2) shifts in the availability of mobilization resources, (3) changes in the political opportunity structure, and (4) rise of an internal commitment to change.

The hypothesis advanced in the previous chapters links the emergence of an active political wing with both the institutional pressure to accommodate and expand. This is further heightened by a concrete threat to a given's group relevancy and legitimacy, as well as the decline in a group's available mobilization resources. In the case of the republican movement in the early 1980s, the group, after having expanded and gone through a process of internal reorganization in the previous decade, was still in a precarious position. Particularly, the group's legitimacy and relevance were both threatened, which affected its ability to mobilize supporters and obtain resources. The UK's shifting political climate, marked by the election of the conservative Thatcher government of 1979 signaled a dramatic change in Northern Ireland policies. The new government's priority, arguably, was to destroy the republican movement and aimed to do so by pursuing two separate strategies: military defeat for the IRA and political isolation of Sinn Féin. Militarily, the government, through intelligence and undercover operations, became more aggressive in targeting IRA members and in infiltrating the organization, in Northern Ireland, the United Kingdom, and abroad.[93]

The government inflicted considerable damage to the IRA through its law-enforcement system and the reliance on the "Ulsterization and criminalization policy." Since the mid-1970s, the UK government had revoked the previous policy of internment without trial for IRA suspects and substituted it with a new policy that relied on the Northern Ireland Police to identify and arrest IRA members ("Ulsterization"). The second pillar of this new policy aimed to remove them from circulation and weaken the movement through the judiciary system ("criminalization").[94] In particular, this new policy relied on "Diplock courts," nonjury courts active since the mid-1970s with special jurisdiction to deal with terrorism cases, which often employed confessions from arrested IRA members to identify and arrest other Republican volunteers.[95]

Although all the elements of this system had been in place since the mid-1970s, the main judicial blow to the IRA came only in 1981 with the "supergrass system." The supergrass trials began in November 1981, following the arrest and trial of Christopher Black in North Belfast. This led to a series of trials where the key, if not sole, evidence provided against the defendants was the confession of other arrested IRA members.[96] These statements, often obtained in special interrogation centers and in breach of common law rules and procedures, led the UK government, between 1981 and 1983, to arrest more than six hundred alleged paramilitary members, based on only thirty-five statements by internal informants.[97] As a result, the supergrass trials managed to seriously harm the IRA.

External pressure, combined with a series of major operational setbacks and internal rifts, led to an increased threat to the group's relevancy and legitimacy.[98] This produced a sense of insecurity over the group's access to human and material resources, as an IRA spokesperson admitted in late 1982, that the organization was experiencing "a number of problems, logistical problems or problems with material and supplies."[99] This crisis was to be solved partially with the arrival of a conspicuous amount of weapons coming from Libya, shipped to the Provos in 1985 and 1986.[100]

The arrival of weapons did not reverse the trend of the previous few years, where the increasingly aggressive UK campaign against the IRA, coupled with the internal rifts, organizational setbacks, and decline in available resources, led to a stalemate and to a decline in the group's relevancy.

Along with these problems, the republican movement was also under threat because of the Thatcher campaign to politically isolate and marginalize Sinn Féin. The government's main tools to achieve this goal would be renewed cross-border cooperation with the government of Ireland as well as the increased support for the constitutional nationalist party within Northern Ireland, the SDLP.

Starting in the early 1980s, the UK and the Irish governments held a series of bilateral summits to enhance security and political cooperation on the Northern Ireland Conflict. The result was the Anglo-Irish Agreement of 1985. The document represented an important departure in British policy on Northern Ireland, which had previously refused to involve any external actor in the conflict by maintaining the role of sole arbiter of the Northern Ireland affairs.[101]

With the Anglo-Irish Agreement, this strategy was replaced with a cross-border partnership, centered on the Anglo-Irish Intergovernmental Council and based on the two governments' commitment not to attempt any change to the status quo in Northern Ireland without the consent of the majority of the people living in the six counties.[102]

From a republican perspective, the agreement indicated Ireland's public renunciation to any pursuit of a future reunification, an interpretation that was backed in a statement of the British secretary of state Tom King who declared that "for all practical purposes there will never be a united Ireland."[103] This further strengthened the perception that there had been a strategic change in the outlook of the Northern Ireland question in Ireland. It showed that most of the population in the south had accepted the status quo as final, indicating that the future of republicanism was severely under threat.

The beginning of the Irish-British dialogue also served to empower the SDLP, the main political competitor of Sinn Féin in its campaign to gain the support of the nationalist community in Northern Ireland. The Anglo-Irish Agreement was heavily influenced by the SDLP and its leader, John Hume, who had shaped Dublin's views and demands on Northern Ireland through the New Ireland Forum of 1983–1984.[104]

The Anglo-Irish Agreement represented a political victory for the SDLP, especially as some of the language of the agreement, including the explicit recognition of the identity and interests of the nationalist community, and its right to pursue reunification though peaceful means was perfectly in line with SDLP's policies and aspirations.[105] Strengthening the nationalist alternative to Sinn Féin was clearly in the United Kingdom's interest, as it fit with its strategy to achieve the political isolation of Sinn Féin. Yet, it equally conformed to Dublin's interests to curtail the political influence of Sinn Féin south of the border.

By the early 1980s, both the IRA and Sinn Féin were under attack, both north and south of the partition border. Their role had been further crippled in the late 1970s, following the stricter application of a complete broadcast censorship on IRA and Sinn Féin representatives in media within Ireland.[106]

Sinn Féin's ongoing political isolation and the decline in popularity in the Republic of Ireland, which were further confirmed through the poor electoral performance of the February 1982 general Irish elections,[107] pushed the organization to rethink its political strategy, pushing it toward the end of abstentionism in 1986 and toward assuming a more active role in Irish institutional politics. Both the military attacks on the IRA and the political campaign against Sinn Féin amounted to threats to the group's legitimacy, relevance, and capacity to mobilize resources. At the same time, in the early 1980s, an important shift in the republican movement's potential constituency produced a change in the political opportunity structure and resulted in an incentive to compete in local elections, as well to take office if elected. A shift in the distribution of the voters along the political scale created a political opening for the Sinn Féin.

By October 1981, when Sinn Féin decided to compete and assume office in Northern Ireland's local elections, the republican movement's potential number of political supporters had grown dramatically in the previous two years. This growth had offered an important reason to strengthen the political wing and to attempt translating this backing into political power and influence. Reasons behind this increased support, despite the ongoing stalemate and military strain, can be found in the rise of a parallel political campaign for prisoners' rights, which in turn drew support for Sinn Féin and the republican movement. Republican prisoners under British detention became a prominent issue after 1976 when the government, as a by-product of the new "criminalization" policy, revoked the special category status previously awarded to republican and loyalist prisoners.[108]

This act spurred a series of internal protests by the detainees in the H-blocks of Her Majesty's Prison Maze (the Maze) in Northern Ireland. At first, the measures taken in protest of this new policy ranged from a rejection of prison uniforms, the "blanket protest," to the refusal to leave their cells, the "no-wash" protest. These acts were sanctioned by Sinn Féin together with the prisoners' families and a number of local civil society organizations, who became directly involved in the movement to support the prisoners through the H Block/Armagh campaign.[109] Being part of this broader, issue-based alliance with other organizations reduced Sinn Féin's political isolation.

The turning point in the prisoners' struggle came in October 1980, when the prisoners began a series of hunger strikes, which would ultimately lead to the death of ten republican detainees, including one of the prisoners' leaders, Bobby Sands,[110] following the UK government's refusal to grant them the special status they were demanding.

The hunger strikes mobilized public opinion to support the prisoners and the republican movement, as shown by the surprising electoral victory of Bobby Sands in April 1981. Only a few weeks before his death after sixty-six days of fasting, Sands, gained a seat at Westminster through the Anti-H Block coalition, backed by Sinn Féin and a number of civil society groups.[111] Bobby Sands's election served as a powerful lesson to the republican movement and shifted its focus and organizational efforts on strengthening its political wing and expanding the movement.

This trend was further strengthened with the election of two more detainees, Kieran Doherty and Paddy Agnew, in the Irish general elections in June 1981. The existence of a broad and cross-border backing behind the prisoners and their struggle led the republican movements to attempt to translate the support for the prisoners' rights into a backing of their political and armed struggle.[112]

By the end of prisoners' protests in October 1981 the political climate and balance of power within Northern Ireland was beginning to shift to favor the republican movement. This change also corresponded with the October 1981 decision to compete in the upcoming Northern Ireland local elections and to assume office if elected. This decision was later validated by the electoral results of October 1982, when Sinn Féin surprised many by gaining 10 percent of the total preferences in the Northern Ireland assembly elections, and capturing approximately 20 percent of the Catholic votes.[113]

Another by-product of the prisoners' movement was to increase Sinn Féin's profile and political activism, and to draw renewed international and domestic support for the party, resulting in a powerful incentive to focus on contending elections and assuming office.[114] Sinn Féin's role in the political prisoners' movement pushed the group to cooperate with local, civil society organizations, to become further involved with community politics, and to focus on broadening its support bases. An example of this trend included the increased focus on running and expanding a network of "advice centers," previously called "incident centers" that were set up in 1975 to monitor the effective implementation of the IRA cease-fire. With the end of the cease-fire and the rise in its potential constituency, Sinn Féin managed to use these centers to become involved in community politics and in social and economic issues, indicating the group's increased interest in acting as an ordinary political party.[115]

By the end of 1981, when Sinn Féin—backed by the IRA Army Council—sanctioned full political participation in the Northern Ireland local elections, the republican movement was experiencing a temporary drain in its resources, along with a military decline and a stalemate of the IRA, and a political campaign to isolate and discredit Sinn Féin. These challenges all resulted in a direct threat to the group's relevancy and provided an incentive for political expansion. At the same time, the group had a new potential constituency thanks to the political turmoil generated by the prisoners' struggle, which generated a tangible, political opening for Sinn Féin to increase its role in the political system.

In reality, this was not the only political shift that resulted in an opening in the political system for Sinn Féin and that informed its decision to take part in the 1983 and 1985 local elections and take office if elected. By 1982, the United Kingdom decided to reestablish a local assembly for legislative and executive functions in Northern Ireland and to hold elections in October 1982 though a proportional electoral system.[116]

Although the assembly, boycotted first by nationalist forces and then by unionist forced, collapsed in June 1986, the UK decision to reestablish the Northern Ireland assembly indicated the renewed importance of the local political arena and provided a further incentive for Sinn Féin to focus on institutional politics in parallel with the continuation of the armed struggle.

In the previous chapters, it has been also reiterated how political change is also related to an internal commitment to reform the organization. In the case of the republican movement, the increased interest in institutional politics relates to the rise of a new group of internal leaders and with their fresh approach to the overall political and military strategy of Sinn Féin and the IRA.

One by-product of the internal changes within the IRA in the latter part of the 1970s was the gradual replacement of the "southern" traditional leadership of the movement with a new group of young leaders born and raised in Northern Ireland. This group of men had grown up amid the conflict. They were aware of the daily realities of Northern Ireland and were in touch with the feelings of the Catholic community in the six counties.

The new republican leadership was more pragmatic than the traditional one, with a renewed interest in gaining the "hearts and minds" of the local population. The new leadership focused on grassroots mobilization and on building a political constituency. The commitment to raise Sinn Féin's political profile and role was not seen as an alternative to the armed struggle, but rather as a means to strengthen the republican movement through diversifying its approaches in achieving an independent and united Ireland.

This new leadership, particularly through leaders like Gerry Adams, Danny Morrison, and Martin McGuinness, gradually gained control of some key posts within the republican movement, with Adams being elected as Sinn Féin president in 1983.[117]

With the rise of the new republican leadership the beginning of the 1980s was the development of the Armalite and ballot box strategy, an expression first coined by Morrison in 1981 but which reflected a political strategy already advocated by a group of new republican leaders, led by Gerry Adams, since the mid-1970s. This new paradigm, aimed at transforming Sinn Féin into a fully fledged political party, led to the decision to take part in local elections in Northern Ireland in 1981 and to the official end of abstentionism in Ireland in 1986.

Between 1981 and 1986, the internal commitment to reform the organization grew even stronger, first spurred by the positive electoral performance of the republican detainees in 1981, and then by Sinn Féin's results in 1982, when Morrison, Adams, and McGuinness won the electoral contest in their respective district, albeit they still adhered to abstentionism regarding Stormont, a policy that was not revoked until after the GFA was signed in 1998.[118]

This shift, however, was not the result of a unanimous internal decision to adopt a policy of full political participation and to end abstentionism. An animated internal debate preceded between the "traditionalists," led by Sinn Féin's earlier president Ruairí Ó Brádaigh, who argued that abstentionism was the core principle behind political republican ideology and that it should not be revoked short of achieving a thirty-two-county Ireland, and those who claimed abstentionism was only a tactic, based on the external political circumstances.[119]

The "traditionalists" objected to the end of abstentionism, which was viewed as the eventual decline in the movement's armed struggle, a claim that "reformers" consistently objected, affirming their absolute commitment to support the IRA and its armed campaigns. Reformers were able to state these views publicly because of their solid relation with both Sinn Féin and the IRA. In addition, the IRA had de facto backed the reformers, by lifting the ban on "discussing or advocating the taking of parliamentary seats" in October 1986.

Marking the political ascent of the Adams-McGuiness line, in November 1986, 429 out of 628 Sinn Féin delegates voted in favor of ending abstentionism, just eleven votes over the needed two-thirds majority to take this decision, defeating those who objected to full political participation in the Dáil.[120]

The result of this vote was Sinn Féin's official entry into institutional politics as a fully fledged party in the Republic of Ireland and the creation of a permanent, internal split. The defeated faction led by Ó Brádaigh immediately left the organization and created a separate political group, Republican Sinn Féin, which had from the beginning minimal political impact and initially lacked support from a military wing. Subsequently, the Continuity IRA emerged to back the splinter group; however, the military support failed to increase the political influence of the group.[121] Despite the internal frictions created by Sinn Féin's transformation into a fully fledged political party, the party preserved their core constituency and supporting bases and the overall organizational strength of the movement was not severely damaged.

In the aftermath of the split, Sinn Féin paid special attention to preserve internal unity and to prevent further internal clashes. An example is the isolation and marginalization of those who disagreed with the end of abstentionism but had nonetheless remained within the ranks of Sinn Féin.[122] These measures, together with the links between Sinn Féin and the IRA Army Council leadership, and the unequivocal support expressed by the "reformed" Sinn Féin for the IRA's armed struggle, preserved unity within the republican movement.

The next section delves into the political evolution of Sinn Féin following the decision to fully participate in the political system, first at the municipal level in Northern Ireland and then at the parliamentary level in the Dáil. The section focuses on the relations between Sinn Féin and IRA and on the effect of the military activities on the group's political development.

1981–2012: The Ballot and the Armalite, Explaining the Transition

1981–1987: Early Political Activism and Organizational Change

The previous section discussed how Sinn Féin's political growth in the early 1980s was the result of the party's decision to become more involved in institutional politics. This was first done by agreeing to contest local elections and take office if elected in 1981, and second, by dropping the policy of abstentionism with respect to elections in the Republic of Ireland in 1986.

The period between 1981 and 1987 can be described as partial political involvement for Sinn Féin. The party reorganized itself and amended its platform to increase political appeal and potential constituency. At the same time, political participation was partial, falling short of interacting with the political system and its representatives. The group used political participation as a secondary tool to boost popular support for the armed struggle, not as a way to influence the political reconciliation process, which the Provos only wanted to derail.[123] Nevertheless, the early 1980s did see a great deal of internal change, within the organizational, strategic, and ideological level of the IRA and Sinn Féin. At the organizational level, there was a conscious effort to invest and boost the republican movement's political party, Sinn Féin.

This led to an internal reorganization of the party and its structure, for instance, by abolishing the ineffective provincial councils, which mirrored Sinn Féin's defunct federalist aspirations. Furthermore, Sinn Féin strengthened the role and function of the advice centers, while expanding their numbers in major urban areas.[124] This reorganization reflected the republican movement's new emphasis on supporting local campaigns for economic and social rights, crime prevention, and neighborhood policing, which was a by-product of the group's renewed interest in institutional politics.

While the republican movement fell short of building working relations with constitutional authorities in the United Kingdom and the Republic of Ireland, it emphasized creating a network of grassroots supporters and reaching out to like-minded organizations, for example, the H-Block/Armagh Committee to support the prisoners' protest in the Maze. This committee constituted a powerful lesson for Sinn Féin, stressing the importance of maintaining a supporting network and creating grassroots alliances.

The renewed emphasis on building alliances in the early 1980s did not lead to collaborations with other nationalist forces, such as SDLP, as the relation between the two groups was at the time still marked by competition and ideological hostility, rather than cooperation.[125] However, the group improved its external relations both domestically as well as internationally, with Sinn Féin maintaining contact with a number of radical parties throughout Europe, as well as with other armed organizations, including the PLO, the Basque ETA, and the Sandinistas.[126]

While these organizational changes during the early 1980s transformed Sinn Féin into a more functional political party, the group also revised its political platform and campaigning strategy to improve its electoral appeal. An example of this trend is the increased emphasis on the group's social and economic agenda, openly promoting concepts like "community work" and "local democracy." This broadened its platform beyond creating a united Ireland and supporting the IRA's armed struggle. This process was accompanied by the gradual modernization of the group's policies, for instance, by removing federalist principles from its constitution and by becoming stronger advocates of a decentralized socialist model.[127]

It would be wrong to interpret these changes and the rise of the political status of Sinn Féin as an indication of an internal rift between the political and the armed branches of the republican movement, or as a reflection of an internal decision to abandon the armed struggle against the United Kingdom and its institutions. Indeed, these changes occurred without creating a rift between the logic of armed struggle and that of political accommodation. At the organizational level, IRA and Sinn Féin were still largely intertwined, with an overlap in members, both at the base and at the leadership levels. At this stage, it was clear that the IRA, and the Army Council in particular, was the senior partner in the relationship. There was consensus that "the Irish Republican Army offers the only resolution to the present situation . . . we know that elections while important in that they show public support, will not achieve a British withdrawal."[128]

At the strategic level, the armed struggle and the electoral participation—Morrison's Armalite and ballot box—were considered part of the same campaign. The IRA worked to weaken the British government's will to stay in Northern Ireland, while Sinn Féin mobilized a pro-republican constituency both at the north and at the south of the border.

Sinn Féin's objective was clear: to increase the level of support for the IRA and to create a viable political alternative to the "moderate" SDLP, ensuring a "republican veto" on any political arrangement that concerned Northern Ireland.[129]

This strategic outlook was largely shaped by the experience of the hunger strikes. It also indicated a greater and more sophisticated understanding of the Northern Ireland conflict, shifting from an uncompromising confrontation with the United Kingdom and its political system, to a more subtle approach that mixed armed struggle, confrontation, and conventional politics.[130] The IRA's military efforts were not diminished to sustain Sinn Féin's political activism but rather modified to fit the "long war" strategy, which shifted the emphasis to fighting a war of attrition through sporadic, yet more sophisticated attacks.[131]

In the early 1980s, the IRA carried out a number of "high prestige" target attacks that took place mostly within the United Kingdom, including the Hyde Park attack in 1982 and the Harrods attack in 1983.[132] Another example is the infamous 1984 attack at the Brighton Grand Hotel during a Conservative Party conference,[133] exemplifying the IRA's will to bring the war to the British mainland and to inflict a deadly blow to the British government.

During the early 1980s it seemed that the Armalite and ballot box strategy was working. The IRA campaigns were carrying on high-profile attacks against the United Kingdom, and Sinn Féin was beginning to emerge as a surprisingly strong political actor. In the 1982 elections for the resurrected Northern Ireland assembly, Sinn Féin nominated twelve candidates in the twelve districts and attracted more than sixty thousand votes, gathering roughly 10 percent of the electoral preferences and winning five seats in the seven-eight-member assembly.[134] This was an important test of electoral strength for the party, which had chosen to nominate very high-profile members, including Adams, McGuinness, and Morrison, who all ran (and won) on an abstentionism platform.[135]

Similar encouraging results appeared in the Westminster elections of 1983, where Sinn Féin gained 13.4 percent of the votes, securing Adams's election in the West Belfast district, with Morrison losing in the Mid-Ulster district by only seventy-eight votes.[136] By the time the European parliament elections took place in 1984, Sinn Féin had rapidly expanded and had become a serious political force to be reckoned with. However, after the 1985 local government electoral the beginning of a reversal of Sinn Féin's electoral fortunes began. This trend that would peak in 1989 first questioned the feasibility of the armed struggle and political participation strategy.[137]

In 1984, Sinn Féin still obtained 13.3 percent of the votes for its candidate, Danny Morrison, an important electoral result, although not enough to beat SDLP's leader, John Hume, who obtained 22.1 percent of the electoral preferences.[138] Even during these early years of successful political participation, Sinn Féin was consistently outpolled by the SDLP.

Although Sinn Féin had started to become an important political force within Northern Ireland, it still failed to gain presence in Ireland. Despite the elections of the two republican prisoners in the 1981 Irish elections, this initial success had not been translated into stable support for Sinn Féin, as it had in Northern Ireland. Even after abstentionism was officially dropped regarding Leister House, Sinn Féin had only gained 2 percent of the total votes in the Irish parliamentary elections of 1987.

Following these initial political successes and early setbacks, by the mid-1980s Sinn Féin had started to grapple with the reality of its new paradigm. The initial optimism toward the feasibility of the Armalite and ballot box strategy gradually faded.

While the party was tightly connected with the IRA at the ideological, and likely organizational and strategic level, it was now becoming more obvious that the cooperation between the two groups was not always mutually beneficial. In particular, following the 1984 and 1985 elections, Sinn Féin began to fear the negative effects of the IRA's armed struggle on the party's electoral performance, especially in Ireland, where the level of public tolerance for the IRA's violent actions was much lower.[139] Without distancing itself from the IRA campaigns or criticizing its military campaigns, Sinn Féin leader Gerry Adams urged the Provos to "continue to refine its operations" to minimize "any conflicts between what we are doing and what they are doing."[140]

The actions of the IRA were not always perceived as detrimental to the political advancement of Sinn Féin. For example, the group's leadership, referring to the 1984 Brighton bombing as a "propaganda coup," stressed that the attack had been quite popular among their nationalist constituency.[141] Whether this perception was grounded in reality or whether the republican movement was downplaying the negative publicity of the attack is a separate matter. What matters is that, despite a general feeling that the political advancement of Sinn Féin might have decreased because of the ongoing violence, such perception had not yet been elaborated into a coherent political strategy.

Following the 1987 electoral defeat in Ireland, Sinn Féin was forced to analyze and reevaluate in-depth the relation between the armed and political struggle. This ultimately questioned the Armalite and ballot box strategy and led the group to undergo substantial internal change.

1987–1994: Political Crisis and the Momentum for Change

The first half of the 1980s was characterized by the simultaneous growth of Sinn Féin and the IRA under the banner of the Armalite and ballot box strategy. However, by the end of the decade, a shift occurred for the republican movement. First, the republicans' political landscape seemed negative. The ongoing Thatcher campaign to isolate Sinn Féin began to yield results, particularly since the ratification of the Anglo-Irish Agreement of 1985. This resulted in lower support for the republicans in Ireland, while boosting the SDLP in Northern Ireland. Sinn Féin was increasingly isolated and, most important, the electoral performance of the party underwent a period of decline.

In Ireland, following the mediocre outcome of the 1987 Irish parliamentary elections, the level of support for Sinn Féin dropped even lower. Specifically, in 1989, the party lost more than one-third of the votes it had obtained in 1987, and all but two of the fourteen Sinn Féin candidates lost in the general Irish elections. These gloomy results were repeated in the 1989 Irish elections for the European parliament, in which Sinn Féin performed only slightly better than in the general elections.[142]

On the other side of the border, in Northern Ireland, Sinn Féin's political advance had also stalled. Since 1984 the party's level of electoral support had failed to improve, shattering the leadership's vision to become the main nationalist political force in the six counties. The peak of this process was the local and European elections of 1989, when the party only gained, respectively, 69,032 and 48,914 votes.[143] Meanwhile, the IRA campaigns did not create a momentum in support of the armed struggle, and there was a general perception that the situation had reached both a military and a political stalemate.

The political stalemate resulted in stagnation for Sinn Féin, which was incapable of outperforming SDLP in the north and of gaining political strength in the south. In addition, the high number of operational "mistakes" by the IRA, resulting in a substantial number of civilian casualties, seemed to further discredit Sinn Féin.[144]

Between 1989 and 1992, the Brooke initiative, led by British secretary of state for Northern Ireland Peter Brooke, resumed direct talks between the unionist forces and the nationalist community. This included the explicit exclusion of Sinn Féin due to its connections with the IRA, and thus it further marginalized and excluded the republican movement and Sinn Féin in particular.[145]

Militarily, the IRA was also suffering from a number of failed operations, a temporary drain in its material resources, and an increase in the number of IRA members either killed or detained.[146] These factors contributed to the generalized perception that the situation had reached a "hurting stalemate," where the group did not envision victory and where even the continuation of the status quo, in the long term, would affect the group's effectiveness and relevance.[147] By the end of the 1980s, there was a perception that change, both at the strategic and operational level, was necessary for the movement to overcome its increasing isolation and loss of legitimacy, as well as to match the new organizational and strategic reality. In particular, the principles behind the Armalite and ballot box strategy had to be reevaluated to fit the new political environment. Military struggle and political accommodation were beginning to clash.

Although the organizational partnership between the IRA and Sinn Féin remained unchanged, the status of Sinn Féin and its leaders had become more prominent during the 1980s because of its early electoral results.[148] Sinn Féin had developed its own constituency. Although in most cases this constituency overlapped with that of the IRA, this was not always the case. As a result, the party's political strategy and its organizational needs started to play a greater role in shaping the republican movement's strategic outlook.

The increased importance of the previously less relevant Sinn Féin meant that, when its political performance began to decline, the challenge was taken seriously. The group started to discuss ways to minimize the negative effect from the armed struggle on Sinn Féin's political engagement, at the same time shifting its electoral strategy to challenge its political competitor, SDLP.

From a military standpoint, the organization debated on ways to "recalibrate" the use of force. Within the IRA, there were several calls for the organization to take greater care in trying to minimize civilian casualties. This concern was voiced clearly in 1989 by a member of the IRA General Headquarters who stated that the group had come to a "greater realization than ever of the need for the IRA to avoid civilian casualties." The same IRA member further added that the large number of collateral damages had "dented the confidence of some of our supporters."[149] These same ideas were also expressed by Gerry Adams, who asked the military wing in 1989 to be "careful and careful again."[150] Both the political and the military leaderships recognized the negative effect of the IRA campaigns on the group's political development and asserted the necessity to rectify the situation.

Even so, patterns of violence did not change significantly in the early 1990s and neither was there a reduction in the number of civilian casualties. Casualties, between 1980 and 1991, remained between 25 percent and 40 percent of the total victims, but then escalated to roughly 50 percent between 1991 and 1993, also in response to a rise in loyalist attacks.[151] The IRA did not manage to turn the aims for greater restraint into reality, as exemplified by its infamous use of so-called human bombs in 1990. On those occasions, the group forced civilians to drive a vehicle packed with explosives against a designated targeted. This tactic was hugely unpopular and was quickly dropped.[152] Furthermore, the internal debate on reducing civilian casualties did not result in a decline of the armed struggle in favor of political participation. IRA bombing campaigns in the United Kingdom rose in the early 1990s.[153]

The IRA targeted political targets within the United Kingdom and invested heavily in hitting economic targets. Examples of these attacks included the London Stock Exchange attack in 1990, the 1993 Bishopsgate NatWest tower attack, which hit the British capital's financial district, and the mortar attack in Downing Street in 1991.[154] Within Northern Ireland, the IRA proceeded under a business-as-usual paradigm, continuing to focus on intracommunal "policing" by punishing collaborators, as well as those engaged in behavior deemed by the IRA as "antisocial." Between 1982 and 1997 were at least 755 episodes that included intimidation, beatings, and summary executions.[155] Furthermore, in 1992, the IRA stepped up its involvement in community politics by deciding to forcibly dismantle one of its military rivals, the IPLO.[156]

The IRA did not significantly change its modus operandi in response to Sinn Féin's political rise. Although the logics of military confrontation and political accommodation had started to develop in different directions, this had not produced a serious internal conflict along the politico-military line. What had changed, however, was the purpose behind the use of force. Whereas at the beginning of the 1980s the main idea was to fight a war of attrition to lead the United Kingdom to withdraw from Northern Ireland, by the early 1990s, force was seen as a tool to increase the group's leverage on the political process and to negotiate with its main enemy.[157] This strategic change in using force reflected the beginning of an internal shift in the group's balance of power.

While the campaign to minimize the effects of violence on Sinn Féin's legitimacy was not very successful, the party's strategy of revitalization, namely, a shift in its electoral strategy, yielded much better results along with concrete change. By the beginning of the 1990s, Sinn Féin had reached a political impasse and understood that, to compete and steal votes from the SDLP, they had to secure the votes of at least part of the nonmilitant constituency. Sinn Féin was already successful in obtaining the electoral preferences of the "ultra-nationalist" electorate, but it was failing to reach out to the rest of the Catholic community. To attract votes from these potential supporters, it was necessary for the party to shift toward a more mainstream version of nationalism, thus getting closer to SDLP's constitutional nationalism.[158] The ideological, tactical, and political changes undertaken by Sinn Féin between 1989 and 1994 appear as logical consequences of this strategic shift to attract the "moderate" electorate and remove itself from a political dead end.

The first important changes the group undertook to move in this direction occurred at the ideological and programmatic level between 1987 and 1992. In 1987, amid Sinn Féin's political crisis, the party published *A Scenario for Peace*, in which Sinn Féin laid out a peaceful strategy to reunify Ireland. According to the document, the Protestants then would then recognized as a "national minority."[159] This hardly represented an acceptable outcome for the unionist forces but nevertheless signaled that the republican movement was analyzing options other than armed struggle to achieve its goals and recognized that a military victory was not attainable in the immediate future.

This first political framework was later expanded and enriched in 1992, with the publication of *Towards a Lasting Peace in Ireland.* This document contained several new key ideas, such as describing the conflict as internal and asserting that the British government had the responsibility to persuade "the unionists to look toward a united Ireland."[160] The United Kingdom went from main enemy to being described as the potential persuader of the unionist community, a sign that Sinn Féin was de facto opening the door to direct political negotiations without rejecting armed struggle as a means to "push" the British government to take on the role of "persuader." The document showed Sinn Féin's transition to accepting a political peace process as beginning before the United Kingdom's withdrawal from Northern Ireland.[161] The final reunification of Ireland was seen as an evolutionary process that would begin with direct negotiations and a political peace process, with no guarantee of an immediate British withdrawal. In addition to these changes in the group's political discourse, Sinn Féin aimed to remove itself from political isolation by creating new alliances with other civil society groups and political parties.

In the late 1980s, Gerry Adams developed a concept known as "nationalist consensus," which asserted the importance to create a "Pan-nationalist" front that would include both the SDLP and the government of Ireland.[162] This groundbreaking notion for Sinn Féin led to an initial dialogue with SDLP. This step was incredibly significant, even though it did not produce a concrete agreement or plans of future cooperation. This was mostly due to the existing disagreements between the parties over the role of the armed struggle, as well as their different outlook on the conflict.[163]

Still, the failure of these preliminary talks did not mean the complete cessation of dialogue between the two nationalist forces. On the contrary, the two parties' leaders, Gerry Adams and John Hume, began a stable, yet secretive, dialogue to attempt to bridge their differences. The results of such political exchanges were only made public in April 1993, when the two parties issued a first joint statement, calling to "change the political climate away from conflict and towards a process of national reconciliation," accepting that "the Irish people as a whole have a right to national self-determination."[164]

Sinn Féin renewed its image and broke out of political isolation as a result of the talks with SDLP leader John Hume, along with the progressive shift in the party's political discourse. The beginning of more direct communications between the British government and the republican movement, through Sinn Féin, also contributed to the group's "rebranding." At the end of 1989, Peter Brooke, secretary of state for Northern Ireland, stated that a military defeat of the IRA seemed unlikely. He stressed the importance to find a political solution to the conflict and expressed hopes for the UK government to be "flexible" and "imaginative" in dealing with the armed republican movement once the latter decided to pursue political negotiations and renounce violence.[165]

This opening to the Provos was followed by another speech, in November 1990, in which Brooke stated that the United Kingdom had no "selfish strategic or economic interest in Northern Ireland," a declaration that influenced the republicans in moving somewhat closer to the British government.[166] In addition, the conservative government led by John Major, who had replaced Margaret Thatcher as Tory leader and prime minister in 1990, sought to overcome the stalemate in Northern Ireland and to engage more directly with the IRA.

An example of this trend is the preliminary contacts between the UK government and Sinn Féin in the early 1990s, which led London to seek a more direct, yet still secretive, political confrontation with the republican party during 1993.[167] These political back talks gained momentum after December 15, 1993, following the publication of a second Anglo-Irish joint declaration, known as the Downing Street Declaration. The document reiterated the need to resolve the conflict, while at the same time recognizing the right of self-determination of the Irish people and stating that unity would only be pursued in accordance with the will of the majority of the population in Northern Ireland. The declaration ratified the message conveyed by Brooke in 1990 that the United Kingdom had no "selfish" interest in Northern Ireland and claimed the role of the United Kingdom as "facilitator" of the peace process between the unionist and the nationalist communities.[168]

Although the republican movement was overall unimpressed with the declaration's terms, still it acknowledged the document as a stepping-stone toward the potential resolution of the conflict. The 1993 declaration also led Sinn Féin to remain involved in the emerging peace process, investing in direct political involvement.

In looking at Sinn Féin's journey between 1989 and 1993, it is evident that the group underwent significant changes, most notably in its political discourse, political alliances, and relations with the British government. These steps were necessary to break the political isolation of the republican movement and to raise its profile and influence within Northern Ireland.

This process was not accompanied by a significant decline in the armed struggle, as the bombing campaigns continued in parallel with the political dialogue. By the early 1990s, Sinn Féin was more vocal in distinguishing between its political activism and the IRA campaigns, without however criticizing or distancing itself from the Provos and their resort to violence. For example, in early 1992, Gerry Adams declared that Sinn Féin and the IRA had "no organic links,"[169] a statement that was likely directed to an external rather than an internal audience, as the IRA–Sinn Féin partnership had not been altered.

These measures were not immediately successful. Talks with SDLP improved the public's perception of Sinn Féin but did not translate into an electoral advantage. Consequently, the party's performance in the 1992 Westminster elections was particularly poor, with Sinn Féin gaining no seats and with Gerry Adams losing his West Belfast seat. The same disappointing results were repeated in the 1993 council elections, in which Sinn Féin obtained 12 percent of the electoral preferences, and in the 1994 European parliament elections, in which the party gathered only 9.9 percent of the votes, one of the lowest ever obtained by Sinn Féin since its initial participation in the EU elections.[170] Sinn Féin's electoral performance in Ireland was also disappointing. In the 1992 general elections, Sinn Féin obtained only eight thousand votes more than in 1989, although it had nominated more than three times as many candidates.[171] These electoral defeats would be only temporary setbacks for Sinn Féin. As the peace process gained momentum in the second half of the 1990s and as Sinn Féin's involvement in this dialogue increased, the situation would start to change.

Adams's public campaign to separate between Sinn Féin and the IRA, along with other measures undertaken to shift the group's electoral strategy, ultimately led Sinn Féin to achieve something previously unthinkable: to brand a vote for Sinn Féin as a vote for peace. To accomplish this, the political leadership of the republican movement had to redefine the relation between armed struggle and political activism. The Armalite would have to be put aside in favor of the ballot box.

1994–1998: The Road to Peace and the Good Friday Agreement

By the mid-1990s, there was a general understanding that the armed struggle was detrimental to the political advancement of the republican movement. The conflict between the logic of political accommodation and violent confrontation had not led to an internal rift along the politico-military line. Instead, the republican movement dealt with the growing tension between armed struggle and political activism by choosing the path of differentiation.

Although Sinn Féin never criticized or opposed the IRA and its modus operandi, the organization nevertheless tried to adopt an electoral strategy that underlined its differences with the Provos. At the same time, they created bridges with the SDLP and constitutional nationalism, while asserting their desire to employ an "unarmed strategy." Eventually, the growing internal consensus toward Sinn Féin's political strategy, and the favorable political conditions led the IRA to agree to an unconditional cease-fire in August 1994, showing the group's will to give the political venue a chance.[172]

Before this announcement on August 31, 1994, a number of important signals and events had indicated the group's increased confidence in a peace process. Internally, as early as April 1994, the IRA had announced a three-day cease-fire as a sign of goodwill, then followed by the IRA leadership's Easter message stating that it was "the responsibility of all involved to overcome the obstacles on the road to peace."[173] Around this same time, an internal IRA report called TUAS (Tactical Use of Armed Struggle) was released. The document indicated that the movement's short-term goals were "to construct an Irish nationalist consensus with international support on the basis of the dynamic contained in the Irish peace initiative."[174]

The IRA wanted to create a more stable alliance with SDLP, the Irish government, and the Irish-American lobby in the United States. To them, this coalition would have a powerful effect on any future peace talks and—according to the group's internal analysis—to be a part of such an alliance, the IRA would have to "recalibrate" its military campaigns.

This analysis had been influenced by the secret dialogue with Hume and the British government in the early 1990s but also by the election of President Bill Clinton in the United States, seen by the IRA as the first president "to be substantially influenced" by the Irish-American lobby.[175]

The Clinton administration had further shown its intentions to raise republicans' interest in the peace process as early as January 1994, when the President opened the diplomatic channels to Sinn Féin by granting Gerry Adams a visa to visit the United States and fund-raise for the republican movement.[176] This gesture strengthened Adams and those within the republican movement who advocated pursuing the struggle for a united Ireland through political means.

While the 1970s cease-fires had provided the chance for the IRA to regroup and rearm, the 1994 cessation of violence was not really a response to a drain in the resources of the group. Rather, the cease-fire was linked to a changed perception of the political and security environment.[177] In 1994, there was no threat to the group's access to weapons. However, the IRA decided to implement a temporary cessation of military activities due to changes in Sinn Féin's strategy but also in response to a political "opening" that offered the group the opportunity to be involved in political negotiations.

In August 1994, the IRA stated that by "recognizing the potential of the current situation and in order to enhance the democratic peace process and underline our definitive commitment to its success . . . there will be a complete cessation of military operations."[178] The announcement of the cease-fire was followed by a meeting between Gerry Adams, John Hume, and Irish prime minister Albert Reynolds.[179]

The cease-fire did not immediately create peace. By 1995, Patrick Mayhew, secretary of state for Northern Ireland, who had succeeded Peter Brooke, had made clear that there would be no direct involvement of Sinn Féin in the negotiation process short of IRA decommissioning. The IRA immediately rejected this request as a "new and unreasonable demand."[180]

To overcome this political impasse, which threatened the cease-fire, the UK and Irish government agreed to move forward with a twin-track process that would have the two governments setting up "preparatory talks" to precede substantial negotiations among the parties. The UK-Irish joint communiqué of November 1995 also led to the creation of a three-person International Body tasked to report on the decommissioning issue. The International Body, which was composed of former senator George Mitchell, former prime minister of Iceland Harri Holkeri, and Canada's chief of the defense staff John de Chastelain, reported in January 1996 that decommissioning should be considered in the course of the peace process but that it should not be a precondition to entering the talks.[181]

The British government's initial reaction to the International Body's report was not as the Provos wished. The government seemed to disregard the recommendations for withholding the demand to disarm. This added to the frustration of the republican movement, which maintained that the cease-fire had not led to an increased involvement of the group in the political process. The Provos found it particularly difficult to absorb the issue of prior decommissioning. It was seen as a British attempt to have them announce their unconditional surrender before the political negotiation process even began.[182]

The lack of progress on the political track was indeed an explosive issue within the IRA, and it would lead to an internal debate over the value of preserving the cease-fire. The senior leadership was divided on this question, but the balance tipped in favor of those who objected preserving the cease-fire, especially after the discovery of an increasing number of defections to republican Sinn Féin.[183] The

IRA leadership decided to end the eighteen-month cease-fire and renew its bombing campaign in February 1996, by hitting London's Canary Wharf district.

This resort to violence should not be seen as a by-product of a strategic shift within the republican movement. The IRA was not seeking to revert to the use of force as its principal means to achieve its goals. Instead, it used the attacks as a tactical tool to pressure the British government to begin inclusive peace talks where the issue of decommissioning would not be treated as a precondition for dialogue, as well as to avoid an internal split. Violence was used as a hard-bargaining tactic, employed to better the group's position at the negotiating table, in parallel to Sinn Féin's political campaign.

In the aftermath of the attack, John Major asked Sinn Féin to publicly distance itself from the IRA and the group's attacks. Gerry Adams refused to speak against the IRA, as obviously this would have raised the internal tensions and possibly even led to an internal feud. Instead, the Sinn Féin leader continued with the "separation" strategy, investing in Sinn Féin's outreach efforts and in its political campaign to portray the party as committed and ready for peace.[184]

Malachi O'Doherty claims that Sinn Féin's constant denial of organizational links with the IRA, along with its assertion of being incapable of constraining the Provos's behavior and with its refusal to criticize or condemn its actions are all part of the same strategy. Accordingly, the IRA at times employed violence in parallel to Sinn Féin's political openings. The Provos wanted to show the British government that it could not be constrained by the results of the peace process, while it also intended to pressure the United Kingdom to act more swiftly and to agree to republican demands.[185]

The separation strategy failed to convince the British government, which set up political talks for June 1996 but declared that Sinn Féin would again be excluded from the negotiating table unless the IRA agreed to declare a new cease-fire. Unsurprisingly, this hard-bargaining tactic did not succeed in obtaining a new cessation of the IRA attacks, and it resulted in another political stalemate, which would last until the new cease-fire in July 1997.[186]

Nevertheless, despite Sinn Féin's exclusion from the negotiating table in June 1996, the "separation strategy" succeeded at the grassroots level. During the cease-fire, public support for the republican movement increased substantially on both sides of the border, and this rise in support survived until the end of the cease-fire, largely because of the successful campaign to brand Sinn Féin as a party committed to peace.

In the May 1996 elections for the Northern Ireland Forum—set up to allow for multiparty negotiations—Sinn Féin finally broke the 10 percent electoral ceiling by gaining the 15.5 percent of the votes and winning seventeen seats, indicating an improvement in the group's electoral performance.[187] Sinn Féin's performance also improved in Ireland. In the June 1997 parliamentary elections, the party obtained 2.4 percent of the votes and managed to win its first seat in Leister House, after having been excluded from the parliament for the previous decades.[188]

Sinn Féin's positive electoral results gave confidence to those within the republican movement—such as Sinn Féin leader Gerry Adams—who were advocating for boosting the unarmed strategy. Such voices were further consolidated following the elections of a new Labour government in the United Kingdom in May 1997 led by Tony Blair and with the relinquishment of the decommissioning requirement as a precondition to talks.

In response to such developments, the IRA announced a second cease-fire in July 1997. This renewed cessation of hostilities was preceded by a peak in the armed struggle in the first half of 1997, again maintaining parallel armed and political tracks and attempting to separate the two as much as possible. However, even if the IRA had been extremely active at the beginning of 1997, Sinn Féin had by then become an equal partner in the relationship between the two groups. The momentum provided by the peace process would further push its agenda and its unarmed strategy at the forefront of the republican movement.

In September 1997, Sinn Féin agreed to the Mitchell principles on democracy and nonviolence and officially entered the multiparty talks at Stormont, also ensuring that the political talks would not demand decommissioning as a precondition for talks. Rather, disarmament talks would be held simultaneously to peace negotiations and would involve both unionist and nationalist paramilitary groups.[189]

This step toward institutional politics and the peace process would increase internal tensions over how to accommodate the organizational imperatives of political participation and armed struggle. Ultimately, the internal conflict would escalate and lead to an internal split and the creation of the Real IRA in October 1997.[190]

A minority group within Northern Ireland, the Real IRA is responsible for a number of bloody attacks, including the Omagh town center bombing of August 1998, where more than 29 people were killed and hundreds were injured.[191] Despite this split, the vast majority of the IRA and its supporters stood behind the group's decision to call for a cease-fire and backed the peace negotiations, which would run from September 1997 to April 1998. The process culminated with the Good Friday Agreement, or Belfast Agreement, of April 10, 1998. The agreement recognizes the right to self-determination for the people of Northern Ireland. It also contains provisions for establishing local institutions based on the principles of power sharing, and it includes the creation of cross-border consultative bodies that grant a larger role for the Irish government in Northern Ireland.[192]

Although the document would indeed mark a watershed in the context of the conflict—shifting the dynamic from violent confrontation to political dialogue and reconciliation—the provisions of the Good Friday Agreement are not so substantially different from those contained in the 1973 Sunningdale Agreement. SDLP MP Seamus Mallon famously summarized the situation by asserting that the GFA was just "Sunningdale for slow learners."[193]

The Good Friday Agreement was ratified by a double referendum in Northern Ireland and the Republic of Ireland. It was overwhelmingly accepted on both sides of the border, with 71 percent of voters in Northern Ireland and 94 percent in Ireland who voted in favor of the GFA. This shifted the conflict toward a new phase, forcing the IRA and Sinn Féin to further evolve and adapt to meet the new political environment.[194]

1998–2012: "Normalization" and Disarmament

Since the mid-1980s, the logic of military confrontation and the logic of political participation began to clash within the republican movement, as the armed campaigns of the IRA were seen as detrimental to the Sinn Féin's electoral performance. Through the 1990s, Sinn Féin devised a strategy to deal with the negative effect of the IRA campaigns on its electoral popularity. The party shifted its political strategy and began to draw a very clear separation between its actions and those of the IRA without condemning or criticizing them. By the mid-1990s, Sinn Féin acquired a new and broader constituency that voted in support of its unarmed strategy. Branding a vote for Sinn Féin as a vote for peace, the party built its credibility and popularity. The group also gradually became entrenched in the peace process and in institutional politics. The rise of Sinn Féin's leverage and influence in the Northern Ireland political arena was taken by the IRA as an incentive to "give peace a chance" and to allow the process that would lead to the Good Friday Agreement.

The republican movement's prolonged conflict between political participation and armed struggle led to two major splits along the politico-military line, in 1986 and 1997, but also to an internal restructuring to solve the Armalite and ballot box dilemma. Ultimately, as Sinn Féin became a more influential political party, the costs became higher in maintaining both the armed and political struggle. Following the Good Friday Agreement, timing forced the republican movement to permanently choose between the ballot box and the Armalite.

In April 1998, following the signing of the Good Friday, the IRA was confronted with a new reality. The agreement aimed to restructure the political arena in Northern Ireland, while the peace process, strengthened regionally by the development of an increasingly more integrated Europe,[195] had finally taken off. The organization initially did not endorse the agreement and added that it would not agree to disarm, in accordance with the agreement's provisions on decommissioning. The IRA still accepted the agreement as an important stepping-stone asserting it would be "monitoring" the developments on the ground.[196]

Sinn Féin's analysis of the agreement was similar, albeit more positive: "[the Belfast Agreement] represents what is possible at this time; not the preferred option for any of the participants—certainly not Sinn Féin's. That is the political reality. The Good Friday Agreement is the essential compromise for this phase of the peace process."[197] However, despite these skeptical reactions to the Good Friday Agreement, both IRA and Sinn Féin underwent a series of important strategic changes in its aftermath. As early as May 1998, the Sinn Féin Ard Fheis modified its stand with regard to the participation in the Stormont government. Ninety-seven percent of the delegates supported the end to abstentionism, and numerous IRA commanders and leaders endorsed the decision by taking part in the meeting.[198] The party's strategy following the Good Friday Agreement stressed the importance of "dialogue" and "reconciliation," while specifying a full commitment to the peace process and to maintaining an unarmed strategy.[199]

Sinn Féin strongly insisted on distinguishing between the party and the IRA, a trend that culminated when Sinn Féin's McGuinness declared in 2004 that "the days of Sinn Féin interpreting IRA statements are over; they're gone. . . . We're going to defend our democratic mandate against all comers."[200]

The group began to openly describe violence as a by-product of the conflict between the unionist and the nationalist communities, and as an obstacle to political progress, rather than as a tool to attain political ends.[201] Within Sinn Féin's new political discourse, violence was portrayed as counterproductive. By formulating this analysis of the conflict and becoming involved in the implementation of the Good Friday Agreement, the post-1998 Sinn Féin strengthened its "a vote for Sinn Féin is a vote for peace" strategy.

The decline of the IRA's armed attacks after 1998 and its progressive acceptance of the disarmament process also supported Sinn Féin's electoral performance. For example, in the pre-2005 years, voting for Sinn Féin was seen as a means to encourage the decommissioning process.[202]

Despite this positive association between supporting Sinn Féin and encouraging disarmament, the link between Sinn Féin and the IRA still caused the political party a series of problems that negatively affected both its credibility and its capacity to effectively take part in institutional politics within Northern Ireland. This is easily understood by analyzing the local political process post-1998.

In April 1998, the GFA reestablished the 108-member Northern Ireland assembly, granting it executive and legislative power devolved from Westminster. The assembly, elected by proportional representation, was devised on the principle of power sharing. For example, this system established the principle of cross-community support by the loyalist and nationalist members of the assembly to adopt any significant political measure. The elections to set up the local assembly took place as early as June 1998, only a month following the political referendum on the GFA.[203] The 1998 results were encouraging for Sinn Féin, which obtained eighteen of the total votes and gained eighteen seats in the Stormont assembly, against the twenty-four won by SDLP.[204] For Sinn Féin to translate this positive electoral performance into political power and influence, the party needed to rely on functioning political institutions and productive political relations with the other existing political forces. As early as 1999, it was evident that both aspects were seriously impaired by the IRA and its weapons. The unionist forces in Northern Ireland assured that they were unwilling to engage in a long-term power-sharing arrangement with "political representatives of an unlawfully armed organization which is committed to bringing about change by either the use or threat of acts of terrorism."[205] Meanwhile, the IRA modified its original stance on disarmament and accepted and began discussions with the ad hoc Independent International Commission on Decommissioning set up by the British and Irish governments in 1997. Yet disarmament unfolded extremely slowly.

By December 1999, when the assembly was finally given devolved powers, pressure mounted from the unionist forces to demand the IRA's complete decommissioning by May 2000.[206] In the following months, the new Northern Ireland assembly took powers and set up a power-sharing executive. However, after the lack of progress on IRA disarmament, London suspended the assembly and the executive from February to May 2000, in response to the demands of the unionist parties within Northern Ireland.[207]

The crisis was resolved following an IRA announcement that "the IRA leadership will initiate a process that will completely and verifiably put IRA arms beyond use."[208] This declaration was crucial to restore the Northern Ireland assembly, a sign that the group's organizational priority was to guarantee Sinn Féin's advancement in institutional politics. It was obvious that Sinn Féin had transitioned to become a senior partner from a marginal and subordinate part of the republican movement.

In June 2000, the IRA allowed two international inspectors to access some of the groups' arms dumps. The inspectors later confirmed that the group had decommissioned and secured a large part of its arsenal. Despite this initial progress, by 2001, the IRA had stalled the disarmament process, which once again led to the temporary suspension of the local assembly in the summer of 2001.[209] In this context, two main events contributed to reversing this process and speeding up the disarmament of the Provos.

First, in August 2001, was the arrest of three IRA militants in Colombia, where they allegedly received and provided training to the FARC.[210] The discovery of the IRA-FARC connection deeply angered the United States and contributed a decrease in patience for the Provos, a feeling that was then deeply enhanced after 9/11. The embarrassment following the discovery of the IRA's Colombian connections helped push forward the agenda of those, like Sinn Féin leader Gerry Adams, who internally advocated a speedy decommissioning, and in obtaining the first public act of decommissioning in October 2001.[211]

In addition, the Sinn Féin political leader had an additional factor to sell the pro-decommissioning strategy internally: the continuous political ascent of Sinn Féin. In the June 2001 Westminster elections, the party overtook the SDLP for the first time, obtaining 21.7 percent of the votes and winning four seats.[212] This historic result for Sinn Féin did not necessarily provide political power. The lack of progress of the disarmament track, combined with the failure of all the political parties to establish a functioning local government led the assembly to be suspended again in October 2002. This freeze lasted until May 2007.

The political crisis did not affect Sinn Féin's electoral fortunes. In the November 2003 elections for the assembly, Sinn Féin confirmed its newly acquired dominance over SDLP, after gaining twenty-four seats, against the eighteen awarded to their historic political opponent. This made Sinn Féin the second-largest party in Northern Ireland, after the Democratic Unionist Party (DUP).[213] The 2003 election further confirmed the shift in Northern Ireland's electorate from the traditional "moderate" parties such as the SDLP and Prime Minister David Trimble's Ulster Unionist Party to the traditionally more 'militant' nationalist parties such as DUP and Sinn Féin.

Sinn Féin's electoral success was linked to its effective campaigning around socioeconomic themes, to the performance of its two elected ministers (Martin McGuinness as minister of education and Bairbre de Brun as head of the health portfolio), as well as to the progress of the IRA disarmament.[214] Sinn Féin's electoral rise in Northern Ireland continued in 2004 with the party winning 26.31 percent of the votes against the 15.94 percent obtained by SDLP 2004 in the European parliament elections.[215]

The lack of progress within Northern Ireland prevented the party from having a more direct role in local politics. Following the 2003 and 2004 electoral victories of Sinn Féin and the DUP, the two parties attempted negotiations on a power-sharing arrangement to move beyond the political impasse. Talks failed to overcome the stumbling block represented by IRA weapons, especially following Sinn Féin's refusal to comply with the DUP's requests to provide concrete evidence of the ongoing disarmament.[216]

Following Sinn Féin's refusal to give the DUP what it defined as a "Kodak moment," the negotiations between the two parties collapsed in December 2004. That same month, Sinn Féin was again in the eye of the political storm because of the IRA and its weapons. The Provos were suspected of having carried out a multi-million-pound robbery at the Northern Bank in Belfast on December 20, 2004.[217] Sinn Féin vehemently denied any connections or knowledge of the crime, and the IRA reacted by denying any involvement with the robbery, withdrawing its decommissioning proposal, and asserting that the consequences of the situation and the repeated "attacks" against the IRA should not be "underestimated."[218] The robbery produced an important backlash. Both the UK government and the local unionist forces reacted by speaking harshly of the group's "paramilitary and criminal" activities and by refusing to "accept the farce that Sinn Féin and the IRA are separate."[219]

The robbery also negatively highlighted the IRA's criminal activities post-1998, as well as its continuing "local community policing," which resulted in many attacks, beatings, and summary executions within the Catholic community.[220] The accusations following the robbery, together with the failure of negotiations with the DUP led to an internal debate over the "Adams-McGuinness" strategy of political compromise and disarmament.[221] The republican leadership noticed that the general level of support for Sinn Féin seemed affected by the IRA's glacial pace of disarmament and by its involvement in criminal activities. Even public opinion was negative toward the robbery. January and March 2005 newspaper polls showed that a growing number of the group's constituency openly desired an official separation between Sinn Féin and the IRA, which suggested that Sinn Féin's electorate was starting to lose patience.[222]

With this, Sinn Féin leader Gerry Adams spoke out against the armed activities of the IRA on the eve of the May 2005 Westminster elections. This strategy paid off and Sinn Féin was rewarded by the electorate, winning a fifth seat in the British parliament. Three months after Adams's appeal to depose the weapons, in July 2005, the IRA leadership announced that "all Volunteers have been instructed to assist the development of purely political and democratic programmes through exclusively peaceful means."[223] This historic statement was followed in September 2005 by the international commissioners' ratification of the satisfactory completion of the decommissioning process.

By 2005, the political costs of maintaining an armed wing had become too high for the republican movement, affecting its capacity to become directly involved in government and started to erode its electoral gains. The final decommissioning act of the IRA had a profound effect on the political landscape of Northern Ireland, contributing to the process of "normalization" of political life and intercommunity relations. Despite the complete IRA disarmament, the process toward the restoration of the Northern Ireland assembly and executive would continue to proceed at a rather slow pace until the end of 2006.

In October 2006, the British and Irish governments announced a plan to restore devolution by spring 2007, threatening to dissolve the local political institutions and establish a joint direct administration if the parties had not managed to create a power-sharing government by that deadline.[224] This time, the political forces in Northern Ireland rose up to the challenge, and, with the St. Andrews Agreement, they committed to power sharing, participated in a transitional assembly since November 2006, and met the spring 2007 deadline by setting up a new executive in May 2007.[225]

In achieving this historical result, all local political parties would have to compromise on "core issues." Specifically DUP would have to agree to the principle of power sharing with Sinn Féin, while the republican party would have to agree to legitimize the institution that, for decades, had symbolized the unionist politics of oppression of the Catholic community: the former RUC, renamed Police Service of Northern Ireland (PSNI).[226]

The reform of the Northern Ireland police, along with the issue of the release of republican prisoners from Irish and British jails, had been the most important political campaign conducted by Sinn Féin in the post-GFA period. However, while the GFA provisions regarding the release of the prisoners were implemented without much controversy, reforming the RUC proved to be a political minefield.

Sinn Féin insisted on reforming the local police based on the 1999 Patten report written by the Independent Commission on Policing for Northern Ireland. The commission had recommended the complete organizational restructuring of the RUC, as well as the creation of an ad hoc unionist-nationalist police board to oversee the new organization.[227] The adoption of a diluted version of the report in 2001 led Sinn Féin to refuse to take the newly created seat on the police board and to initiate a political campaign to obtain the full implementation of the organizational reforms recommended in the Patten report.[228]

The boycott of the new police force ended in January 2007, as part of the process to restore devolution of powers to Northern Ireland. Endorsing the PSNI had become the main condition that Sinn Féin needed to meet to bring the devolution process forward. The British and Irish insistence of this issue was largely grounded in the need for Sinn Féin to take a stand with respect to the continuation of republican violence and criminality post-2005 by supporting the new police.[229] The reversal of the boycott is an important example of the role and strategy of Sinn Féin in the post-decommissioning years. The party had to compromise on a series of core issues to take part in the Stormont political system, while it had to still find a way to brand these choices as consistent with its republican aspirations to create a thirty-two-county Ireland.

Reconciling these principles was not always easy, and—as cleverly put by DUP Member of Parliament Gregory Campbell, Sinn Féin was at times appearing to be trying to deny the existence of the country in which it held office.[230] Conscious of this dilemma, Sinn Féin has been adamant in reassuring its constituency that its political goals remained unchanged, while they increasingly invested in diversifying its electoral platform, for example, by stressing its role as opposition and protest party, and by championing socioeconomic campaigns centered on the idea of equality.[231] This post-2005 soul-searching process did not change the political role of Sinn Féin in Northern Ireland: the March 2007 elections for the new devolved assembly confirmed Sinn Féin's position as the largest nationalist party. On that occasion, Sinn Féin gained an impressive 26.1 percent of the votes, against the 15.2 percent of SDLP.[232]

With this mandate from the nationalist constituency, Sinn Féin felt it had the popular legitimacy and political backing to take part in the DUP–Sinn Féin government, with Martin McGuinness serving as deputy prime minister to DUP's Ian Paisley. Both the 2009 European elections and the 2010 Westminster elections confirmed the popularity of Sinn Féin in Northern Ireland, with the party winning, respectively, 26 and 25.5 of the votes, against roughly 16 percent won by SDLP.[233] In Ireland, however, Sinn Féin's popularity has not risen dramatically: in the May 2007 general elections, the party only secured 6.9 percent of the votes, only a 0.4 increase since 2002.[234]

The steady rise of Sinn Féin in Northern Ireland, along with its continuous marginal role south of the border currently represent the main challenge to the party's traditional republican strategy of mobilizing a prounification constituency on both sides of the border. The political journey of Sinn Féin from marginal actor to central political player in Northern Ireland serves a powerful example of the potential power and influence of political wings of armed groups. The analysis of the political development of Sinn Féin showed that, as the group started to gain political influence and acquire a more prominent role in the political system, the logic of political accommodation gradually clashed with that of armed struggle. Specifically, and unlike the cases of Hamas and Hezbollah, with the republican movement, the IRA military campaigns became detrimental to the political advancement of Sinn Féin, thus forcing the group to choose between the Armalite and the ballot box strategy.

In the end, the gradual transition of the group toward institutional politics and the adoption of a totally unarmed strategy were related to a significant opening in the political system, which gave Sinn Féin and its leaders the necessary boost to tilt the internal balance of power towards full political participation.

Assessing the Political Development of the Republican Movement

The IRA—offering one of the most notorious examples of an armed group that permanently gave up violence to join the political process—represents an important case study to analyze the dynamics behind armed groups' participation in institutional politics. The literature on political participation of armed groups consistently relies on this case study to validate the linear "armed-to-political" development model, asserting that the increased involvement in politics was the primary factor that led the IRA to relinquish its military apparatus. Therefore, focusing on the political and military evolution of the IRA is particularly useful to test the cyclical development model.

The first part of the chapter looked at the political rise of Sinn Féin and its role in the republican movement. This shift in the group's organizational strategy began in 1981 with the decision to compete in the Northern Ireland municipal elections and to assume office if elected. This process eventually led to officially abolishing abstentionism with regards to the Irish parliament—the Dáil—in 1986.

As in the previously discussed case studies, the republican movement's shift toward increased involvement in institutional politics was related to four main factors: (1) the group's need to expand to respond to threats to its legitimacy and relevancy, (2) a decline in the group's resources, (3) an opening in the political opportunity structure, and (4) a significant internal commitment to reform the organization.

With the republican movement, the strategic shift toward increased involvement in institutional politics occurred when the group's legitimacy and relevance were both threatened. By the early 1980s, the military war on the IRA and the political war to isolate Sinn Féin were both yielding results. The Thatcher government's policies to defeat the IRA militarily had seriously harmed the organization, and it had managed to impair its access to human and material resources. Politically, Sinn Féin was also in serious difficulties: marginalized and isolated on both sides of the border and increasingly less relevant, especially in the aftermath of the 1985 Anglo-Irish Agreement.

The decision to increase Sinn Féin's political profile and to compete in local elections would help to break in part the isolation of the group, while providing a means to accommodate with the shifting political environment, allowing the group to stay relevant.

At the same time, the early 1980s saw an important shift in the distribution of the voters along the political scale, increasing the republican movement's potential constituency and thus creating an opening in the political opportunity system. The political campaign for the republican prisoners' rights in the early 1980s had mobilized an important sector of the public opinion behind the republican movement. Sinn Féin's increased involvement in institutional politics allowed the group to expand and incorporate these new supporters, building on its increased popularity on both sides of the border. Finally, the increased interest in institutional politics was also related to an internal change in the group's leadership. This younger generation of men, born and raised in Northern Ireland, showed a more pragmatic outlook on the conflict and were much more interested in building a local political constituency and in winning the hearts and minds of the local population. The interplay of these organizational, institutional, and external factors led to the political rise of Sinn Féin and to its participation in the local Northern Ireland municipal elections since the early 1980s.

The second part of the chapter analyzed the political development of Sinn Féin and its evolving relationship with the IRA in the years following the group's decision to end abstentionism with respect to municipal elections in Northern Ireland and parliamentary elections in Ireland. In tracing the shifts in the relation between Sinn Féin and the IRA, the focus of the chapter is on testing the main hypothesis of the study, asserting that strategic change—implying a transition toward completely embracing institutional politics and relinquishing an armed group's armed strategy—is related to a prolonged internal conflict between the organizational logics of political accommodation and military confrontation. Absent such tensions along the politico-military line, armed organizations have very little incentive to choose between bullets and ballots, as the cases of Hezbollah showed in the previous chapters.

Applying this hypothesis to the IRA is particularly interesting, as the conventional wisdom on this case study claims that political participation played a key role in ensuring the group's transition from violence to dialogue,[235] implying that competing in elections was a sufficient factor to stir the group away from the armed struggle.

A closer look to the political and military evolution of the republican movement seems to point in a different direction. At the beginning of the 1980s, when Sinn Féin became more involved in institutional politics, this participation was perceived as part of the new Armalite and ballot box strategy. Politics and the creation of an unarmed strategy were devised as auxiliary tools to complement, not substitute, the military struggle, while Sinn Féin and the IRA worked on the basis of an unequal partnership, dominated by the IRA and its Army Council. By the late 1980s, there were signs that the Armalite and ballot box strategy was not working as effectively as the republican movement had hoped. The group's military campaigns were starting to collide with its political endeavors. The political growth of Sinn Féin had reached a stalemate.

As the logic of political accommodation and of armed struggle started to clash in the early 1990s, the group attempted to minimize the negative effects of the IRA's armed struggle on the party's electoral performance, while still struggling to maintain its Armalite and ballot box strategy. This led Sinn Féin to adopt a strategy of differentiation: the party started to progressively assert its separate identity from the IRA, by creating a more pragmatic political discourse and by reaching out to the more mainstream nationalist party, the SDLP. While Sinn Féin was pursuing this political strategy and increasing its political status and power within Northern Ireland, the IRA did not substantially change its modus operandi or diminish its reliance on violence.

The beginning of an organizational shift away from violence did not come as a result of an increased participation in the political process but rather from the shift in the internal perception of the relation between the Armalite and the ballot box.

After 1994—in parallel with the opening of the political system and the beginning a peace negotiation process in Northern Ireland—the logics of political participation and of armed struggle from separate yet related strategic tools gradually became mutually exclusive alternatives. In the period leading to the Good Friday Agreement the republican movement attempted to maintain its hybrid politico-military strategy, but the costs of preserving this double strategy increased, in terms of public support and in relation to the group's capacity to influence the political negotiation process and gain access to power.

As the internal tensions along the politico-military lines increased on the eve of the agreement, eventually leading to the 1997 internal split and to the creation of the

RIRA, it would also become more obvious that the internal balance of power had changed during the 1990s, leading Sinn Féin from subordinate to stronger partner within the republican movement.

In the aftermath of the GFA the organizational dominance of Sinn Féin and its political leadership would become even more obvious, and when the process of disarmament would again expose the conflict between armed struggle and political participation, the group would naturally drift toward protecting its political achievements, eventually distancing itself from armed struggle. In turn, this process was crucial in leading to the permanent demise of the IRA's armed strategy and its military apparatus.

When looking at the political development of Sinn Féin, it is possible to appreciate how the party's political growth was from the beginning limited by the IRA's military campaigns. As the party rose in status and power, this trend was only strengthened, since the armed struggle threatened the group's popularity within its political constituency and its access to political dialogue and, ultimately, political power. Short of this strategic clash between the logic of armed struggle and the principle of political participation, it is unclear whether the group would have had the same incentives to relinquish its military apparatus following the Good Friday Agreement.

Armed Groups and Political Integration

Findings and Policy Implications

This book focuses on the relationship between armed groups and institutional politics, in particular looking at the reasons behind an armed group's decision to establish a political wing and to compete in elections. The main assumption is that armed groups, as social organizations pursuing a political agenda, are rational players interested in surviving and guaranteeing their "organizational maintenance."[1]

An armed group's calculated decision to establish a political wing, according to the working hypothesis, is directly related to the interplay of four necessary but not sufficient factors. These factors are (1) institutional pressures to expand and accommodate in response to a threat, (2) the external openness of the political system, (3) temporary drains in the availability of mobilization resources, and (4) an internal commitment to change. The selected case studies test the theoretical framework, as the rest of the chapter analyzes. They also permit taking a closer look at the dynamics of political wing development after the initial creation of the political front.

The research examines the political development of the Irish Republican Army (IRA), Hamas, and Hezbollah. The research looks at whether the main assumptions in the literature, asserting that political participation leads to progressive "moderation" of armed groups and to their ultimate transition into solely political organizations, is universally valid. The preliminary results drawn from the case studies—although not sufficient to be the basis for a general theory on political wing formation and development—do serve the useful purpose of questioning the dominant linear armed-to-political paradigm and provide a first alternative explanatory framework. The study examines the development of political wings by focusing on the internal power distribution within a particular group and on the nature of the relationship between that group's political and military apparatuses.

The hypothesis asserts that an organization's potential to undergo strategic change and "moderation" is related to a prolonged and intense disequilibrium between the group's military and political wings. This ultimately leads the group to judge the two logics of military struggle and political accommodation as mutually exclusive. Under these conditions, the research expects an organization to be at its ripest moment for strategic internal change, especially if the political wing of the armed-political group possesses a high degree of autonomy as well as the capacity to spearhead internal change, along with a level of legitimacy and relevance within the political arena. This process, unlike the one described by the dominant "linear moderation paradigm," is expected to be cyclical, with the organization alternating phases of cooperation between armed and political wings, and stages of open internal competition. The case studies seem to support this cyclical development model, while also offering important policy insights on how best to regulate and integrate armed groups into a political system.

Hypotheses and Case Studies: Analytic Explanation of the Key Findings

Common and Diverging Patterns: Political Wing Formation

The selected case studies show very different conditions under which political wings develop and groups start to compete in elections. In all cases, the entry into institutional politics is related to the interplay of four main institutional, internal, and political factors.

1. Institutional pressures to expand and accommodate, in response to a legitimacy and relevancy threat. In each of the three examined case studies, the entry into institutional politics follows an important shift in the group's security and political environment. This results in a threat to the organization's legitimacy and pushes it to rely on a political wing as an accommodation tool. With Hezbollah in 1992, the group had to prove its relevance in the post–civil war political climate, while also reasserting its autonomy and distinctiveness from its main political opponent, Amal. Hamas's legitimacy and appeal, both in 1994 and 2004, were threatened. In 1994, the establishment of the Palestinian Authority empowered Fatah and lowered the general level of support for Hamas and its armed struggle. Similarly, in 2004, the progressive easing of the second intifada following the fall of 2002 resulted in declining rates of approval for the group within the Palestinian population, while prospects of renewed political negotiations further threatened to marginalize the Islamists. The republican movement during the early 1980s experienced similar problems. Since 1979 the Conservative Thatcher government succeeded in weakening the IRA militarily while isolating Sinn Féin politically. This occurred through renewed cross-border cooperation with the government of Ireland as well as through increased support for the constitutional nationalist party within Northern Ireland, the SDLP.

In each case, the direct legitimacy and relevancy threat pushed the armed groups to invest in institutional politics to regain legitimacy and to cope with their security and military environment. Simultaneously, the creation of a political wing became the main expansionary tool used to increase the supporting bases of the organization and to improve its position with respect to its political competitors. This paved the way to absorb the rising number of potential supporters, which, together with a shift in the political opportunity system, constituted the second main factor that led to the creation of a political front: an opening of the political system.

2. *An "opening" in the political opportunity system.* The main commonality between the three cases is that these groups entered into institutional politics following a modification of the political system. Such change resulted in either a favorable shift in the distribution of the voters from the groups' perspective, or in a higher level of permeability within the structures of power. Hezbollah joined the political system following a double opening. First, after the civil war, Hezbollah could count on a newly acquired constituency, because of the political decline of Amal, the popularity achieved fighting the Israeli occupation, and the support obtained among the Shia community for its social welfare services.

At the same time, elections resumed following the ratification of the Document of National Accord and the official end of civil war, and Hezbollah found concrete incentives to take part in institutional politics, since the restructured political system ensured greater access to power to the Shia community. Last, the Syrian military and political presence in post-Taif Lebanon improved the permeability of the structures of power for Hezbollah, both by reducing political volatility and by counterbalancing the power of the Maronite Christians.

The same "double opening" was present for Hamas in 2004. Fatah's popularity was in decline, spurred by the failure of negotiations with the Israel. Internal organizational rifts within Fatah, and the poor performance in governing the PA, also contributed to weakening Hamas's main political competitor. All these factors combined generated an increase in the number of potential supporters for the Palestinian Islamists. The death of Arafat in 2004 resulted in a dramatic opening of the Palestinian political system previously characterized by high centralization, low separation of powers, and the de facto control of the system by Fatah's historic leader.

Both factors were largely absent in 1994 when Hamas, despite facing a legitimacy threat and a drain in its availability of mobilization resources, decided not to take part in the Palestinian parliamentary elections.

In 1981, Sinn Féin's decision to run in the Northern Ireland local elections and to assume office if elected was a response to an important shift in the republican movement's potential constituency. Although the political system did not become more permeable for Sinn Féin, the group could count on a new potential constituency created in the aftermath of the hunger strikes. This generated a tangible political opening for Sinn Féin as well as an incentive to increase its role in the political system.

3. A decline in the availability of mobilization resources. Another common pattern with Hamas, Hezbollah, and the IRA is that their decisions to invest in institutional politics came during a temporary decline in their access to human and material resources. The groups chose to create a political wing to increase their autonomy as well as to diversify their sources of revenue and support.

The creation of a political wing in Hezbollah came in response to important changes in Iranian foreign policy after 1989 and the death of Ayatollah Khomeini, which resulted in a temporary decline in the level of logistical and financial support offered to Hezbollah. The military wing's autonomy and freedom of action were also increasingly constrained by Syria and by the domestic post–civil war political process.

Hamas's access to resources was threatened in both 1994 and 2004. In the mid-1990s, the repeated crackdowns on Hamas's armed wing and financial revenues by Israel and by the newly formed PA strained the group's finances. Ten years later, in the post-9/11 world, Hamas's resources were also under pressure as both Israel and the international community aggressively tried to crack down on the group's sources of funding. The decline in Hamas's ability to fund-raise was accompanied by a deterioration in the capacity of the group's military wing. In the early 1980s, the IRA also experienced external pressure combined with a series of major operational setbacks and internal rifts, which produced a decline in the success of the military wing as well as a sense of insecurity over the group's access to human and material resources.

4. An internal commitment to change. The formation of a political wing coincides with the emergence of an internal coalition within the armed organization that supports entry into institutional politics. As the case studies show, this development is accompanied by the promotion of a political ideology and programmatic platform that favors political accommodation and participation in the political system, while attempting to maintain ideological continuity within the group's original goals and values, thus preserving internal cohesion.

Despite the initial organizational conflict over pursuing political power, Hezbollah's decision to take part in institutional politics was in the end strongly supported by the majority of its internal leadership and simultaneously backed by Iran. This ensured the existence of a dominant coalition that promoted political participation. Regarding Hamas, the decision to compete in the municipal and parliamentary elections following Arafat's death was similarly supported by its local and external leaderships, and while the group's military leaders were not directly involved in the electoral process, they did not attempt to jeopardize it. Sinn Féin's increasing political activism was also backed internally within the party and sanctioned by the IRA's Army Council, thus ensuring strong support for pursuing the path of institutional politics.

When looking at the process of political wing formation and the decision to compete in institutional politics, the case studies appear to provide preliminary evidence that supports the initial hypothesis: An armed group's decision to form a political wing is the result of a rational calculation and a response to shifts in the group's mobilization and political opportunity structure, as well as institutional challenges and internal changes in the organizational balance of power. Although the number of case studies falls short of allowing the construction of a model to predict political wing formation in armed groups, the findings are significant and can serve as an important stepping-stone for further large-N studies on the topic. Understanding what may drive armed groups to create a political wing can and should assist decision makers when devising policies designed to regulate political participation and encourage the integration of armed groups in the political system.

Common and Diverging Patterns: Political Wing Development

The second part of the study focuses on the dynamics that occur after the creation of a political wing by an armed organization and to the group's participation in electoral politics. The first important finding from the case studies suggests that the dominant paradigm in the literature, which asserts that political participation ensures a linear transition of an armed group into an unarmed one, does not fit all major cases of armed groups' involvement in institutional politics.

The conventional wisdom that "there is ample evidence that participation in an electoral process forces any party, regardless of ideology, to moderate its position if it wants to attract voters in large numbers"[2] is not strongly backed by the analysis of the political development of Hamas, Hezbollah, and the IRA. According to this dominant thesis, once these armed groups become involved in the political process through contending elections, there should be a linear development toward "moderation."

As analyzed in chapter 1, *moderation* refers to, at the very least, a gradual relinquishment of the armed strategy in favor of an unarmed one, and to the group's progressive integration into the political system. This should lead to greater acceptance of the rules and constraints of institutional politics, as well as to an increased interest in bargaining and negotiating with other political actors. This process should also produce a shift in the group's violent ideology, giving way for one that is more accommodating.

When looking at the political development of Hezbollah, the notion of a linear "armed-to-political" transformation is seriously challenged. Since its initial involvement in institutional politics in 1992, the group has not transformed in a way that is consistent with the above-described parameters of moderation. While the organization has halted some of its most violent practices since 1992, including the kidnapping of Western hostages, and diminishing its involvement in international terrorism, Hezbollah's military apparatus and its "resistance" remain at the center of its strategy and ideology. The group's reliance on violence has not ceased over the years. On the contrary, as the July 2006 war against Israel and the May 2008 temporary takeover of West Beirut demonstrate, Hezbollah continues to employ its military strength whenever it deems convenient to do so.

Over the past decades the group has become increasingly integrated at the political level, and this in turn has led to important changes and to the adoption of a more accommodation-seeking attitude. For example, in the aftermath of the group's decision to contend the 1992 parliamentary elections, Hezbollah focused on recasting its identity as a national movement, while softening its stance with respect to creating an Islamic state in Lebanon, and became open to cross-sectarian alliances.

It is possible to see how adopting a more nuanced political discourse and participating in cross-sectarian political alliances should be viewed as a sign of the group's growing political pragmatism, rather than as a transition toward becoming an "ordinary" political party. Even if the group has become a mainstream and integrated political party, Hezbollah's acceptance of the rules and constraints of the political system has not substantially increased over the years. While participating in the political process, Hezbollah continues to maintain and develop its armed wing, refusing to submit its military strategy or its weapons to the scrutiny and constraints of the government.

Moreover, Hezbollah's main strategy of being an opposition party focuses on employing all available political tools to guarantee and protect the group's military apparatus and its weapons. When these political tools are insufficient to achieve core organizational goals, Hezbollah does not hesitate to place the logic of political accommodation on hold and resume direct armed confrontation, as demonstrated by the May 2008 internal clashes.

Hamas's political development shows a more blurry picture than Hezbollah, where the political wing and the military apparatus have developed and grown simultaneously during the years. This simultaneous development of both wings contrasts with the notion of a linear transition toward politics and away from armed struggle.

However, Hamas also fails to comply with the parameters of linear moderation. Since its entry into institutional politics in the aftermath of Arafat's death in 2004, Hamas's reliance on armed force to increase its political leverage has not diminished, although the number and intensity of its armed campaigns against Israel somewhat declined.

The group's reliance on force remains a central element of its strategy (both domestically as well as with respect to Israel), as demonstrated by the repeated clashes with Fatah. These clashes culminated with the 2007 armed takeover of Gaza, and Hamas has subsequently relied on force to police and eradicate internal dissent from within the Gaza Strip.

Hamas's political development has not increased integration with other Palestinian political actors or with the local political system. On the contrary, the lack of agreement on a mutually satisfactory division of power between Hamas and its main political opponents triggered the current de facto separation of the West Bank and Gaza and led to Hamas's sole ruling in Gaza. Both issues constitute important evidence against the transformation of Hamas into an ordinary political party with a more accommodation-prone attitude in regards to domestic political negotiations and power sharing.

These findings do not dismiss the fact that the organization has transformed to participate in institutional politics, nor do they deny that the group has the potential to transition toward a hybrid organization that places greater reliance on unarmed politics. Indeed, an analysis of the internal dynamics of the organization reveals an ongoing tension along the politico-military line along with a process of political adaptation. Nevertheless, the findings also express doubt over the deterministic idea that political participation must automatically bring integration and accommodation at the expense of armed confrontation.

The analysis of the political development of the IRA similarly demonstrates how political participation does not automatically lead to "moderation." This is the case even though the IRA has often been cited in literature as an example of a linear transition toward unarmed contentious politics, and despite its status as an armed group that relinquished violence and integrated into the political system.

Although ultimately Sinn Féin's political activities and the IRA's military campaigns became mutually incompatible, forcing the republican movement to relinquish its armed strategy to pursue full political integration, the Sinn Féin's participation in the political process did not automatically reduce the IRA's perception of the utility of force. Politics did not reduce the actual reliance on force until other factors materialized, such as the existence of a committed leadership, a prolonged disequilibrium between armed and political activities, and the existence of a concrete opportunity to access power and not just take part in the political process. For example, between 1981 and 1994, the level of violence and the type of targets chosen by the IRA did not substantially change or decline as Sinn Féin 's involvement in institutional politics increased. Similarly, the number of killings and attacks did not diminish preceding the electoral contests, showing that the group was not effectively restrained by contending the elections.[3]

Rather, the progressive integration into the political system, which in the case of the republican movement brought about a progressive ideological shift, the adoption of a more pragmatic political discourse, and a growing interest in creating political alliances with other actors, seemed triggered not only by the process of political participation but rather by the internal dynamics created by such participation, and by the shifting levels of external support for the group and its agenda, again questioning the quasi-deterministic linear development model.

The analysis of the political development of Hezbollah, Hamas, and the IRA seems to confirm that political participation does not automatically lead to disarmament and full political integration, and that an alternative explanatory framework might instead be necessary to understand this phenomenon. The research suggests that a closer look at the internal relationship between a group's military and political wing is crucial in assessing the organization's potential for strategic change and "moderation," a hypothesis validated by the case studies. An examination of the political development of the IRA points to a few additional elements, which seem also crucial in ensuring an armed organization's transition into an ordinary political party.

Hezbollah proved to be a useful case to test and validate the initial hypothesis regarding the relationship between interorganizational conflict and the potential for strategic change. The organization is characterized by a high degree of internal cohesion and by a strong vertical chain of command: The group's political and armed wings are both directly overseen by the same group of leaders, and all the organization's policies and strategies are closely shaped by the charismatic secretary-general, Hassan Nasrallah.

Thus, since Hezbollah's entry into institutional politics, there is a strong focus on simultaneously developing its political party and its military apparatus, while asserting a "zero-tolerance" policy with respect to internal dissent. The research expected this organization to have a very low potential for strategic change and for transitioning from hybrid armed-political group to unarmed organization. An in-depth analysis of Hezbollah's political and military development confirmed this initial hypothesis.

Over the past decades the group evolved from a marginal militia into a powerful hybrid army and from a political outcast to a mainstream political party. The group's political strategy evolved to complement and support the military one, and the different organizational branches developed a solid relationship of strategic complementarity. Under these conditions and in the absence of internal conflict along the politico-military line, Hezbollah is highly unlikely to have any strategic interest in relinquishing its hybrid politico-military status, a trend that is confirmed by the analysis of the current strategy of the organization. The cases of Hamas and the IRA, however, revealed the existence of internal conflicts along the politico-military line, thus raising these groups' potential for strategic change.

In classic theory of guerrilla movements, a given group's armed apparatus and political front are meant to evolve simultaneously and reciprocally strengthen each other. However, in reality, often this relationship is not as smooth as described by the case of Hezbollah. As Hamas and the IRA highlight, the military and political wings of a given organization can have different imperatives: the military apparatus is concerned with maintaining secrecy and maximizing operational effectiveness. The political party, meanwhile, focuses on grassroots mobilization and external recognition, tasks that require the group to be more open and susceptible to shifts in public opinion. As such, the political party's activities and success at times may be impaired by the operations of the military wing, if these activities are not popular among the party's constituency, or if they contribute to lower its domestic and international legitimacy. As the IRA highlights, this is particularly true when the public starts to question the legitimacy and credibility of the group's modus operandi by regarding its armed actions as criminal and corrupt.[4]

Hamas's development and operational activities reveal that—in contrast to Hezbollah—the group has a less integrated structure, due to the leadership's geographical dispersion, its higher internal turnover, and because of recurrent internal conflicts. Hamas, unlike Hezbollah, has two distinguishable armed and political cores. As the case study highlights, internal conflicts along the politico-military and local-external lines tend to occur cyclically within Hamas. When such internal conflicts arise, such as following the 2006 parliamentary elections, the organization finds itself at its ripest moment for strategic change. Until now, Hamas's internal politico-military crises have always been temporary, and the organization has consistently been able to repair internal rifts and reestablish the balance of power inside the group without having to relinquish its hybrid nature.

The analysis of the republican movement in Northern Ireland, in contrast, reveals a much deeper level of internal dissonance between the logic of political accommodation and that of armed confrontation. Although the "Armalite and ballot box" strategy aimed at simultaneously develop armed and political activities and to create a relation of complementarity, the reality on the ground soon questioned the feasibility of this dual strategy. As early as the late 1980s, the logics of military struggle and political accommodation began to clash, as the IRA's military operations started to be perceived as detrimental to the political advancement of Sinn Féin.

Unlike with Hamas, the conflict along the politico-military line was managed by creating a strategy of official separation between Sinn Féin and the IRA, although the tension between the two institutional logics of accommodation and confrontation was never fully resolved. As such the republican movement found itself in a position of prolonged internal conflict between the two logics of institutional politics and armed struggle. Thus, it had the highest incentives to pursue strategic change and fully transition to an unarmed political party.

There are a few significant factors that facilitated such transformation in the IRA's case, which are absent in the previously analyzed case of Hamas. First, in ensuring a political transition, the republican movement was internally pushed by the charismatic leadership of Sinn Féin leader Gerry Adams, who was personally responsible for shaping the group's policies and for its gradual full-fledged entry into institutional politics. Second, in the two decades preceding the IRA's complete relinquishment of its weapons, Sinn Féin had managed to develop a separate and autonomous identity from the IRA and managed to gain a solid constituency. Sinn Féin's power and status bolstered, creating a valid and credible alternative to armed struggle. Third, Sinn Féin's political consistency proved to be highly influenced by the IRA's military campaigns. Violence was detrimental to the popularity of Sinn Féin, and the public's preferences soon became an important constraint in shaping the behavior of the group and its reliance on force. This popular opposition to the military wing's use of violence appears to have been present in the case of Hamas, albeit in a weaker form.

In explaining this significant difference, there is an important element that led Sinn Féin's constituency to be more negatively influenced by the armed campaigns of the IRA. Unlike Hamas and Hezbollah, the republican movement in Northern Ireland never maintained or provided an array of social and political goods to its constituency. This made the group's political constituency more susceptible to shifts in the group's policies and strategies. When analyzing the supporting bases of Hamas and Hezbollah, it is important to factor in the role of their clientelist network as an additional source of legitimacy that is not influenced by the popularity of the group's armed struggle. As a result, these groups are more impervious to short-term shifts in the level of acceptance for violence.

Finally, and this last point is going to be analyzed more in-depth in the last section, the republican movement found itself under different external conditions. Sinn Féin was being recognized domestically and internationally and simultaneously offered concrete integration in the political system with potential access to power and decision making. Thus, an opening was created for the political wing to develop and assert its primacy.

When looking at the political development of the three chosen case studies, it is possible to observe a relationship between the presence of interorganizational conflict along the politico-military line and the potential for strategic change and transition toward unarmed politics. Each analyzed case study falls into one of three different points in an ideal spectrum that ranges from low to high potential for strategic change.

Hezbollah, with its highly integrated structure and strategic military and political cooperation, would fall on the lowest end of the spectrum; it has the smallest chance for political transition. Hamas, with its cyclical conflicts along the politico-military dimension, would fall in the middle of the spectrum. Last, the IRA, with its prolonged and intense disequilibrium between the logic of military struggle and political accommodation, would fall on the other extreme of the spectrum; it has the highest potential for transition.

Far from representing a general theory, these findings serve as a useful and innovative starting point to analyze the political trajectory of other hybrid politico-military organizations. They also offer a basis to analyze and evaluate the effectiveness of current policy frameworks designed to regulate and integrate political wings of armed groups. The next section attempts to detail some preliminary policy implications of the findings.

Political Integration of Armed Groups: Lessons Learned

Even though the findings are preliminary, the policy implications that can be derived from them are significant and can contribute to reshaping the dominant view on how to integrate armed groups into a given country's political system. First, the study indicates that an armed group's decision to create a political wing and to participate in elections is a rational and strategic choice that depends on a variety of internal, institutional, organizational, and external factors.

The main implication of this finding is that, contrary to the dominant view expressed in the literature, simply allowing armed groups to participate in the political system is not enough to guarantee their actual participation. Other factors, such as the level of internal commitment, the existence of strong institutional pressures to grow and expand, or the presence of a political constituency to support the armed group's entry into politics, may not be entirely controllable by government policies.

This is not to say, however, that the decision of armed groups to compete in elections is impermeable to governmental policies. On the contrary, the case studies show a correlation between favorable shifts in the political opportunity structure (for example, reforms that make the political system more open, permeable, stable, and reliable) and a group's entry into institutional politics.

Political reforms that increase minorities' access to power, such as power-sharing agreements, or changes in the electoral system toward the proportional representation model, can contribute to encouraging the official entry of armed groups into institutional politics by creating an opening for participation. Shifts in the political and security environment can trigger a switch in the predominant mind-set, away from confrontation and toward reconciliation, thereby increasing the cost of fighting and providing a powerful incentive toward entering institutional politics (as was the case in Lebanon's post–civil war environment, following the Taif Agreement).

Government policies can also target an armed group's dependencies and try to crack down on its capacity to fund-raise and recruit. Aside from successfully weakening the military apparatus of the group, this measure may also contribute to the organization's decision to adapt to the shifting environment by joining the political system. However, and this is the second main finding of the study, encouraging an armed group to create a political wing and to join the political system is not a panacea for ensuring its progressive integration and "moderation."

The study shows how the political development of armed groups is not necessarily a progression from armed to unarmed and from military to political. Based on this finding, one can question a number of important assumptions behind the policies designed to promote political participation and integration of armed groups.

The notion that providing access to the political system and facilitating integration will lead to a political transition does not stand the test of the case studies. For example, the Lebanese Hezbollah has obtained over the years increasing access to the political system, while its integration in the national political arena has led the group to obtain virtual veto power, along with its allies, over any substantial national policy decisions. However, as examined previously, integration and participation have not necessarily led to "moderation" or transition toward relinquishing the military apparatus. Hezbollah shows that providing an alternative political channel for voicing the group's grievances may not be enough to bring about its transition to the realm of unarmed politics.

What's more, addressing the underlying concerns of the armed organization may also not guarantee its disarmament. An example is the IRA and its disarmament process, which was not connected with the group's achieving its historical political objective of reunification. Rather, the IRA's disarmament stemmed from a shift in the internal relationship between the group's political and military activities, accompanied by a favorable political opportunity system.

The study, by focusing on the internal relations within a given group as a key variable to analyze the potential for strategic change, also discredits the idea that there can be a one-size-fits-all policy to deal with armed groups that have decided to participate in elections. The study paves the way for a critical look at the dogmatic policies adopted to deal with the political participation of armed groups: for example, as a policy of concessions and integration may fail to persuade a given armed organization to pursue disarmament, a policy solely based on repression and systematically denying concessions, including political ones, can also backfire.

The research suggests that governmental policies need to avoid this deterministic approach. They need to employ a different combination of tools to deal differently with groups, like Hezbollah, which have high internal cohesion and strategic cooperation between the political and armed wings, while devising a separate framework when engaging groups with interorganizational tensions along the politico-military line.

When approaching these two separate types of hybrid armed-political organizations, governments should rely on a number of different tools: the first should be designed to discourage the armed struggle by increasing the costs of fighting, while the second should be aimed at improving the political and economic environment, thereby driving greater involvement of the armed-political group. Drawing on Ross and Gurr's study on the decline of terrorism in the United States and Canada,[5] the distinction should be drawn between deterrence and preemption policies to discourage violence and operations designed to crackdown on the organization and its leaders (the "military repression"), backlash measures to diminish the group's external level of legitimacy ("political isolation"), and burnout strategies to lower the internal level of cohesion and commitment ("internal disagreements").

To these policies, the research adds political reforms and dialogue to increase the status of the group's political wing ("concessions"). The next sections analyze, based on the lessons learned from the case studies, how these four broad strategies should be applied to different types of hybrid armed-political organizations.

The "Hezbollah Paradigm": Unitary and Mutually Reinforcing Political and Military Wings

For groups such as Hezbollah, where the political and the military wings consistently cooperate and their respective activities are mutually reinforcing, measures designed to target the former will inevitably have a negative effect on the latter and vice versa.[6] Because of the internal cohesion and unity of purpose between the group's military and political wings, weakening the group's military apparatus serves to undermine the entire organizational structure, including its political party.

The opposite is also true, namely, actions that weaken the political wing also undermine the military wing. It follows that when governments use a "security approach" to target a group's armed apparatus, this measure can at the same time weaken the organization's overall strength. In addition, such measures can be complemented with policies designed to undermine the political wing by increasing its political isolation, thus creating a simultaneous political and military process to weaken the group.

Direct attacks on the political wing by cracking down on its members or by restricting its right to take part in the political process, however, is a substantially more controversial and far less recommendable measure. This is so even if it may weaken the armed-political group in the short term. Once a given political wing has been initially recognized at the domestic level and allowed to participate in the political system, reversing this initial decision and proscribing the group's political activities may lead to a number of detrimental effects.

The exclusion of the political wing can increase the hybrid armed-political organization's incentive to rely on violence and become a proper antisystemic revolutionary party. At the same time, political exclusion may increase the popular legitimacy of the group's armed struggle, thus backfiring.[7]

Such provisions can also undermine the population's trust in the fairness and democratic commitment of the political system, and, especially, if the banned political wing has a substantial political constituency, it can lead to broader questions about the legitimacy of the system.[8] This could raise the potential for internal strife and violence as the proscribed group may seek to redress its exclusion from institutional politics. In other words, while cracking down on a hybrid armed-political organization's armed wing can be useful in weakening the group, the political party affiliated with the organization should be targeted mainly through policies aimed at maximizing its isolation and eroding its legitimacy. This can be achieved by attempting to lower the level of institutional and grassroots support for the group's political wing, while refraining from proscribing the group's political activities of electoral participation.

For Hezbollah, the best tool available is to target the group's reputation of credibility and integrity. Hezbollah counts on a large constituency of supporters who back both the group's political agenda and its "resistance" against Israel. The high approval rating behind the group's "resistance" is largely grounded in the Shia constituency and enhanced by the assumption that Hezbollah does not employ force against other Lebanese actors and that its actions are shaped by integrity and honesty.

Cracks in these assumptions could highly damage the level of support for the group, an important reason Hezbollah's current political campaign is centered on denying the alleged accusations of its role in the assassination of former prime minister Rafik Hariri. If proved, these accusations would damage both the group's reputation of integrity and its self-portrayed image of "national defense against Israel."

Even in groups with high internal cohesion and cooperation along the politico-military line, such as Hezbollah, policies designed to factionalize the group from within may be useful, albeit it may be difficult to achieve positive results in the short term. In general, caution must be noted against strategies that encourage internal factionalism. Policies to impair recruitment, remove leaders, and encourage sedition may backfire, as noted by Martha Crenshaw, who explains that internal disagreement is not synonymous with the decline in using violence as a strategy.[9]

Internal disagreement may lead to defections and the creation of new armed terrorist cells, thus obtaining the propagation, rather than the decline of terrorism.[10] Moreover, by increasing the number of groups who rely on violence, one creates a more competitive environment for the original hybrid armed-political organization. This may result in a general escalation of violence, as old and newly created groups compete to outbid one another and establish their monopoly on "resistance." Policies that encourage internal dissent therefore should be carefully regulated and aimed at generating disagreement along the politico-military line, for example, by increasing the level of popular disapproval for the group's violent campaigns. However, with groups such as Hezbollah, the likelihood of success is slim, as the group's level of internal cohesion and unity is extremely high.

The last set of policies designed to deal with political participation of armed groups—those involving public recognition, increased accommodation, and enhanced dialogue—also may not be particularly well suited to deal with groups such as Hezbollah. As the case study shows, hybrid political-military organizations characterized by high internal cohesion and mutual reinforcement between the political and military wings do not react to increased access to political representation and power by automatically transitioning toward unarmed politics.

Because the relationship between the political and the military wings is one of cooperation and mutual reinforcement, the growth and increased success of the political party only strengthens the armed apparatus. As Hezbollah case study shows, the organization has low incentives to choose between its arms and its political activism, and thus it will attempt to use increased openings in the political system to consolidate its position and power while retaining its dual military and political structure.

Increased international and domestic acceptance is also unlikely to shift this dynamic, unless such acceptance is conditioned on the group embarking on real, strategic change and gradually renouncing violence. This finding goes against the assumption summarized by Rudolph and Van Engeland,[11] who argue that when armed groups decide to join the political system "the international community should embrace, without conditions, those who are attempting to make the transition."

This is the case because for groups with high internal unity and mutual politico-military cooperation, the "transition" may not be a transition at all, and the task of the domestic actors as well as the international community should be to generate external constraints and opportunities that create internal dissonance between the group's logic of political accommodation and that of armed struggle. The group is then forced to begin a transition instead of continuing to operate at the dual armed-unarmed level.

The "IRA Paradigm": Internally Divided Hybrid Politico-military Organizations

For organizations with a higher potential for strategic change, such as Hamas and, to a higher degree, the IRA, the case studies suggest employing a substantially different approach to the one outlined earlier that tackle groups with high internal cohesion, such as Hezbollah.

In groups where internal conflict is present along the politico-military line, the main task of policies aimed at these groups should be to encourage and heighten such division. They should also ensure that the political wing acquires internal credibility and external support to become the dominant faction within the organization.

First, this implies working at the law-enforcement and military level to undermine and weaken the group's military wing. With Hezbollah, operations against its military wing can be expected to weaken its political wing because of the strategic complementarities between the two wings; while this is not necessarily the case of more internally divided groups. This strategy may potentially spark a different process in internally divided organizations. For example, in relation to the IRA, Peter Neumann notes that the government's security efforts against the group were instrumental in strengthening the republican political leadership and in backing their call to pursue political engagement as the only viable route of confrontation.[12] By focusing on defeating the group militarily, the "security approach" had the effect of facilitating the rise of republican leaders who argued for the necessity of relying on institutional politics, rather than on bullets. Even if targeting the weapons and armed apparatus of the hybrid politico-military organization may strengthen the political wing and its activities, the opposite statement is also true. Policies specifically designed to target the political wing, either by proscribing its political activism or by targeting its members, may backfire. For example, proscribing a group may increase its reliance on violence by weakening the credibility of the political leaders and empowering the more "hard core" and hawkish internal militants.

Isolating the political wing, a key tool in dealing with groups under the "Hezbollah paradigm" and to push them to choose between bullets and ballots, can backfire when implemented against internally divided organizations, as this can ultimately discredit the political party and lead to a shift in the internal balance of power towards the military wing. Instead, governments that deal with these types of groups should rely on security efforts to target the military wing, combined with policies designed to increase the internal disagreement and tip the balance of power toward the political wing. On the basis of the case study findings, there are two main tools that can facilitate the move to disarmament.

These measures are increasing the political cost of armed struggle and raising the level of political integration and access to both representation and power (thus lowering the incentives to attain political goals through armed struggle). Increasing the cost of armed struggle is highly correlated with shifts in the public's acceptance and support for the use of armed force, because, as highlighted by the IRA and Hamas, a decline in the popular support for the military force can lead the hybrid politico-military organization to question the utility of such a tactic. Such questions may arise when the military campaigns are perceived as detrimental to the group's progress within the realm of institutional politics. This realignment in public perception of the morality and utility of force needs to be accompanied by a series of measures aimed at increasing the level of participation and access of the political wing, raising its stakes and interests in the political system.

Such policies of integration and dialogue can benefit internally divided organizations. Unlike with Hezbollah, these policies can raise the internal disagreement between the political and the military leadership while empowering the former at the expense of the latter. Again, drawing on the case studies, it is possible to identify a number of policies designed to achieve such result.

First, a policy of domestic and international recognition of the political wing may have a positive effect and strengthen its separate identity and political agendas, encouraging its progressive involvement in the political system. Second, inclusion in the political dialogue or "peace process" is an important step to increase internally the level of power and status of the political wing. For the IRA, opening political negotiations to Sinn Féin and allowing the group to influence the process were crucial steps in facilitating the republican movement's transition. Applying this framework to Hamas implies arguing for recognizing the group and including its political leadership in future negotiations. Third, together with implementing policies of recognition and inclusion, the case studies indicate the importance of creating a political opportunity system that is equally conducive to the increased integration of the political wing. This includes the existence of a stable and transparent political system where access to representation can deliver potential access to power and decision making. Furthermore, the internal power relations need to ensure that power-sharing arrangements can be implemented. This is particularly true in cases of ethnically divided or politically polarized societies.

It is also important to foster elite cooperation within such systems, another means to raise the level of integration and direct stake of the hybrid politico-military organization in the country's political system. While fostering domestic integration and external recognition of the political wing, it is also crucial to request a gradual commitment from the group's political leaders in respecting and upholding the results of the political process where they have been allowed to participate.

Inclusion and integration of the political wing has to be balanced with the need to create constraints on political participation that provide an incentive for the group to choose between its armed and its political activities. For example, with the IRA, while Sinn Féin became increasingly integrated in the political process preceding the Good Friday Agreement, its presence at the negotiating table and in the process that would lead to the agreement was conditional on delivering an IRA cease-fire as well as a commitment to the Mitchell Principles on democracy and nonviolence. These demands forced the group to choose between the logic of armed struggle and that of political accommodation, while still providing high political incentives to rely on the latter.

Finally, the balance between concessions and constraints on political participation of the political wing must allow for political leaders to present political participation to the rest of their organization as mutually advantageous and not diametrically opposite to the group's agenda. The level of commitment requested needs to be both firm and realistic while still allowing the group not to lose its credibility regarding the majority of supporters. For example, in the case of Sinn Féin and the IRA, negotiations moved towards achieving preliminary results after disarmament became an issue to be dealt at the negotiating table, rather than a precondition to the talks.

When devising a policy approach to deal with hybrid politico-military groups that are internally divided along political and military lines, there are a series of important tools that can be employed. These include effective containment of the military wing and its operations together with policies to increase the internal frictions along the politico-military line, as well as political tools to empower the political wing. The case studies reveal the importance of domestic and international recognition, domestic political integration, and a political system that maximizes power sharing and encourages elite cooperation. The study also showed the prominent role of mechanisms that increase the level of commitment of the political leadership to the political process, gradually forcing a divorce between the internal logic of accommodation and that of armed struggle.

Again these tools are different from those designed for organizations that operate under conditions of internal strategic cooperation, such as Hezbollah, showing the importance of avoiding a one-size-fits-all policy when dealing with political wings of armed groups.

These very preliminary considerations, based on the observation of the political development of Hamas, Hezbollah, and the IRA, can constitute the basis for further studies on the role of normative and political constraints on the political participation of political wings of armed groups. Such studies are not just relevant but also timely, given the evolving political dynamics arising from the so-called Arab Awakening.

Despite the important policy insights that emerged from the first analysis of the case studies, a few questions still arise. What is the role and impact of the international community in ensuring the transition from armed militia to political party? How much do the processes and dynamics of the political negotiations that precede such transition matter? What specific policies have been employed so far in constraining and regulating the political participation of violent or nondemocratic parties, and what can be learned from these experiences?

Chapter 1 • *Introduction*

1. The literature on terrorism studies has produced a series of noteworthy works on the peaceful transition of former armed-terrorist organizations. See Jones and Libicki, *How Terrorist Groups End*; Gupta, *Understanding Terrorism and Political Violence*; Horgan, *Walking Away from Terrorism.* Also, on how political wings affect the decision to relinquish violence, see Siqueira, "Political and Militant Wings"; Dayton and Kriesberg, *Conflict Transformation and Peacebuilding*; Soberg Shugart, "Guerrillas and Elections"; and Deane, "Crime Corrupting Credibility."

2. See Allison, "Transition from Armed Opposition to Electoral Opposition"; Deonandan, Close, and Prevost, *From Revolutionary Movements to Political Parties.*

3. See chapter 3. Siqueira, "Political and Militant Wings," 219.

4. Van Engeland and Rudolph, *From Terrorism to Politics*; Weinberg, Pedahzur, and Perliger, *Political Parties and Terrorist Groups.*

5. Van Engeland and Rudolph, *From Terrorism to Politics*, 7–9, 183–185.

6. Weinberg, Pedahzur, and Perliger, *Political Parties and Terrorist Groups*, 21–22, 75–78.

7. Downs, *Inside Bureaucracy*, 16–17.

8. See, for example, Brathwaite, "Other Side of the Coin," 1–2, 6.

9. Van Engeland and Rudolph, *From Terrorism to Politics*, 5.

10. See, for example, Phillips, *From Bullets to Ballots*, 1; Allison, "Transition from Armed Opposition to Electoral Opposition," 139.

11. Goodwin and Skocpol, "Explaining Revolutions," 495.

12. Ibid.

13. Quoted by McClintock, *Revolutionary Movements in Latin America*, 26.

14. Gurr, "Causal Model of Civil Strife," 1105.

15. Wood, *Forging Democracy from Below*; Goodwin, *No Other Way Out*; McClintock, *Revolutionary Movements in Latin America.*

16. Crenshaw, "Causes of Terrorism," 383–384.

17. Deane, "Crime Corrupting Credibility," 447; Neumann, "Bullet and the Ballot Box," 945–946.

18. Neumann, "Bullet and the Ballot Box," 947.

19. Ottaway, "Islamists and Democracy."

20. Finn, "Electoral Regimes and the Proscription of Anti-democratic Parties," 52–53.

21. Hislope, "Ethnic Conflict and the Generosity Moment."

22. Neumann, "Bullet and the Ballot Box," 948.

23. For a more in-depth description of the "mainstream" understanding of political parties and armed groups as polar opposites, see Weinberg, "Turning to Terror," 423–424.

24. Sinn Fein leader Danny Morrison famously declared in 1981: "Who here really believes we can win the war through the ballot box? But will anyone here object if, with a ballot paper in this hand and an Armalite in the other, we take power in Ireland?" (English, *Armed Struggle: History of the IRA*, 224–225).

25. Eubank and Weinberg, "Does Democracy Encourage Terrorism?," quoted in Neumann, "Bullet and the Ballot Box," 944.

26. Rapoport and Weinberg, "Elections and Violence," 17.

27. De Zeeuw, *From Soldiers to Politicians*, 19–23.

28. Van Engeland and Rudolph, *From Terrorism to Politics*, 7.

29. Historical institutionalism is a specific approach to political sciences, one that focuses on understanding the shifts in political behavior and outcomes based on the analysis of the evolution of political institutions (see Steinmo, "Historical Institutionalism?").

30. Maney et al., "Past's Promise," 186.

31. Smooha, "Control of Minorities," 256.

Chapter 2 • The Power of Politics

1. DeFronzo, *Revolutions and Revolutionary Movements*, 7.
2. Milnor, ed. *Comparative Political Parties*, 19–22.
3. Siqueira, "Political and Militant Wings," 219.
4. Broom and Selznick, *Sociology*, 238.
5. Wellhofer and Hennessey, *Party Development*, 136–137.
6. Panebianco, *Political Parties*, 17–20.
7. Scott, *Organizations*, 13.
8. Downs, *Inside Bureaucracy*, 16–17.
9. Kriesi, "Political Context and Opportunity," 81.
10. Klandermans, "Mobilization and Participation," 586–588.
11. Clark and Wilson, *Incentive Systems*, 143.
12. Downs, *Inside Bureaucracy*, 9.
13. Wilson, *Political Organizations*, 30–31.
14. Rucht, "Movement Allies, Adversaries, and Third Parties," 197.
15. Clark and Wilson, "Incentive Systems," 158.
16. Pugh and Hickson, *Writers on Organizations*, 62.
17. Scott, *Organizations*, 69.
18. Wilson, *Political Organizations*, 263.
19. Clark and Wilson, *Incentive Systems*, 158.
20. Kriesi, *Political Context and Opportunity*, 69–70.
21. Weinberg, Pedahzur, and Perliger, *Political Parties and Terrorist Groups*, 19.

22. Lijphart, *Electoral Systems and Party Systems.*

23. Ibid., 10–12; Lijphart, "Political Consequences of Electoral Laws," 482.

24. Lijphart, *Democracies*, 23–30.

25. *Malapportionment* is when there is a high level of discrepancies in the number of voters in each district, which concretely means that candidates running in districts with a higher number of voters need substantially more preferences to be elected, thus violating the principle of effective representation. *Gerrymandering* refers to the intentional drawing of electoral boundaries in ways that consistently favor a given party (Taagepera and Soberg Shugart, *Seats and Votes*, 14–15).

26. Robertson, "The Return to History," 20.

27. Kriesi, "Political Context and Opportunity," 71–72.

28. Downs, *An Economic Theory of Democracy*, 128–131.

29. Greenwood and Hinings, *Understanding Organizational Change*, 1025.

30. Abell, *Organizations as Bargaining and Influence Systems*, 11.

31. Greenwood and Hinings, "Understanding Organizational Change," 1033.

32. Pfeffer, *Power and Organizations*, 3.

33. Bacharach and Lawler, *Organizational Politics*, 135.

34. Christensen and Molin, "Origin and Transformation of Organizations," 81–82.

35. US House Permanent Select Committee on Intelligence, *The Use of the Internet by Islamic Extremists*, testimony by Bruce Hoffman, May 4, 1996, 19; quoted in Moghadam and Fishman, "Debates and Divisions within and around Al-Qa'ida," 3–4.

36. Siqueira, "Political and Militant Wings," 220.

37. Crenshaw, "Theories of Terrorism," 13–31.

38. Moghadam and Fishman, *Self-Inflicted Wounds*, vi.

39. Gurr, "Causal Model of Civil Strife," 107.

40. Goldman, *From Warfare to Party Politics*, 9.

41. Della Porta, "Left-Wing Terrorism in Italy," 107.

42. Ibid., 122.

43. Downs, *Inside Bureaucracy*, 237.

44. Hira and Hira, "The New Institutionalism," 272.

45. Della Porta, "Left-Wing Terrorism in Italy," 109; Beitler, *Path to Mass Rebellion*, 11–12.

46. Lustick, "Terrorism in the Arab-Israeli Conflict," 514–515.

Chapter 3 • The Lebanese Hezbollah

1. Hezbollah denies any involvement in these attacks.

2. Azani, "Testimony on 'Hezbollah's Global Reach,'" 55.

3. US Department of State, Office of the Coordinator for Counterterrorism, "Foreign Terrorist Organizations," July 7, 2009, http://www.state.gov/s/ct/rls/other/des/123085.htm (accessed August 24, 2009).

4. US Department of the Treasury, "Treasury Targets Hizballah Network in Africa," May 27, 2009, http://www.treas.gov/press/releases/tg149.htm (accessed August 24, 2009).

5. Byman, "Should Hezbollah Be Next?," 55.

6. Official Journal of the European Union, "Council Common Position 2009/67/Cfsp," http://eur-lex.europa.eu/LexUriServ/LexUriServ.do?uri=OJ:L:2009:023:0037:0042:EN:PDF (accessed August 24, 2009).

7. Ritzmann, Testimony on "Adding Hezbollah to the EU Terror List."

8. Chalabi, *The Shi'is*, 162.

9. Olmert, "Shi'is and the Lebanese State," 189–191.

10. Norton, "Changing Actors and Leadership," 110–111.

11. Malik, "Experiment in Multicultural Independence," 19.

12. The Jafari school is the dominant school of jurisprudence—or *fiqh*—adopted by Shia Muslims. Chalabi, *The Shi'is of Jabal*, 139, 145.

13. Mackey, *Mirror of the Arab World*, 161.

14. Producing convincing demographic data on the Lebanese population is particularly challenging because the country has not had an official census since 1932.

15. Hamzeh, "Clan Conflicts, Hezbollah," 434.

16. Norton, "Changing Actors and Leadership," 112–113.

17. Mackey, *Mirror of the Arab World*, 162.

18. Qassem, *Hizbullah*, 17.

19. Harik, "Between Islam and the System," 43–44.

20. Ibid.

21. Winslow, *Lebanon*, 161.

22. Norton, "Changing Actors and Leadership," 115.

23. Norton, *Hezbollah*, 30–31.

24. Ibid., 31–32.

25. Ahman Nizar Hamzeh, *In the Path of Hizbullah*, 23–24.

26. Mackey, *Mirror of the Arab World*, 169–170.

27. Harik, *Hezbollah*, 34–37.

28. Kramer, "Hizbullah," 27.

29. Qassem, *Hizbullah*, 19–20.

30. Kramer, "Hizbullah," 21.

31. Ibid., 34.

32. Hamzeh, *In the Path of Hizbullah*, 101.

33. Norton, *Hezbollah*, 43.

34. Kramer, "Hizbullah," 33.

35. Phillips, Testimony on "Adding Hezbollah to the EU Terrorist List."

36. Winslow, *Lebanon*, 250–251.

37. Byman, *Should Hezbollah Be Next?*, 56–57.

38. Sobelman, "New Rules of the Game," 67–69.

39. Arkin, *Divining Victory*, 28–31.

40. Hamzeh, *In the Path of Hizbullah*, 122–123.

41. See Alagha, "The Shifts in Hizbullah's Ideology."

42. Norton, "Hizballah and the Israeli Withdrawal," 32–33.

43. Saad-Gorayeb, *Hizbu'llah*, 94.

44. Norton, "Hizballah and the Israeli Withdrawal," 29.

45. Hamzeh, *In the Path of Hizbullah*, 45.

46. Saad-Gorayeb, *Hizbu'llah*, 43.
47. Harik, *Hezbollah*, 54.
48. Qassem, *Hizbullah*, 62–63.
49. Ibid.
50. Saad-Gorayeb, *Hizbu'llah*, 43.
51. Ranstorp, "Hezbollah's Command Leadership," 330; Hamzeh, *In the Path of Hizbullah*, 48–70.
52. Hamzeh, *In the Path of Hizbullah*, 327, 66–67.
53. Ibid., 70–74.
54. Harel and Issacharoff, *34 Days*, 32–33.
55. Qassem, *Hizbullah*, 58.
56. http://www.alintiqad.com/ and http://www.alnour.com.lb/ (accessed October 1, 2010).
57. Harb and Leenders, "Know Thy Enemy, 188.
58. http://www.almanar.com.lb/newssite/AboutUs.aspx?language=en (accessed October 1, 2010).
59. Ibid.
60. Kalb, *Israeli-Hezbollah War of 2006*.
61. Hamzeh, *In the Path of Hizbullah*, 49.
62. Harb and Leenders, "Know Thy Enemy," 188.
63. Judith Palmer Harik, interview by the author, Beirut, July 11, 2009.
64. Khashan and Mousawi, "Hizbullah's Jihad Concept."
65. Hamzeh, *In the Path of Hizbullah*, 55–57.
66. Harik, interview by the author, Beirut, July 11, 2009.
67. Harik, *Hezbollah*, 83–86. See also http://almashriq.hiof.no/lebanon/300/320/324/324.2/hizballah/jihad-el-binna/ (accessed October 12, 2010).
68. Harik, interview by the author, Beirut, July 11, 2009.
69. Ranstorp, *Hizb'allah in Lebanon*, 83.
70. US Department of the Treasury, "Fact Sheet: Designation of Iranian Entities and Individuals for Proliferation Activities and Support for Terrorism," October 25, 2007, http://www.treasury.gov/press/releases/hp644.htm (accessed September 3, 2009).
71. Hamzeh, *In the Path of Hizbullah*, 63.
72. Slavin, *Mullahs, Money, and Militias*.
73. Berti, "Reassessing the Transnational Terrorism-Criminal Link."
74. Harik, "Between Islam and the System," 62–63.
75. Qassem, *Hizbullah*, 60–62.
76. The Twelfth Imam, who Shiites believe to be the leader of the community who will one day return as the *Mahdi*, a Messiah-like figure, who will appear in the years before the Day of Judgment.
77. Norton, *Hezbollah*, 37–40.
78. Saad-Gorayeb, *Hizbu'llah*, 34–36.
79. "The Hizballah Program: An Open Letter," February 16, 1985. Reprinted in *Jerusalem Quarterly* 48, 1988, www.standwithus.com/pdfs/flyers/hezbollah_program.pdf_(accessed December 20, 2010).
80. Saad-Gorayeb, *Hizbu'llah*, 49.

81. Harb and Leenders, "Know Thy Enemy," 179.

82. Saad-Gorayeb, *Hizbu'llah*, 57.

83. *The Political Document (Manifesto) of Hezbollah 2009 AC /1430 H*, November 30, 2009, Hezbollah Press Statement.

84. Harb and Leenders, "Know Thy Enemy," 189–190.

85. Kramer, "Sacrifice and 'Self-Martyrdom.'"

86. Ibid.

87. Norton, *Hezbollah*, 72.

88. Ranstorp, "Hezbollah's Command Leadership," 317–322.

89. Salloukh, "Syria and Lebanon," 14.

90. The Taif Agreement (signed on October 22, 1989 and ratified on November 4, 1989), http://www.mideastinfo.com/documents/taif.htm (accessed August 25, 2009).

91. Ibid.

92. Jaber, *Hezbollah*, 34–35.

93. Norton, "Lebanon after Ta'if," 458–460.

94. Gambill, "Syria's Triumph in Lebanon."

95. Qassem, *Hizbullah*, 104–105.

96. Mackey, *Mirror of the Arab World*, 148–150.

97. Cleveland, *History of the Modern Middle East*, 219–222.

98. Winslow, *Lebanon*, 80–81.

99. Norton, "Lebanon after Ta'if," 462.

100. Latif Abul-Husn, interview by author, Beirut, July 10, 2008; Maktabi, "Lebanese Census," 219.

101. Qassem, *Hizbullah*, 124–125.

102. Norton, *Hezbollah*, 105–107.

103. Kramer, "The Oracle of Hizbullah," 147.

104. Qassem, *Hizbullah*, 124–125.

105. Ibid., 187–191.

106. Ranstorp, "Hezbollah's Command Leadership," 314–315.

107. Ibid., 315.

108. "Interview with Hassan Nasrallah," *As-Safir*, February 27, 1992, in Noe, ed., *Voice of Hezbollah*, 74.

109. Hamzeh, "Lebanon's Hizbullah," 334.

110. Qassem, *Hizbullah*, 189.

111. "Interview with Hassan Nasrallah," in Noe, ed., *Voice of Hezbollah*, 67.

112. Palmer Harik, *Hezbollah*, 73–74.

113. Qassem, "Appendix: Hezbollah 1992 Election Programme," in *Hizbullah*, 217–277.

114. Latif Abul-Husn, interview by the author, Beirut, July 10, 2008.

115. Karam Karam, interview by the author, Beirut, July 9, 2008.

116. Youssef Mouwad, interview by the author, Beirut, July 14, 2008.

117. Paul Salem, interview by the author, Beirut, July 10, 2008.

118. Hamzeh, "Lebanon's Hizbullah," 750–751, 333.

119. Hamzeh, "Lebanon's Islamist and Local Politics," 745–746.

120. Saad-Gorayeb, *Hizbu'llah*, 54.

121. Wiegand, "Reformation of a Terrorist Group," 676.

122. Hamzeh, "Lebanon's Hizbullah," 334.

123. "Interview with Secretary General Hassan Nasrallah," in Noe, ed., *Voice of Hezbollah*, 88.

124. "Interview with Hassan Nasrallah," in Noe, ed., *Voice of Hezbollah*, 156.

125. Norton and Schwedler, "(In)security Zones in South Lebanon," 61–69.

126. Eisenberg, "Israel's South Lebanon Imbroglio."

127. Norton and Schwedler, "(In)security Zones in South Lebanon," 71.

128. Alagha, *Shifts in Hizbullah's Ideology*, 45.

129. Harris, "Lebanon," 527–528.

130. Alagha, *Shifts in Hizbullah's Ideology*, 46.

131. Phares, "Liberating Lebanon."

132. Eisenberg, "Israel's South Lebanon Imbroglio."

133. Harik, *Hezbollah*, 118–122.

134. Alagha, *Shifts in Hizbullah's Ideology*, 44.

135. Usher, "Hizballah, Syria, and the Lebanese Elections," 59, 64–65.

136. "Syria Steps in to Ensure 'Balance' at Lebanese Municipal Polls," *Mideast Mirror*, May 20, 1998, available from LexisNexis.

137. "4 Lebanese Wounded in Hezbollah-Amal Clashes," Xinhua News Agency, May 8, 1998, available from LexisNexis.

138. "Lebanon: Government Slogan Aims to Undermine Hezbollah, Leader Nasrallah Says," Radio of Islam—Voice of the Oppressed (transcript), May 24, 1998, BBC Worldwide Monitoring, available from LexisNexis.

139. Hamzeh, *In the Path of Hizbullah*, 127.

140. Sam F. Ghattas, "Beirut Votes for Religious Harmony," Associated Press Worldstream, June 8, 1998, available from LexisNexis.

141. "Hezbollah Suffers Electoral Defeat in Main Stronghold," Agence France Presse, June 15, 1998, available from LexisNexis.

142. "Lebanon's Hizbollah Seeks to Placate Bekaa Supporters," *Mideast Mirror*, July 30, 1998, available from LexisNexis.

143. "Interviews with Hassan Nasrallah," in Noe, ed., *Voice of Hezbollah*, 208.

144. Hajjar, *Hizballah*, 23.

145. UN Security Council. "Report of the Secretary-General on the Implementation of Security Council Resolutions 425 (1978) and 426 (1978)," May 22, 2000, http://www.unhcr.org/refworld/docid/3ae6afbb0.html%20%28accessed%2029%20November%202009 (accessed July 25, 2009).

146. "In Focus: Shebaa Farms," *BBC News*, May 25, 2000, http://news.bbc.co.uk/2/hi/middle_east/763504.stm (accessed November 1, 2010).

147. Kaufman, *The Shebaa Farms*, 12–17.

148. Hajjar, *Hizballah*, 21.

149. "Nasrallah 'Victory' Speech," in Noe, ed., in *Voice of Hezbollah*, 237.

150. Sobelman, *New Rules of the Game*, 67.

151. Ibid., 60–61.

152. David Rudge, "Criticism Grows in Lebanon over Hizbullah Attacks," Jerusalem Post, July 6, 2001, available from LexisNexis.

153. Sobelman, *New Rules of the Game*, 52.

154. "Hezbollah Chief Defends Syrian Presence in Lebanon as Shiites Mark Holiday," Agence France Presse, April 4, 2001, available from LexisNexis.

155. "Lebanon," *Al Manar*, May 25, 2001, BBC Monitoring Middle East, available from LexisNexis.

156. Norton, "Hizballah and the Israeli Withdrawal," 34.

157. Simon and Stevenson, "Declawing the 'Party of God,'" 39.

158. "Hariri Has Three-Hour Meeting with Hizbollah Boss Nasrallah," *Mideast Mirror*, November 16, 2000; available from LexisNexis.

159. Simon and Stevenson, "Declawing the 'Party of God,'" 34.

160. "Premier in France Says Fears More Violence in Region," February 17, 2001, BBC Summary of World Broadcasts, available from LexisNexis.

161. Sam F. Ghattas, "Israeli Soldier Killed in Guerrilla Attack Near South Lebanese Border," Associated Press, February 16, 2001, available from LexisNexis.

162. "Lebanese Premier Responds to Remarks by Hezbollah Leader," Voice of Lebanon, February 19, 2009, BBC Worldwide Monitoring, available from LexisNexis.

163. "Hariri Denounces 'Monopoly' of Anti-Israel Resistance," Agence France Presse, February 19, 2001, available from LexisNexis.

164. "Hariri Enforces Truce with Hezbollah after Overnight Talks," Xinhua News Service, February 22, 2001, available from LexisNexis.

165. Norton, *Hezbollah*, 107.

166. Dr. Karam Karam, interview with the author, Beirut, July 9, 2008.

167. UN Security Council, "Resolution 1559 (2004)," September 2, 2004, http://www.un.org/News/Press/docs/2004/sc8181.doc.htm (accessed July 25, 2009).

168. "Hezbollah Calls on UNSC to Reject US Draft on Syrian Troops in Lebanon," Lebanese National News Agency, September 1, 2004, BBC Worldwide Monitoring, available from LexisNexis.

169. "Lebanese Parliament Votes to Extend President's Term," al-Manar Television, September 3, 2004, provided by BBC Monitoring Middle East, available from LexisNexis.

170. Salloukh, "Syria and Lebanon," 21.

171. European Union Election Observation Mission, "Parliamentary Elections," 20.

172. Alagha, "Hizballah after the Syrian Withdrawal," 34.

173. The battle of Karbala (680 CE), which led to the martyrdom of the son of Ali and third Shia Imam Hussein is a central event in the Shia narrative, commemorated every year with the Ashura. "Speech by Hassan Nasrallah," in Noe, ed., *Voice of Hezbollah*.

174. Alagha, "Hizballah after the Syrian Withdrawal," 35.

175. "Election Tracker: Lebanon," Angus Reid Global Monitor, June 19, 2005, http://www.angus-reid.com/tracker/view/6962 (accessed November 1, 2010).

176. European Union Election Observation Mission, "Parliamentary Elections," 35.

177. Alagha, "Hizballah after the Syrian Withdrawal," 3.

178. Schweitzer, "'Divine Victory' and Earthly Failures," 125.

179. Joseph Panossian, "Hezbollah Says It Has Captured 2 Israeli Soldiers in Clashes," Associated Press, July 12, 2006, available from LexisNexis.

180. "Timeline of the July War 2006," *Daily Star*, http://www.dailystar.com.lb/July_War06.asp (accessed September 23, 2010).

181. "Israel Begins Freeing 400 Palestinians as Part of Prisoner Exchange with Hezbollah," Associated Press, January 29, 2004, available from LexisNexis.

182. Ze'ev Schiff, "Kidnap of Soldiers in July Was Hezbollah's Fifth Attempt," *Haaretz*, September 19, 2006, http://www.haaretz.com/hasen/spages/764450.html (accessed November 1, 2010).

183. "Interview with Hassan Nasrallah," in Noe, ed., *Voice of Hezbollah*, 390.

184. "Hezbollah Hands Syria 114 Bodies of Arab Fighters," Agence France Presse, July 23, 2008, available from LexisNexis.

185. Harik, interview by the author, Beirut, July 11, 2009.

186. Ibid.

187. "Lebanese Official: Hezbollah Must Surrender Weapons," Associated Press Worldstream, August 14, 2006, available from LexisNexis.

188. Sam F. Ghattas and Zeina Karam, "Lebanon Avoids Issue of Hezbollah's Arms," Associated Press Online, August 16, 2006, available from LexisNexis.

189. http://www.un.org/en/peacekeeping/missions/unifil/ (accessed November 1, 2010).

190. "Hezbollah MP Demands Lebanon Government Step Down," Agence France Presse, September 11, 2006, available from LexisNexis.

191. "Hezbollah to Join Talks on Lebanon Unity Government," Agence France Presse, October 26, 2006, available from LexisNexis.

192. "Lebanon's PM Rejects Resignation of Hezbollah and Other Shiite Cabinet Ministers," Associated Press Worldstream, November 11, 2006, available from LexisNexis.

193. Lebanese Constitution, article 95 [National Committee].

194. Harris, "Lebanon's Day in Court."

195. Hilal Khashan, interview with the author, Beirut, July 8, 2009; Elie Khoury, interview with the author, Beirut, July 14, 2008.

196. Hussein Dakroub, "Hezbollah's Leader Calls for Mass Demonstrations to Oust Lebanon's Western-Backed Government," Associated Press, November 19, 2006, available from LexisNexis.

197. "Hezbollah Militants Take Over West Beirut," CNN, May 9, 2008, http://edition.cnn.com/2008/WORLD/meast/05/09/beirut.violence/index.html (accessed November 1, 2010).

198. "The Doha Agreement," *Now Lebanon*, May 21, 2008, http://www.nowlebanon.com/NewsArticleDetails.aspx?ID=44023&MID=115&PID=2_(accessed November 1, 2010).

199. Michael Slackman, "U.S.-Backed Alliance Wins in Lebanon," *New York Times*, June 7, 2009, http://www.nytimes.com/2009/06/08/world/middleeast/08lebanon.html?_r=1 (accessed November 1, 2010); "March 14 Bloc Wins Lebanon Election," *Al Jazeera (English)*, June 8, 2009, http://english.aljazeera.net/news/middleeast/2009/06/20096813424442589.html (accessed November 1, 2010); Hussein Assi, "'Popular Majority' Goes to. . . Opposition

with 55% of Votes," *al-Manar*, June 9, 2009, http://almanar.com.lb/NewsSite/NewsDetails.aspx?id=89269&language=en (accessed November 1, 2010).

200. "PM Al-Sanyurah after Cairo Meeting: Third Blocking Experience Failed . . . ," Lebanese National News Agency, June 14, 2009, http://www.nna-leb.gov.lb/phpfolder/loadpage_ar.php?page=14–06–2009/JOU81.html (in Arabic) (accessed November 1, 2010).

201. "Without National Consensus New Cabinet Will Achieve Nothing," Agence France Presse, November 11, 2009, available from LexisNexis.

202. "Lebanon's New Government," *International Foundation for Electoral Systems*, November 9, 2009, http://www.ifes.org/publication/38e87b372599cdff387c76fd022fb123/Lebanons_new_government.pdf (accessed November 1, 2010).

203. *The Political Document (Manifesto) of Hezbollah.*

204. Ibid.

205. Schenker, "Now Comes the Hard Part."

206. Na'im Qasim, "Interview with Ghassan Bin-Jiddu," *Al Jazeera (Arabic)*, May 28, 2009, translation by and available from MidEast Wire.

207. *The Political Document (Manifesto) of Hezbollah.*

208. Harik, interview with the author, Beirut, July 11, 2009.

209. Harris, "Lebanon's Day in Court."

210. Ian Black, "Accusing Syria of Killing PM Was Wrong, Says Lebanon Leader," *The Guardian*, September 7, 2010, available from LexisNexis.

211. Hussein Dakroub and Hassan Lakiss, "Uncertainty Grips Lebanon: Western Powers Accuse March 8 of Subverting Justice after Government Toppled," *The Daily Star*, January 13, 2011, http://www.dailystar.com.lb/article.asp?edition_id=1&categ_id=2&article_id=123602#axzz1AuA3QVHF (accessed November 18, 2012).

212. Kiwan Fadia, interview by the author, Beirut, July 11, 2008.

213. Berti, "Hizb Allah's Domestic Containment."

214. "Speech Delivered by Hezbollah Secretary General Sayyed Hassan Nasrallah during the Solidarity Rally with Egypt That Was Held in Ghobairy Municipality Square—Jnah," Hezbollah Press Statement, February 7, 2011.

215. Rafic Hariri Statement, Lebanese National News Agency, August 13, 2011.

216. Hanin Ghaddar, "A New Resistance, A New Enemy," Now Lebanon, October 24, 2011, http://www.nowlebanon.com/NewsArticleDetails.aspx?ID=325376#ixzz1cv6lf9Av (accessed November 18, 2012).

Chapter 4 • The Palestinian Hamas

1. US Department of State, "Patterns of Global Terrorism: 1992. Appendix B. Background Information on Terrorist Groups," April 30, 1993, http://www.fas.org/irp/threat/terror_92/backg.html (accessed July 25, 2009).

2. US Department of State, *Foreign Terrorist Organizations*, 2009; "Prohibiting Transactions with Terrorists Who Threaten to Disrupt the Middle East Peace Process: Executive Order 12947," *Federal Register* 60, no. 16, January 25, 1995, http://www.ustreas.gov/offices/enforcement/ofac/legal/eo/12947.pdf (accessed September 1, 2010).

3. "EU Blacklists Hamas Political Wing," *BBC News*, September 11, 2003, http://news.bbc.co.uk/2/hi/middle_east/3100518.stm (accessed March 12, 2010).

4. Official Journal of the European Union, "Council Common Position 2008/586/Cfsp updating Common Position 2001/931/CFSP on the Application of Specific Measures to Combat Terrorism and Repealing Common Position 2007/871/CFSP," July 16, 2008, http://eurlex.europa.eu/LexUriServ/LexUriServ.do?uri=OJ:L:2008:188:0071:0076:EN:PDF (accessed October 31, 2010).

5. Jamal, *Media Politics and Democracy*, 4.

6. Nusse, *Muslim Palestine*, xi.

7. Bregam, *Israel's Wars*, 193.

8. El-Awaisi, *Muslim Brothers*, 34–39.

9. Mishal and Sela, *Palestinian Hamas*, 574.

10. Hroub, *Hamas, Political Thought and Practice*, 17–18.

11. Abu-Amr, "Hamas," 7.

12. Abu-Amr, "Shaykh Ahmad Yasin," 228–229, 229.

13. Knudsen, "Crescent and Sword," 1375.

14. Abu-Amr, "Shaykh Ahmad Yasin," 230–231.

15. *Dawa* means "the call," and it originally referred to proselytizing. Today, it also refers to Islamic preaching and education within the Muslim world and with the objective of restoring a more Islamic lifestyle and identity.

16. Abu-Amr, "Hamas," 7–8.

17. Zuhur, "Hamas and Israel," 20–21.

18. Abu-Amr, "Shaykh Ahmad Yasin," 239.

19. Freund, *Looking into HAMAS*, 30.

20. Abu-Amr, "Hamas," 10–11.

21. Dolnik and Bhattacharjee, "Hamas," 109.

22. Professor Asher Susser, interview by the author, Tel Aviv, March 23, 2010.

23. Kristianasen, "Challenge and Counterchallenge," 20.

24. Tamimi, *Hamas*, 59–60.

25. Zeid al-Keylani, *Islamic Movement in Jordan*, 164.

26. Alexander, *Palestinian Religious Terrorism*, 1.

27. "Clinton, Israel, and the Hamas Expulsion," 37; Israeli, "Manual of Islamic Fundamentalist Terrorism," 27–29.

28. Knudsen, "Crescent and Sword," 1381.

29. Hroub, *Hamas, Political Thought and Practice*, 119.

30. Israeli Ministry of Foreign Affairs, "Fatal Terrorist Attacks in Israel since the DOP," http://www.mfa.gov.il/mfa/terrorism%20obstacle%20to%20peace/palestinian%20terror%20before%202000/fatal%20terrorist%20attacks%20in%20israel%20since%20the%20dop%20-s (accessed December 5, 2006).

31. Shikaki, "Peace Now or Hamas Later," 30–31.

32. Qassam rockets were developed by Hamas during the Al-Aqsa Intifada. They are made from a section of lamppost filled with explosive material and they have no guidance system. See Israel Ministry of Foreign Affairs, "Four Years of Conflict: Israel's War against-

Terrorism," October 3, 2004, http://www.mfa.gov.il/MFA/Terrorism+Obstacle+to+Peace/Terrorism+and+Islamic+Fundamentalism-/Four+Years+of+Conflict+3-Oct-2004.htm (accessed December 5, 2006).

33. Mishal, "Pragmatic Dimension," 577–580.

34. Hroub, "Hamas after Shaykh Yassin," 30.

35. Mishal, "Pragmatic Dimension," 582.

36. Gunning, *Hamas in Politics*, 98–99.

37. Abu-Amr, *Hamas*, 13.

38. Dr. Gershon Baskin, interview by the author, Jerusalem, March 7, 2010.

39. Gunning, *Hamas in Politics*, 99–100, 244.

40. Muslih, *Foreign Policy of Hamas*, 15.

41. Zuhur, *Hamas And Israel*, 53.

42. Mishal and Sela, *Palestinian Hamas*, 158, app. 1.

43. Abu-Amr, *Hamas*, 6.

44. Mishal and Sela, *Palestinian Hamas*, app. 1.

45. Dr. Margret Johannsen, interview by the author, March 13, 2010.

46. Dr. Gershon Baskin, interview by the author, Jerusalem, March 7, 2010.

47. Mishal, "Pragmatic Dimension," 581–583.

48. Zuhur, *Hamas and Israel*, 39.

49. Tamimi, *Hamas*, 60.

50. Hroub, "Hamas after Shaykh Yassin," 31.

51. Shane Bauer, "Hamas: We Will Win War in Gaza," *Al Jazeera News*, January 13, 2009, http://english.aljazeera.net/news/middleeast/2009/01/2009181553331111890.html (accessed March 12, 2010).

52. Jamal, *Media Politics and Democracy*, chap. 4.

53. Peter Adams, "Hi-Tech Hamas: Reporting from the Gaza Strip," *IslamOnline.net*, January 22, 2006, http://www.islamonline.net/servlet/Satellite?c=Article_C&cid=1156077834864&pagename=Zone-English-Muslim_Affairs%2FMAELayout (accessed March 12, 2010).

54. Jensen, *Political Ideology of Hamas*, 142, 92–102; Malka, "Forcing Choices," 39.

55. Ibid.

56. Roy, "Hamas and the Transformation(s)," 16.

57. Malka, "Forcing Choices," 39.

58. Levitt, "Financial Setbacks for Hamas."

59. Maqdsi, "Charter of the Islamic Resistance Movement," 122–134.

60. Baskin, interview by the author, Jerusalem, March 7, 2010; Johannsen, interview by the author, March 13, 2010.

61. Knudsen, "Crescent and Sword," 1378.

62. Hafez, "Review: Muslim Palestine," 140.

63. Knudsen, "Crescent and Sword," 1379.

64. Scham and Abu-Irshaid, "Hamas," 8.

65. Tamimi, *Hamas*, 166–167.

66. Scham and Abu-Irshaid, "Hamas," 7.

67. Gunning, *Hamas in Politics*, 57–60.

68. Electoral platform of the Change and Reform block, November 2004. Quoted in Hroub, "'New Hamas,'" 10–11.

69. Dr. Meir Litvak, interview by the author, Tel Aviv, April 21, 2010.

70. Maqdsi, "Charter of the Islamic Resistance Movement," art. 22, 9.

71. Hroub, *Hamas, Political Thought and Practice*, 49–50.

72. Ibid., 147–154.

73. Gunning, *Hamas in Politics*, 109–110.

74. Hroub, *Hamas, Political Thought and Practice*, 219.

75. Shikaki, "Peace Now or Hamas Later," 30–32.

76. Ibid., 35.

77. Roy, "Hamas and the Transformation(s)," 14.

78. Jamal, *Media Politics and Democracy*, chap. 1.

79. Ibid.

80. Mishal and Sela, "Participation without Presence," 5, 7–8.

81. Kristianasen, "Challenge and Counterchallenge," 25–27.

82. Hroub, *Hamas, Political Thought and Practice*, 65, 223–226.

83. Weinberg and Pedahzur, *Political Parties and Terrorist Groups*, 93.

84. Kristianasen, "Challenge and Counterchallenge," 27.

85. Weinberg and Pedahzur, *Political Parties and Terrorist Groups*, 93; Mishal and Sela, "Participation without Presence," 21.

86. Kristianasen, "Challenge and Counterchallenge," 27.

87. Mishal and Sela, "Participation without Presence," 15.

88. Roy, "Hamas and the Transformation(s)," 15.

89. Gunning, *Hamas in Politics*, 228–229; Palestinian Center for Policy and Survey Research (PSR), "Survey Research Unit: Public Opinion Poll # 8," June 19–22, 2003, http://www.pcpsr.org/survey/polls/2003/p8a.html (accessed December 2, 2012).

90. Usher, "Letter from the Occupied Territories," 48.

91. Gunning, *Hamas in Politics*, 226–227.

92. Susser, *Rise of Hamas in Palestine*, 45–46.

93. Shikaki, "Palestinians Divided," 93–94.

94. Usher, "Letter from the Occupied Territories," 47–48.

95. US Senate, *Palestinian Legislative Council Elections*, 21.

96. Usher, "Letter from the Occupied Territories," 34–35.

97. Herzog, "Can Hamas Be Tamed?"

98. Hroub, "Hamas after Shaykh Yassin," 32.

99. Mishal, "Pragmatic Dimension," 575.

100. Dr. Meir Litvak, interview by the author, Tel Aviv, April 21, 2010.

101. Ibid.

102. Zahhar and Hijazi, "Hamas," 82.

103. Hroub, *Hamas, Political Thought and Practice*, 216–217.

104. Kristianasen, "Challenge and Counterchallenge," 20–22.

105. Ibid.; Mishal and Sela, "Participation without Presence," 13–14.

106. Hroub, *Hamas, Political Thought and Practice*, 228–229.

107. Haberman, "Between Hudna and Crackdown"; Kristianasen, "Challenge and Counterchallenge," 29.

108. Kristianasen, "Challenge and Counterchallenge," 30–31.

109. Shikaki, "Palestinians Divided," 89, 97–98.

110. Hroub, "Hamas after Shaykh Yassin," 25.

111. Roy, "Hamas and the Transformation(s)," 17–18.

112. Steiz, "Hamas Stands Down?," 5–6.

113. Usher, "Intifada Two Years On," 30–31.

114. Ibid., 32, 36.

115. Milton-Edwards and Crooke, "Elusive Ingredient," 46–47.

116. Ibid., 41.

117. Enderlin, *Lost Years*, 253–255.

118. Hroub, *Hamas, Political Thought and Practice*, 219.

119. Usher, "Letter from the Occupied Territories," 44; Esposito, "Quarterly Update on Conflict and Diplomacy," 148.

120. Central Elections Committee-Palestine, http://www.elections.ps/tabid/814/language/en-US/Default.aspx; "Official Results of Palestinian Municipal Elections Announced," Xinhua General News Service, December 26, 2004, available from LexisNexis; Saud Abu Ramadan, "Hamas Makes Major Election Gains," UPI, January 28, 2005, available from LexisNexis.

121. Ravi Nessman, "West Bank Municipal Election Tests Strength of Islamic Party," Associated Press, December 23, 2004, available from LexisNexis.

122. "Election Officials: Fatah Wins 56 Percent, Hamas 33 Percent of Votes in Municipal Elections," Associated Press Worldstream, May 6, 2005; "Fatah Emerges Biggest Winner in Third Stage of Local Elections," Xinhua General News Service, October 1, 2005, available from LexisNexis.

123. Daniel Williams, "Hamas Wins Control of 3 West Bank Cities; Militant Group's Surprise Victories Shatter PLO Monopoly in Palestinian Politics," *Washington Post*, December 16, 2005, available from LexisNexis.

124. Gunning, *Hamas in Politics*, 146–147.

125. Esposito, "Quarterly Update on Conflict and Diplomacy," 148.

126. "Hamas Leader Says Local Poll Results Show Movement 'Making Progress,'" interview with Hamas West Bank Leader Hasan Yusuf, *Al-Jazeera*, December 26, 2004, available from LexisNexis; "Political Platform of the Reform and Change Movement," Palestinian Information Centre, January 14, 2005, available from LexisNexis.

127. Lara Sukhtian, "Hamas Turns Focus to Political Campaign Ahead of Municipal Elections," Associated Press Worldstream, January 25, 2005, available from LexisNexis.

128. Usher, *Letter from the Occupied Territories*, 43.

129. "1st Lead: New Round of Inter-Palestinian Dialogue Opens in Cairo," Xinhua General News Service, March 15, 2005, available from LexisNexis.

130. "Beach Strike Shakes Hamas Cease-Fire," CNN.com, June 9, 2006; available from http://edition.cnn.com/2006/WORLD/meast/06/09/mideast/ (accessed March 12, 2010).

131. "Cairo Declaration," http://weekly.ahram.org.eg/2005/735/re1.htm (accessed December 2, 2012).

132. "Urgent: Hamas to Run in Palestinian Legislative Elections," Xinhua General News Service, March 12, 2005, available from LexisNexis; "Hamas Urges General Elections, Abbas Reluctant," Islamic Republic News Agency, November 17, 2004, available from LexisNexis.

133. "Khaled Abu Toameh, Abbas Backs Hamas Election Participation," *Jerusalem Post*, November 2, 2005, accessed December 5, 2006, http://www.jpost.com/servlet/Satellite?cid=1129540652080&pagename=JPost%2FJPArticle%2FShowFul (accessed March 12, 2010).

134. Mohammed Daraghmeh, "Palestinian Leader Asks Militant Hamas to Join Cabinet Ahead of Israel's Gaza Pullout," Associated Press Worldstream, July 2, 2005, available from LexisNexis.

135. US Senate, *Palestinian Legislative Council Elections*, 21.

136. "Hamas Rejects Any Amendments to the General Legislative Election Law," Palestinian Information Centre Website, November 23, 2005, available from LexisNexis.

137. "The Final Results of the Second PLC Elections," Central Elections Commission-Palestine, January 29, 2006, http://www.elections.ps/template.aspx?id=291 (accessed March 12, 2010). "The list of Change and Reform obtained 74 seats; the Fatah Movement obtained 45 seats; the list of the Martyr Abu Ali Mustapha obtained 3 seats; the Alternative received 2 seats; Independent Palestine received 2 seats; the Third Way received 2 seats; and the Independents list obtained 4 seats."

138. "Statement to the Masses on the Participation of Hamas in the Municipal and Legislative Elections," Palestinian Information Centre, October 28, 2005, available from LexisNexis.

139. Hroub, " 'New Hamas,' " 8–13.

140. Gunning, *Hamas in Politics*, 151.

141. International Crisis Group, "Inside Gaza," 9–10.

142. US Senate, *Palestinian Legislative Council Elections*, 2.

143. Gwertzman, "Interview: Shikaki."

144. Susser, *Rise of Hamas in Palestine*, 41.

145. Mohammed Shakeel, "Election 2006: Former Ruling Party Rejects Joining Hamas-Led Palestinian Government," World Markets Analysis, January 30, 2006; "Hamas Intends to Form National Coalition Cabinet," Xinhua General News Service, February 12, 2006, available from LexisNexis.

146. Ibrahim Barzak, "Islamic Hamas Leader to Begin Forming New Palestinian Government," Associated Press Worldstream, February 20, 2006, available from LexisNexis.

147. "Hamas Unveils Its Cabinet," *The Economist*, March 20, 2006, available from LexisNexis.

148. International Crisis Group, "After Mecca," 25.

149. Hroub, " 'New Hamas,' " 17.

150. Kurz, "Rise of Hamas in Israel," 24.

151. Shikaki, "With Hamas in Power," 8–9.

152. Ibid.; International Crisis Group, "After Mecca," 16.

153. Associated Press Online, April 7, 2006, available from LexisNexis.

154. Ismail Haniyeh, "Aggression under False Pretense," *Washington Post*, July 11, 2006, http://www.washingtonpost.com/wpdyn/content/article/2006/07/10/AR2006071001108.html (accessed March 12, 2010).

155. Ali Waked, "Hamas: Our Goal—Liberate Jerusalem," YNet News, February 14, 2006, http://www.ynetnews.com/articles/0,7340,L-3215968,00.html (accessed March 12, 2010).

156. Khaled Abu Toameh, "Power Struggle Erupts at the PLC: Abbas Aide Accuses Hamas of Coup Attempt," *Jerusalem Post*, March 7, 2006, available from LexisNexis; "Fatah MPs Boycott Parliament," *Al Jazeera News*, March 16, 2006, http://english.aljazeera.net/news/archive/archive?ArchiveId=19149 (accessed March 12, 2010).

157. Arnon Regular, "Hamas-Fatah Unrest Persists in Territories Despite Bid to End Tension," *Haaretz*, April 23, 2006, http://www.haaretz.com/hasen/pages/ShArt.jhtml?itemNo=708037&contrassID=1&subContrassID=0&sbSubContrassID=0 (accessed March 12, 2010).

158. Ibid.

159. "Chronology—Key Events since Hamas Came to Power," Reuters, February 7, 2007, http://www.reuters.com/article/idUSL09597423 (accessed March 12, 2010).

160. "Israel Justifies Hamas Detentions," *BBC News*, June 29, 2006, http://news.bbc.co.uk/2/hi/middle_east/5129836.stm.

161. Tamimi, *Hamas*, 242–243.

162. Herb Keinon and Yaakov Katz, "Israel Accepts Ceasefire Offer," *Jerusalem Post*, November 25, 2006, http://www.jpost.com/servlet/Satellite?cid=1162378480111&pagename=JPost%2FJPArticle%2FShowFull (accessed March 12, 2010).

163. "Hamas Threatens Intifada If No Agreement on Palestinian State," *Daily Times*, November 26, 2006, http://www.dailytimes.com.pk/default.asp?page=2006%5C11%5C26%5Cstory_26-11-2006_pg7_21 (accessed March 12, 2010).

164. International Crisis Group, "After Mecca," 26.

165. International Crisis Group, "Palestine Divided," 2.

166. Shikaki, "With Hamas in Power," 7.

167. Sarah El Deeb, "Abbas Dissolves Palestinian Government after Hamas Vanquishes Fatah and Takes Control of Gaza," Associated Press, June 15, 2007, available from LexisNexis.

168. International Crisis Group, "Inside Gaza," 14–17.

169. Milton-Edwards, "The Ascendance Of Political Islam," 1591.

170. See Human Rights Watch, "Under the Cover of War," April 2009, http://www.hrw.org/sites/default/files/reports/iopt0409webwcover.pdf (accessed November 25, 2012).

171. Milton-Edwards, "Order without Law?," 670.

172. International Crisis Group, "Ruling Palestine," I, 6–11, 26.

173. Amnesty International, "Occupied Palestinian Territories," October 24, 2007, http://www.Amnesty.Org/En/Library/Info/MDE21/020/2007/En (accessed March 15, 2010).

174. International Crisis Group, "Ruling Palestine," 6–8.

175. Ibid., 26.

176. Berti, "Salafist-Jihadist Activism in Gaza."

177. Ibid.

178. Ibid., 27.

179. Saab, "New Hamas in the Making?"

180. Phoebe Greenwood, "Hamas Moves Away from Violence in Deal with Palestin-

ian Authority," *The Guardian*, December 18, 2011, http://www.guardian.co.uk/world/2011/dec/18/hamas-moves-from-violence-palestinian (accessed November 25, 2012)

Chapter 5 • The Irish Republican Army and Sinn Féin in Northern Ireland

1. In the following chapter, IRA and PIRA (respectively, Irish Republican Army and Provisional Irish Republican Army) will be used interchangeably. When referring to a splinter group of the IRA, such as the Real Irish Republican Army (or Real IRA) or the Continuity Irish Republican Army (Continuity IRA), the chapter will use "RIRA" and "CIRA." The IRA and Sinn Féin are also referred to as the *Republicans* or the *republican movement*, while the term *nationalist forces* is used when referring to both Sinn Féin and the Social Democratic and Labour Party (SDLP).

2. Van Engeland and Rudolph, *From Terrorism to Politics*, 51.

3. Neumann, "Bullet and the Ballot Box," 950.

4. UK Home Office, "Proscribed Terrorist Groups," http://www.homeoffice.gov.uk/publications/counter-terrorism/proscribed-terror-groups/proscribed-groups?view=Binary (accessed October 31, 2010).

5. Council on Foreign Relations, "Provisional Irish Republican Army (IRA) (aka, PIRA, 'the Provos,' Óglaigh na hÉireann) (UK Separatists)," http://www.cfr.org/publication/9240/provisional_irish_republican_army_ira_aka_pira_the_provos_glaigh_na_hireann_uk_separatists.html (accessed October 31, 2010).

6. US State Department of State, Office of the Coordinator for Counterterrorism, "Foreign Terrorist Organization," October 15, 2010, http://www.state.gov/s/ct/rls/other/des/123085.htm (accessed October 31, 2010); Council of Europe, "Council Common Position 2009/67/CfspOf 26, January 2009: Updating Common Position 2001/931/Cfsp on the Application of Specific Measures to Combat Terrorism and Repealing Common Position 2008/586/Cfsp," http://eur-lex.europa.eu/LexUriServ/LexUriServ.do?uri=OJ:L:2009:023:0037:0042:EN:PDF (accessed October 31, 2010); UK Home Office, "Proscribed Terrorist Groups."

7. Stevenson, "Northern Ireland," 126.

8. Bloomfield, *Peacemaking Strategies in Northern Ireland*, 10.

9. Mitchell, "Social Violence in Northern Ireland," 181.

10. Kuusisto-Arponen, "End of Violence," 121.

11. Kalansooriya, *LTTE and IRA*, 11.

12. Northern Ireland Office, *Northern Ireland Constitutional Proposals*, Cmnd. 5259 (London: HMSO, March 20, 1973). Quoted by Bloomfield, *Peacemaking Strategies in Northern Ireland*, 13.

13. Ibid.

14. Mitchell, "Social Violence in Northern Ireland," 182.

15. Thompson, "Deprivation and Political Violence in Northern Ireland," 690–691.

16. Bloomfield, *Peacemaking Strategies in Northern Ireland*, 11.

17. Terchek, "Conflict and Cleavage in Northern Ireland," 52–53.

18. Mitchell, "Social Violence in Northern Ireland," 182.

19. Rafter, *Sinn Féin, 1905–2005,* 44.
20. Maillot, *New Sinn Féin,* 8.
21. Kalansooriya, *LTTE and IRA,* 11.
22. Rafter, *Sinn Féin,* 48–54.
23. Kelley, *Longest War,* 35; Maillot, *New Sinn Féin,* 10.
24. Kelley, *Longest War,* 42.
25. Kalansooriya, *LTTE and IRA,* 30.
26. Kelley, *Longest War,* 44.
27. Ibid., 53–53.
28. Bloomfield, *Peacemaking Strategies in Northern Ireland,* 25–26.
29. Weitzer, "Policing a Divided Society, 41; Ó Broin, *Sinn Féin and the Politics of Left Republicanism,* 127; Kelley, *Longest War,* 46–48.
30. McGladdery, *Provisional IRA in England,* 26–46.
31. Smooha, "Control of Minorities in Israel and Northern Ireland," 258.
32. Terchek, "Conflict and Cleavage in Northern Ireland," 55–56.
33. Foley, *Legion of the Rearguard,* 209–211.
34. Van Voris, "Provisional IRA and the Limits of Terrorism," 414.
35. Bell, *Gun in Politics,* 150–151.
36. Kelley, *Longest War,* 86.
37. Ó Broin, *Sinn Féin and the Politics of Left Republicanism,* 200–205.
38. Foley, *Legion of the Rearguard,* 211.
39. Ibid., 212–213.
40. Ó Broin, *Sinn Féin and the Politics of Left Republicanism.*
41. Augusteijn, "Political Violence and Democracy," 10; Sawyer, "Ending Violence," 34.
42. Van Voris, "Provisional IRA and the Limits of Terrorism," 416–417.
43. O'Doherty, *Trouble with Guns,* 69–70.
44. Bell, *Gun in Politics,* 142.
45. Oppenheimer, *IRA,* 28.
46. Kalansooriya, *LTTE and IRA,* 108–109.
47. Bloomfield, *Peacemaking Strategies in Northern Ireland,* 26–31.
48. Kalansooriya, *LTTE and IRA,* 112.
49. See, for example, the attack on October 5, 1974, at two local pubs in Guildford, which killed 5 people and injured 75; or the November 21, 1974, attacks at the Mulberry Bush and Tavern in Town pubs in Birmingham, leading to 21 deaths and more than 183 injured. Oppenheimer, *IRA,* 79; McGladdery, *Provisional IRA in England,* 86–90.
50. Kelley, *Longest War,* 199–203.
51. McGladdery, *Provisional IRA in England,* 98–101.
52. Oppenheimer, *IRA,* 32–33; O'Doherty, *Trouble with Guns,* 97–98.
53. O'Doherty, *Trouble with Guns,* 98.
54. Kalansooriya, *LTTE and IRA,* 31; Cox, "Bringing in the 'International,'" 679.
55. Oppenheimer, *IRA,* 31; Hannigan, "Armalite and the Ballot Box," 35.
56. Bell, *Gun in Politics,* 182; Oppenheimer, *IRA,* 31.
57. O'Doherty, *Trouble with Guns,* 112.
58. Hannigan, "Armalite and the Ballot Box," 34.

59. Ibid., 35.

60. Richards, "Terrorist Groups and Political Fronts," 74–75; Rafter, *Sinn Féin, 1905–2005*, 24.

61. Maillot, *New Sinn Féin*, 85.

62. O'Doherty, *Trouble with Guns*, 158.

63. Ryan, *War and Peace in Ireland*, 73.

64. Augusteijn, "Political Violence and Democracy," 1–2; English, *Armed Struggle*, 315.

65. Ibid., 296, 316.

66. UK House of Commons, Northern Ireland Affairs Committee, *The Financing of Terrorism in Northern Ireland*, 18.

67. Ibid., 12–13; Moran, "Paramilitaries, 'Ordinary Decent Criminals,'" 265; UK House of Commons, Northern Ireland Affairs Committee, *The Financing of Terrorism in Northern Ireland*, 13.

68. Ibid., 17.

69. Guelke, "United States, Irish Americans," 523.

70. English, *Armed Struggle*, 249; Kalansooriya, *LTTE and IRA*, 35.

71. Ó Broin, *Sinn Féin and the Politics of Left Republicanism*, 72.

72. McGladdery, *Provisional IRA in England*, 11–12.

73. Augusteijn, "Political Violence and Democracy," 17.

74. Bew, Frampton, and Gurruchaga, *Talking to Terrorists*, 73–75.

75. Irish Republican Army, *Green Book (Volumes I & II)*, 1956 and 1977. 8; Bell, *Gun in Politics*, 152–153.

76. Irish Republican Army, *Green Book*, 4.

77. Murray and Tonge, *Sinn Féin and the SDLP*, 36–38.

78. Kelley, *Longest War*, 129; Murray and Tonge, *Sinn Féin and the SDLP*, 36–38.

79. Ryan, *War and Peace in Ireland*, 216.

80. Ó Broin, *Sinn Féin and the Politics of Left Republicanism*, 242.

81. Ibid., 241–242.

82. Neumann, "Bullet and the Ballot Box," 955.

83. O'Doherty, *Trouble with Guns*, 113.

84. Neumann, "Bullet and the Ballot Box," 953.

85. O'Doherty, *Trouble with Guns*, 116–121.

86. *Sinn Féin-Unite Ireland.*

87. Quoted in Ryan, *War and Peace in Ireland*, 14.

88. Neumann, "Bullet and the Ballot Box," 957; Maillot, *New Sinn Féin*, 23.

89. *Towards a Lasting Peace in Ireland*, http://www.sinnfein.ie/contents/15212 (accessed December 2, 2010).

90. English, *Armed Struggle*, 250–251.

91. Ibid., 227.

92. Ryan, *War and Peace in Ireland*, 65.

93. Maillot, *New Sinn Féin*, 29; Bean, *New Politics of Sinn Féin*, 184.

94. Bonner, "Combating Terrorism," 29.

95. Hillyard and Percy-Smith, "Converting Terrorists," 339–340.

96. Ibid., 335–339.

97. Maillot, *New Sinn Féin*, 29.

98. Hannigan, "Armalite and the Ballot Box," 33.

99. English, *Armed Struggle*, 227.

100. Ibid., 250.

101. Bloomfield, *Peacemaking Strategies in Northern Ireland*, 35, 38; The Government of Ireland and the Government of the United Kingdom, *Agreement*, November 15, 1985, http://cain.ulst.ac.uk/events/aia/aiadoc.htm (accessed November 12, 2010).

102. The Government of Ireland and the Government of the United Kingdom, *Agreement.*

103. Quoted by Murray and Tonge, *Sinn Féin and the SDLP*, 150.

104. Bloomfield, *Peacemaking Strategies in Northern Ireland*, 39.

105. Ibid., 39.

106. Maillot, *New Sinn Féin*, 74–75.

107. Rafter, *Sinn Féin*, 98–99.

108. Ó Broin, *Sinn Féin and the Politics of Left Republicanism*, 236.

109. Bew et al., *Talking to Terrorists*, 87; Hannigan, "Armalite and the Ballot Box," 33.

110. Ó Broin, *Sinn Féin and the Politics of Left Republicanism*, 237.

111. Hannigan, "Armalite and the Ballot Box," 33–34.

112. Bew et al., *Talking to Terrorists*, 89.

113. Van Engeland and Rudolph, *From Terrorism to Politics*, 59.

114. Ó Broin, *Sinn Féin and the Politics of Left Republicanism*, 239.

115. Bean, *New Politics of Sinn Féin*, 186; Maillot, *New Sinn Féin*, 24–25.

116. Kalansooriya, *LTTE and IRA*, 114.

117. Hannigan, "Armalite and the Ballot Box," 33. Adams and McGuinness were allegedly also became part of the IRA Army Council, although this claim cannot be ascertained and is denied by the republican leaders (Rafter, *Sinn Féin*, 120).

118. Kelley, *Longest War*, 350.

119. Rafter, *Sinn Féin*, 100–101.

120. English, *Armed Struggle*, 133, 250.

121. Murray and Tonge, *Sinn Féin and the SDLP*, 159–160.

122. English, *Armed Struggle*, 246.

123. Neumann, "The Bullet and the Ballot Box," 954.

124. Hannigan, "Armalite and the Ballot Box," 34; Murray and Tonge, *Sinn Féin and the SDLP,* 129–130.

125. Neumann, "Bullet and the Ballot Box," 954–955.

126. Ó Broin, *Sinn Féin and the Politics of Left Republicanism*, 242.

127. Maillot, *New Sinn Féin*, 88; Murray and Tonge, *Sinn Féin and the SDLP*, 128–130.

128. Martin McGuinness (1984) quoted in English, *Armed Struggle*, 245.

129. Maillot, *New Sinn Féin*, 25.

130. Ó Broin, *Sinn Féin and the Politics of Left Republicanism*, 239.

131. McGladdery, *Provisional IRA in England*, 115.

132. Oppenheimer, *IRA*, 32–33.

133. O'Doherty, *Trouble with Guns*, 97.

134. English, *Armed Struggle*, 244; Rafter, *Sinn Féin*, 119, 154.

135. Rafter, *Sinn Féin*, 119.

136. Ibid., 120–122, 154.

137. Neumann, "Bullet and the Ballot Box," 964.

138. Rafter, *Sinn Féin*, 157.

139. Neumann, "Bullet and the Ballot Box," 958.

140. Gerry Adams, quoted in Murray and Tonge, *Sinn Féin and the SDLP*, 154.

141. McGladdery, *Provisional IRA in England*, 131.

142. Rafter, *Sinn Féin*, 150–151.

143. Neumann, "Bullet and the Ballot Box," 964.

144. McGladdery, *Provisional IRA in England*, 150–151.

145. Bew et al., *Talking to Terrorists*, 111.

146. McGladdery, *Provisional IRA in England*, 150–151.

147. Weinberg, Pedahzur, and Perliger, *Political Parties and Terrorist Groups*, 134.

148. Sawyer, "Ending Violence," 35–37.

149. Quoted in English, *Armed Struggle*, 260.

150. Quoted in Neumann, "Bullet and the Ballot Box," 964.

151. Ibid., 959–963; Rowan, *Behind the Lines*, 33.

152. Rowan, *Behind the Lines*, 19; Bew et al., *Talking to Terrorists*, 108.

153. McGladdery, *The Provisional IRA in England*, 143–152.

154. Ibid., 147; English, *Armed Struggle*, 279.

155. Ibid., 275.

156. Sawyer, "Ending Violence," 37–38.

157. McGladdery, *Provisional IRA in England*, 143.

158. Evans and Duffy, "Beyond the Sectarian Divide," 77.

159. Rowan, *Behind the Lines*, 7–8.

160. *Towards a Lasting Peace in Ireland.*

161. Neumann, "Bullet and the Ballot Box," 956; *Towards a Lasting Peace in Ireland.*

162. Neumann, "Bullet and the Ballot Box," 955.

163. Ó Broin, *Sinn Féin and the Politics of Left Republicanism*, 259.

164. English, *Armed Struggle*, 265; *First Joint Statement Issued by Social Democratic and Labour Party (SDLP) Leader Mr John Hume and Sinn Féin President, Mr Gerry Adams on Saturday 24 April 1993.* http://cain.ulst.ac.uk/events/peace/docs/ha24493.htm (accessed December 2, 2010).

165. Bloomfield, *Political Dialogue in Northern Ireland*, 16.

166. English, *Armed Struggle*, 269.

167. Bew and Gillespie, *Northern Ireland Peace Process, 1993–1996*, 31.

168. Dunnigan, *Deep-Rooted Conflict*, 75–83.

169. Quoted in Bloomfield, *Political Dialogue in Northern Ireland*, 160.

170. Rafter, *Sinn Féin*, 156–157; Bew et al., *Talking to Terrorists*, 291.

171. Ibid., 1523.

172. Neumann, "Bullet and the Ballot Box," 953.

173. English, *Armed Struggle*, 283.

174. *Moloney, A Secret History of the IRA, 498–501; The "TUAS" Document.* http://cain.ulst.ac.uk/othelem/organ/ira/tuas94.htm (accessed December 2, 2010).

175. Ibid.

176. Stevenson, "Northern Ireland," 125.

177. Oppenheimer, *IRA*, 11.

178. "IRA Statement Announcing the Cease-Fire—21 August 1994," in Dunnigan, *Deep-Rooted Conflict*, 65.

179. Oppenheimer, *IRA*, 332.

180. English, *Armed Struggle*, 288.

181. De Chastelain, "The Northern Ireland Peace Process," 155–158.

182. Bew and Gillespie, *Northern Ireland Peace Process*, 162; English, *Armed Struggle*, 289.

183. McGladdery, *Provisional IRA in England*, 191.

184. Bew and Gillespie, *Northern Ireland Peace Process*, 172.

185. O'Doherty, *Trouble with Guns*, 119.

186. Bew and Gillespie, *Northern Ireland Peace Process*, 174–175.

187. English, *Armed Struggle*, 291.

188. Rafter, *Sinn Féin*, 158–159.

189. Brams and Togman, "Cooperation through Threats," 32–37.

190. English, *Armed Struggle*, 296.

191. Sawyer, "Ending Violence," 39.

192. *Agreement Reached in the Multi-Party Negotiations.*

193. Sawyer, "Ending Violence," 3–4; Quoted in Millar, *Northern Ireland*, 194.

194. English, *Armed Struggle*, 299.

195. Stevenson, "Peace in Northern Ireland," 41.

196. "IRA Statement, April 30, 1998," http://news.bbc.co.uk/2/hi/events/northern_ireland/latest_news/85905.stm (accessed December 6, 2010).

197. Quoted in English, *Armed Struggle*, 300.

198. Murray and Tonge, *Sinn Féin and the SDLP*, 217.

199. Bean, *New Politics of Sinn Féin*, 218–219.

200. Quoted in Rafter, *Sinn Féin*, 32.

201. Ibid., 232–233.

202. Richards, "Terrorist Groups and Political Fronts," 76.

203. Kuusisto-Arponen, "End of Violence and Introduction of 'Real' Politics," 125; Hancock, "Northern Irish Peace Process," 204.

204. English, *Armed Struggle*, 302.

205. David Trimble, quoted in English, *Armed Struggle*, 328.

206. Kuusisto-Arponen, "End of Violence and Introduction of 'Real' Politics," 125; Millar, *Northern Ireland*, 111.

207. Hancock, "Northern Irish Peace Process," 204.

208. "IRA Statement in Full, May 6, 2000," http://news.bbc.co.uk/2/hi/uk_news/northern_ireland/738718.stm (accessed December 8, 2010).

209. Oppenheimer, *IRA*, 337–339; Hancock, "Northern Irish Peace Process," 204.

210. English, *Armed Struggle*, 331.

211. Richards, "Terrorist Groups and Political Fronts," 79–80.

212. Maillot, *New Sinn Féin*, 66.

213. Murray and Tonge, *Sinn Féin and the SDLP*, 231.

214. Ibid., 260; Maillot, *New Sinn Féin*, 52–56.

215. Rafter, *Sinn Féin*, 157.

216. Van Engeland and Rudolph, *From Terrorism to Politics*, 64.

217. Rafter, *Sinn Féin*, 28.

218. Bew et al., *Talking to Terrorists*, 161.

219. Ibid.

220. Moran, "Paramilitaries, 'Ordinary Decent Criminals,'" 269–270.

221. Rafter, *Sinn Féin*, 30.

222. Bew et al., *Talking to Terrorists*, 162.

223. "IRA Statement in Full, July 8, 2005," http://news.bbc.co.uk/2/hi/uk_news/northern_ireland/4724599.stm (accessed December 8, 2010).

224. Hancock, "Northern Irish Peace Process," 204.

225. Ibid.

226. Bew et al., *Talking to Terrorists*, 163.

227. Murray and Tonge, *Sinn Féin and the SDLP*, 216–217; *The Patten Report on Policing: Summary of Recommendations*, http://cain.ulst.ac.uk/issues/police/patten/recommend.htm (accessed December 12, 2010).

228. Murray and Tonge, *Sinn Féin and the SDLP*, 216–217.

229. Bew et al., *Talking to Terrorists*, 164.

230. Quoted in Bean, *New Politics of Sinn Féin*, 174–175.

231. Rafter, *Sinn Féin*, 219; Bean, *New Politics of Sinn Féin*, 210.

232. "Who Won What When and Where?," http://www.ark.ac.uk/elections/ (accessed December 12, 2010).

233. Ibid.

234. Bean, *New Politics of Sinn Féin*, 252–253.

235. Neumann, "Bullet and the Ballot Box," 942.

Chapter 6 • Armed Groups and Political Integration

1. See chapter 3. The concept of maintenance is broader than the notion of mere survival as existence, and it includes the capacity to secure a minimal level of resources and contributions, to maintain a membership base and a communication structure, to have a specific organizational purpose or *raison d'etre* that justifies their existence, and to preserve internal unity (Wilson, *Political Organizations*, 30–31).

2. Ottaway, "Islamists and Democracy."

3. Neumann, "The Bullet and the Ballot Box," 959.

4. See Deane, "Crime Corrupting Credibility."

5. Ross and Gurr, "Why Terrorism Subsides," quoted in Crenshaw, "How Terrorism Declines," 80–81.

6. Siqueira, "Political and Militant Wings," 226–227.

7. Finn, "Electoral Regimes," 66.

8. Ibid.

9. Crenshaw, "How Terrorism Declines," 80–81.

10. Ibid.

11. Van Engeland and Rudolph, "From Terrorism to Politics," 190.

12. Neumann, "Bullet and the Ballot Box," 971.

Abell, Peter. *Organizations as Bargaining and Influence Systems.* London: Halsted Press, 1975.

Abu-Amr, Ziad. "Hamas: A Historical and Political Background." *Journal of Palestine Studies* 22, no. 4 (1993): 5–19.

Abu-Amr, Ziad. "Shaykh Ahmad Yasin and the Origins of Hamas." In *Spokesmen for the Despised: Fundamentalist Leaders of the Middle East,* ed. R. S. Appleby, 225–256. Chicago: University of Chicago Press, 1997.

Adding Hezbollah to the EU Terrorist List: Hearing before the Subcommittee on Europe of the Committee on Foreign Affairs. 110th Cong. 19 (2007) (statement of James Phillips, Research Fellow for Middle Eastern Affairs, The Kathryn and Shelby Cullom Davis Institute for International Studies, The Heritage Foundation).

Alagha, Joseph. "Hizballah after the Syrian Withdrawal." *Middle East Report,* no. 237 (Winter 2005): 34–39.

Alagha, Joseph Elie. "The Shifts in Hizbullah's Ideology: Religious Ideology, Political Ideology, and Political Program." ISIM Dissertations. Leiden, the Netherlands: Amsterdam University Press, 2007.

Alexander, Yonah. *Palestinian Religious Terrorism: Hamas and Islamic Jihad.* Ardsley, NY: Transnational Publisher, 2002.

Allison, Michael E. "The Transition from Armed Opposition to Electoral Opposition in Central America." *Latin American Politics and Society* 48, no. 4 (2006): 137–162.

Arkin, William M. *Divining Victory. Airpower in the 2006 Israel-Hezbollah War.* Maxwell Air Force Base, AL: Air University Press, 2007.

Augusteijn, Joost. "Political Violence and Democracy: An Analysis of the Tensions within Irish Republican Strategy, 1914–2002." *Irish Political Studies* 18, no. 1 (2003): 1–26.

Azani, Eitan. *Testimony on 'Hezbollah's Global Reach.'" US House of Representatives, Committee on International Relations, Subcommittee on International Terrorism and Nonproliferation, Subcommittee on the Middle East and Central Asia, September 28, 2006.* 109th Cong. (2006).

Bacharach, Samuel B., and Edward J. Lawler. *Organizational Politics.* Stamford, CT: Jai Press, 2007.

Bean, Kevin. *The New Politics of Sinn Fein.* Liverpool: Liverpool University Press, 2007.

Beitler, Ruth Margolies. *The Path to Mass Rebellion: An Analysis of Two Intifadas.* Lanham, MD: Lexington Books, 2004.

Bell, J. Bowyer. *The Gun in Politics: An Analysis of the Irish Political Conflict. 1916–1986.* New Brunswick, NJ: Transaction Books, 1987.

Berti, Benedetta. "Hizb Allah's Domestic Containment." *Combating Terrorism Center (CTC) Sentinel* 2, no. 11 (November 2009).

Berti, Benedetta. "Reassessing the Transnational Terrorism-Criminal Link in South America's Tri-Border Area." *Terrorism Monitor* 6, no. 18 (2008).

Berti, Benedetta. "Salafist-Jihadist Activism in Gaza: Mapping the Threat." Combating Terrorism Center (CTC) Sentinel 3, no. 5 (May 2010).

Bew, John, Martyn Frampton, and Inigo Gurruchaga. *Talking to Terrorists: Making Peace in Northern Ireland and the Basque Country.* New York: Columbia University Press, 2009.

Bew, Paul, and Gordon Gillespie. *The Northern Ireland Peace Process 1993–1996: A Chronology.* London: Serif, 1996.

Bloomfield, David. *Political Dialogue in Northern Ireland: The Brooke Initiative, 1989–92.* Basingstoke: Macmillan, 1998.

Bloomfield, David. *Peacemaking Strategies in Northern Ireland: Building Complementarity in Conflict Management Theory.* Basingstoke: Macmillan, 1997.

Bonner, David. "Combating Terrorism: Supergrass Trials in Northern Ireland." *Modern Law Review* 51, no. 1 (1988): 23–53.

Brams, Steven J., and Jeffrey M. Togman. "Cooperation through Threats: The Northern Ireland Case." *Political Science and Politics* 31, no. 1 (1998): 32–37.

Brathwaite, Robert. "The Other Side of the Coin: Terror Groups and Political Wing Formation." Presented at the annual meeting of the Western Political Science Association, Manchester Hyatt, San Diego, CA, March 20, 2008.

Bregam, Ahron. *Israel's Wars: A History since 1947.* 2nd ed. London: Routledge, 2002.

Broom, Leonard, and Philip Selznick. *Sociology: A Text with Adapted Readings.* Evanston, IL: Row, Peterson, 1955.

Byman, Daniel. "Should Hezbollah Be Next? *Foreign Affairs* 82, no. 6 (2003): 54–66.

Chalabi, Tamara. *The Shi'is of Jabal 'Amil and the New Lebanon."* New York: Palgrave Macmillan, 2006.

Christensen, Soren, and Jan Molin. "Origin and Transformation of Organizations." In *The Institutional Construction of Organizations. International and Longitudinal Studies,* ed. W. Richard Scott and Soren Christensen, 67–90. London: Sage Publications, 1995.

Clark, Peter B., and James Q. Wilson. "Incentive Systems: A Theory of Organization." *Administrative Science Quarterly* 6, no. 2 (1961): 129–166.

Cleveland, William. *A History of the Modern Middle East.* 2nd ed. Boulder, CO: Westview Press, 2000.

"Clinton, Israel, and the Hamas Expulsion." *Middle East Report,* no. 181 (1991): 37.

Cox, Michael. "Bringing in the 'International': The IRA Ceasefire and the End of the Cold War." *International Affairs* 73, no. 4 (1997): 671–693.

Crenshaw, Martha. "The Causes of Terrorism." *Comparative Politics* 13, no. 4 (1981): 379–399.

Crenshaw, Martha. "How Terrorism Declines." In *Terrorism Research and Public Policy,* ed. Clark McCauley, 73–87. London: Frank Cass, 1991.

Crenshaw, Martha, ed. *Terrorism in Context.* University Park: Pennsylvania State University Press, 1995.

Crenshaw, Martha. "Theories of Terrorism: Instrumental and Organizational Approaches." In *Inside Terrorism*, ed. David C. Rapoport, 13–31. London: Frank Cass, 2001.

Dayton, Bruce W., and Louis Kriesberg. *Conflict Transformation and Peacebuilding: Moving from Violence to Sustainable Peace.* London: Routledge, 2009.

Deane, Shelley. "Crime Corrupting Credibility: The Problem of Shifting from Paramilitaries to Parliamentarians." *Civil Wars* 10, no. 4 (2008): 431–450.

De Chastelain, John. "The Northern Ireland Peace Process and the Impact of Decommissioning." In *From Political Violence to Negotiated Settlement: The Winding Path to Peace in the Twentieth-Century Ireland*, ed. Maurice J. Bric and John Coakley, chapter 10. Dublin, University College Dublin Press, 2004.

DeFronzo, James. *Revolutions & Revolutionary Movements.* Boulder, CO: Westview Press, 1991.

Della Porta, Donatella. "Left-Wing Terrorism in Italy." In Crenshaw, *Terrorism in Context*, 105–159.

Deonandan, Kalowatie, David Close, and Gary Prevost. *From Revolutionary Movements to Political Parties: Cases from Latin America and Africa.* New York: Palgrave Macmillan, 2007.

De Zeeu, Jeroen. *From Soldiers to Politicians: Transforming Rebel Movements after Civil War.* Boulder, CO: Lynne Rienner, 2008.

Dolnik, Adam, and Anjali Bhattacharjee. "Hamas: Suicide Bombings, Rockets, or WMD?" *Terrorism and Political Violence* 14, no. 6 (2002): 109–128.

Downs, Anthony. *Inside Bureaucracy.* Boston: Little, Brown, 1967.

Dunnigan, John P. *Deep-Rooted Conflict and the IRA Cease-Fire.* Lanham, MD: University Press of America, 1995.

Eisenberg, Laura Zittrain. "Israel's South Lebanon Imbroglio." *Middle East Quarterly* 4, no. 2 (1997). http://www.meforum.org/352/israels-south-lebanon-imbroglio.

El-Awaisi, Abd Al-Fattah Muhammad. *The Muslim Brothers and the Palestine Question, 1928–1947.* London: Tauris Academic Studies, 1998.

English, Richard. *Armed Struggle. The History of the IRA.* Oxford: Oxford University Press, 2003.

Esposito, Michele K. "Quarterly Update on Conflict and Diplomacy: Dates 16 May–15 August 2005." *Journal of Palestine Studies* 35, no. 1 (2005): 138–161.

Eubank, William Lee, and Leonard Weinberg. "Does Democracy Encourage Terrorism?," *Terrorism and Political Violence* 6, no. 4 (1994): 417–443.

Evans, Geoffrey, and Mary Duffy. "Beyond the Sectarian Divide: The Social Base and Political Consequences of Nationalist and Unionist Party Competition in Northern Ireland." *British Journal of Political Sciences* 27, no. 1 (1997): 47–81.

European Union Election Observation Mission. "Parliamentary Elections: Lebanon 2005."

Fearon, James D., and David D. Latin. "Violence and the Social Construction of Ethnic Identity." *International Organization* 54, no. 4 (2000): 845–877.

Finn, John. "Electoral Regimes and the Proscription of Anti-democratic Parties." *Terrorism and Political Violence* 12, no. 3 (2000): 51–77.

Foley, Conor. *Legion of the Rearguard: The IRA and the Modern Irish State.* London: Pluto Press, 1992.

Freund, Wolfgang. *Looking into HAMAS and Other Constituents of the Palestinian-Israeli Confrontation.* Frankfurt: Peter Lang, 2002.

Gambill, Gary. "Syria's Triumph in Lebanon: Au Revoir, Les Ententes." *MERIA,* December

3, 2010. http://www.gloria-center.org/2010/12/gambill-2010–12–03/. Accessed December 1, 2012.

Goldman, Ralph. *From Warfare to Party Politics*. Syracuse, NY: Syracuse University Press, 1990.

Goodwin, Jeff, and Theda Skocpol. "Explaining Revolutions in the Contemporary Third World." *Politics Society* 17, no. 4 (1989): 489–509.

Goodwin, Jeff. *No Other Way Out: States and Revolutionary Movements, 1945–1991*. New York: Cambridge University Press, 2001.

Greenwood, Royston, and C. R. Hinings. "Understanding Organizational Change: Bringing Together the Old and New Institutionalism." *Academy of Management Review* 21, no. 4 (1996): 1022–1054.

Guelke, Adrian. "The United States, Irish Americans and the Northern Ireland Peace Process." *International Affairs* 72, no. 3 (1996): 521–536.

Gunning, Jeroen. *Hamas in Politics: Democracy, Religion, Violence*. New York: Columbia University Press, 2008.

Gunning, Jeroen. "Peace with Hamas? The Transforming Potential of Political Participation." *International Affairs* 80, no. 2 (2004): 241–255.

Gupta, Dipak K. *Understanding Terrorism and Political Violence: The Life Cycle of Birth, Growth, Transformation, and Demise*. London: Routledge, 2008.

Gurr, Ted. "A Causal Model of Civil Strife: A Comparative Analysis Using New Indices." *The American Political Science Review* 62, no. 4 (1968): 1104–1124.

Gwertzman, Bernard. "Interview: Shikaki: Since Israeli Withdrawal from Gaza, Palestinians Now Give Top Priority to Improving Living Standard, Not End to Occupation." *Council on Foreign Relations* (October 19, 2005). http://www.cfr.org/publication/9055/shikaki.html. Accessed September 3, 2010.

Haberman, Shoshanah. *Between Hudna and Crackdown: Assessing the Record of Hamas Ceasefires*. Peace Watch 424. Washington, DC: The Washington Institute for Near East Policy, June 2, 2003.

Hafez, Mohammed M. "Review: Muslim Palestine: The Ideology of Hamas by Andrea Nusse." *International Journal of Middle Eastern Studies* 33, no. 1 (2001): 139–141.

Hajjar, Sami G. *Hizballah: Terrorism, National Liberation, or Menace?* Carlisle, PA: Strategic Studies Institute, US Army War College, August 2002.

Hamzeh, Ahmad Nizar. "Clan Conflicts, Hezbollah and the Lebanese State." *Journal of Social, Political, and Economic Studies* 19, no. 4 (1994): 433–446.

Hamzeh, Ahmad Nizar. *In the Path of Hizbullah*. Syracuse, NY: Syracuse University Press, 2004.

Hamzeh, Ahmad Nizar. "Lebanon's Hizbullah: From Islamic Revolution to Parliamentary Accommodation." *Third World Quarterly* 14, no. 2 (1993): 321–338.

Hamzeh, Ahmad Nizar. "Lebanon's Islamist and Local politics: A New Reality." *Third World Quarterly* 21, no. 5 (2000): 739–759.

Hancock, Landon E. "The Northern Irish Peace Process: From Top to Bottom." *International Studies* 10 (2008): 203–238.

Hannigan, John A. "The Armalite and the Ballot Box: Dilemmas of Strategy and Ideology in the Provisional IRA." *Social Problems* 33, no. 1 (1985): 31–40.

Harb, Mona, and Reinoud Leenders. "Know Thy Enemy: Hizbullah 'Terrorism' and the Polities of Perception." *Third World Quarterly* 6, no. 1 (2005): 173–197.

Harel, Amos, and Avi Issacharoff. *34 Days: Israel, Hezbollah, and the War in Lebanon.* New York: Palgrave Macmillan, 2008.

Harik, Judith Palmer. "Between Islam and the System: Sources and Implications of Popular Support for Lebanon's Hizballah." *Journal of Conflict Resolution* 40, no. 1 (1996): 41–67.

Harik, Judith Palmer. *Hezbollah: The Changing Face of Terrorism.* London: I. B. Tauris, 2006.

Harris, William. "Lebanon's Day in Court: The Controversial Life of the Hariri Tribunal." *Foreign Affairs Snapshots.* June 30, 2011. http://www.foreignaffairs.com/articles/67971/william-harris/lebanons-day-in-court. Accessed May 30, 2012.

Harris, William B. "Lebanon." In *Middle East Contemporary Survey: 1993–17,* ed. Ami Ayalon. Boulder, CO: Westview Press, 1995.

Herzog, Michael. "Can Hamas Be Tamed?" *Foreign Affairs* 85 no. 2 (March/April 2006): 83–94.

Hillyard, Paddy, and Janie Percy-Smith. "Converting Terrorists: The Use of Supergrasses in Northern Ireland." *Journal of Law and Society* 11, no. 3 (1984): 335–355.

Hira, Anil, and Ron *Hira.* "The New Institutionalism: Contradictory Notions of Change." *American Journal of Economics and Sociology* 59, no. 2 (2000): 267–282.

Hislope, Robert. "Ethnic Conflict and the 'Generosity Moment.'" *Journal of Democracy* 9, no. 1 (1998).

Horgan, John. *Walking Away from Terrorism.* London: Routledge, 2009.

Hroub, Khaled. *Hamas, Political Thought, and Practice.* Washington, DC: Institute for Palestine Studies, 2000.

Hroub, Khaled. "Hamas after Shaykh Yassin and Rantisi." *Journal of Palestine Studies* 33, no. 4 (2004): 21–38.

Hroub, Khaled. "A 'New Hamas' through Its New Documents." *Journal of Palestine Studies* 34, no. 4 (2006): 10–11.

International Crisis Group. "Palestine Divided." *Middle East Briefing,* no. 25 (December 17, 2008).

International Crisis Group. "Ruling Palestine: I. Gaza under Hamas." *Middle East Report,* no. 73 (March 19, 2008).

International Crisis Group. "After Mecca: Engaging Hamas." *Middle East Report,* no. 62 (February 28, 2007).

International Crisis Group. "Inside Gaza: The Challenge of Clans and Families." *Middle East Report,* no. 71 (December 20, 2007): 9–10.

International Crisis Group. "Syria after Lebanon, Lebanon after Syria." *Middle East Briefing,* no. 39 (April 12, 2005).

Israeli, Raphael. "A Manual of Islamic Fundamentalist Terrorism." Studies in Conflict & Terrorism 23, no. 3 (May/June 2002): 23–40.

Jaber, Hala. *Hezbollah: Born with a Vengeance.* London: Fourth Estate, 1997.

Jamal, Amal. *Media Politics and Democracy in Palestine.* Brighton: Sussex Academic Press, 2005.

Jensen, Michael Irving. *The Political Ideology of Hamas: A Grassroots Perspective.* London: I. B. Tauris, 2009.

Jones, Seth J., and Libicki, Martin C. *How Terrorist Groups End: Lessons for Countering Al Qa'ida.* Santa Monica, CA: Rand, 2008.

Jorish, *Avi. Beacon of Hatred: Inside Hizballah's Al-Manar Television.* Washington, DC: Washington Institute for Near East Policy, 2004.

Kalansooriya, Ranga. *LTTE and IRA: Combating Terrorism and Discussing Peace.* Colombo, Sri Lanka: Sanhinda Printers and Publishers, 2001.

Kalb, Marvin. *The Israeli-Hezbollah War of 2006: The Media as a Weapon in Asymmetrical Conflict.* Kennedy School of Government Faculty Research Working Paper Series, Cambridge, MA, Kennedy School of Government, 2007.

Kaufman, Asher. *The Shebaa Farms: A Case Study of Border Dynamics in the Middle East.* Jerusalem: The Harry S. Truman Research Institute for the Advancement of Peace, Hebrew University, 2002.

Kelley, Kevin J. *The Longest War: Northern Ireland and the IRA.* 2nd ed. Westport, CT: L. Hill, 1988.

Khashan, Hilal, and Ibrahim Mousawi. "Hizbullah's Jihad Concept." *Journal of Religion and Society* 9 (2007). http://moses.creighton.edu/JRS/2007/2007–19.html. Accessed September 2, 2010.

Klandermans, Bert. "Mobilization and Participation: Social-Psychological Expansions of Resource Mobilization Theory." *American Sociological Review* 49, no. 5 (1984): 583–600.

Knudsen, Are. "Crescent and Sword: The Hamas Enigma." *Third World Quarterly* 26, no. 8 (2005): 1373–1388.

Kramer, Martin. "Hizbullah: The Calculus of Jihad." *Bulletin of the American Academy of Arts and Sciences* 17, no. 8 (1994): 20–43.

Kramer, Martin. "The Oracle of Hizbullah. Sayyid Muhammad Husayn Fadlallah." In *Spokesmen for the Despised: Fundamentalist Leaders of the Middle East,* ed. R. Scott Appleby, 83–181. Chicago: University of Chicago Press, 1997.

Kramer, Martin. "Sacrifice and 'Self-Martyrdom' in Shiite Lebanon." *Terrorism and Political Violence* 3, no. 3 (1991): 30–47. Accessed October 10, 2010. http://www.martinkramer.org/sandbox/reader/archives/sacrifice-and-self-martyrdom-in-shiite-lebanon.

Kriesi, Hanspeter. "Political Context and Opportunity." In Snow et al., *Blackwell Companion to Social Movements,* 67–90.

Kristianasen, Wendy. "Challenge and Counterchallenge: Hamas's Response to Oslo." *Journal of Palestine Studies* 28, no. 3 (1999): 19–36.

Kurz, Anat. "The Rise of Hamas in Israel: Continuity and Change." In *The Challenges of Hamas,* ed. Aviva Palter. Conference Transcript. Netanya, Israel: S. Daniel Abraham Center for Strategic Dialogue, 2006.

Kuusisto-Arponen, Anna-Kaisa. "The End of Violence and Introduction of 'Real' Politics: Tensions in Peaceful Northern Ireland." *Geografiska Annaler Series B, Human Geography* 83, no. 3 (2001): 121–130.

"Lebanon's New Government." International Foundation for Electoral Systems. http://www.ifes.org/publication/38e87b372599cdff387c76fd022fb123/Lebanons_new_government.pdf. Accessed November 9, 2009.

Levitt, Matthew. *Financial Setbacks for Hamas.* Policy Watch 143. Washington, DC: The Washington Institute for Near East Studies, 2008.

Lijphart, Arend. *Democracies: Patterns of Majoritarian and Consensus Government in Twenty-One Countries.* New Haven, CT: Yale University Press, 1984.

Lijphart, Arend. *Electoral Systems and Party Systems: A Study of Twenty-Seven Democracies 1945–1990.* Oxford: Oxford University Press, 1994.

Lijphart, Arend. "The Political Consequences of Electoral Laws, 1945–85." *American Political Science Review* 84, no. 2 (1990): 481–496.

Lustick, Ian. "Terrorism in the Arab-Israeli Conflict: Targets and Audiences." In Crenshaw, *Terrorism in Context,* 514–532.

Mackey, Sandra. *Mirror of the Arab World: Lebanon in Conflict.* New York: W. W. Norton, 2008.

Maillot, Agnes. *New Sinn Fein: Irish Republicanism in the Twenty-First Century.* London: Routledge, 2005.

Maktabi, Rania. "The Lebanese Census of 1932 Revisited: Who Are the Lebanese?" *British Journal of Middle Eastern Studies* 26, no. 2 (1999): 219.

Malik, Hafeez. "Overview: Lebanon as an Experiment in Multicultural Interdependence." In *Lebanon's Second Republic. Prospects for the Twenty First Century,* ed. Kail C. Ellis, 14–22 Gainesville: University Press of Florida, 2002.

Malka, Haim. "Forcing Choices: Testing the Transformation of Hamas." *The Washington Quarterly* 28, no. 4 (Autumn 2005): 37–54.

Maney, Gregory M., Ibtisam Ibrahim, Gareth I. Higgins, and Hanna Herzog. "The Past's Promise: Lessons from Peace Processes in Northern Ireland and the Middle East." *Journal of Peace Research* 43, no. 6 (2006): 181–200.

Maqdsi, Muhammad. "Charter of the Islamic Resistance Movement (Hamas) of Palestine." *Journal of Palestine Studies* 22, no. 4 (1993): 122–134.

McClintock, Cynthia. *Revolutionary Movements in Latin America: El Salvador's FMLN and Peru's Shining Path.* Washington, DC: United States Institute of Peace Press, 1998.

McGladdery, Gary. *The Provisional IRA in England: The Bombing Campaign 1973–1999.* Portland, OR: Irish Academic Press, 2006.

Millar, Frank. *Northern Ireland: A Triumph of Politics. Interviews and Analysis 1988–2008.* Dublin: Irish Academic Press, 2009.

Milnor, Andrew J. ed. *Comparative Political Parties: Selected Readings.* New York: Thomas Y. Crowell Company, 1964.

Milton-Edwards, Beverley. "The Ascendance of Political Islam: Hamas and Consolidation in the Gaza Strip." *Third World Quarterly* 29, no. 8 (2008): 1585–1599.

Milton-Edwards, Beverley. "Order without Law? An Anatomy of Hamas Security: The Executive Force (Tanfithya)." *International Peacekeeping* 15, no. 5 (2008): 663–676.

Milton-Edwards, Beverley, and Alastair Crooke. "Elusive Ingredient: Hamas and the Peace Process." *Journal of Palestine Studies* 33, no. 4 (2005): 39–52.

Mishal, Shaul. "The Pragmatic Dimension of the Palestinian Hamas: A Network Perspective." *Armed Force & Society* 29, no. 4 (2003): 569–589.

Mishal, Shaul, and Avraham Sela. *The Palestinian Hamas: Vision, Violence and Coexistence.* New York: Columbia University Press, 2000.

Mishal, Shaul, and Avraham Sela. "Participation without Presence: Hamas, the Palestinian

Authority and the Politics of Negotiated Coexistence." *Middle Eastern Studies* 38, no. 3 (2002): 1–26.

Mitchell, James K. "Social Violence in Northern Ireland." *Geographical Review* 69, no. 2 (1971): 179–201.

Moghadam, Assaf, and Brian Fishman. "Debates and Divisions within and around Al-Qa'ida." In *Self-Inflicted Wounds: Debates and Divisions within al-Qa'ida and Its Periphery*," ed. Assaf Moghadam and Brian Fishman, 1–18. West Point, NY: Combating Terrorism Center at West Point, 2010.

Moloney, Ed. *A Secret History of the IRA*. New York: W. W. Norton, 2002.

Moran, Jon. "Paramilitaries, 'Ordinary Decent Criminals' and the Development of Organised Crime Following the Belfast Agreement." *International Journal of the Sociology of the Law* 32 (2004): 263–278.

Murray, Gerard, and Jonathan Tonge. *Sinn Fein and the SDLP: From Alienation to Participation*. London: Hurst, 2005.

Muslih, Muhammad. *The Foreign Policy of Hamas*. New York: Council on Foreign Relations, 1999.

Napoleoni, Loretta. *Modern Jihad: Tracing the Dollars behind the Terror Networks*. London: Pluto Press, 2003.

Nasr, Vali. *The Shia Revival: How Conflicts within Islam Will Shape the Future*. New York: W. W. Norton, 2006.

Neumann, Peter. R. "The Bullet and the Ballot Box: The Case of the IRA." *Journal of Strategic Studies* 28, no. 6 (2005): 941–975.

Noe, Nicholas, ed. *Voice of Hezbollah: The Statements of Sayed Hassan Nasrallah*. London: Verso, 2007.

Norton, Augustus Richard. "Changing Actors and Leadership among the Shiites of Lebanon." *Annals of the American Academy of Political and Social Science* 482, no. 1 (1985): 109–121.

Norton, Augustus Richard. *Hezbollah*. Princeton, NJ: Princeton University Press, 2007.

Norton, Augustus Richard. "Hizballah and the Israeli Withdrawal from Southern Lebanon." *Journal of Palestine Studies* 30, no. 1 (2000): 22–35.

Norton, Augustus Richard. "Lebanon after Ta'if: Is the Civil War Over?" *Middle East Journal* 45, no. 3 (1991): 441–456.

Norton, Augustus Richard, and Jillian Schwedler. "(In)security Zones in South Lebanon." *Journal of Palestine Studies* 23, no. 1 (1993): 61–69.

Nusse, Andrea. *Muslim Palestine: The Ideology of Hamas*. Amsterdam: Harwood Academic, 1998.

Ó Broin, Eoin. *Sinn Féin and the Politics of Left Republicanism*. London: Pluto Press, 2009.

O'Doherty, Malacho. *The Trouble with Guns: Republican Strategy and the Provisional IRA*. Belfast: Blackstaff Press, 1998.

Olmert, Joseph. "The Shi'is and the Lebanese State." In *Shi'ism, Resistance, and Revolution*, ed. Martin Kramer, 189–201. Boulder, CO: Westview Press, 1987.

Oppenheimer, A. R. "*IRA, The Bombs and the Bullets: A History of Deadly Ingenuity*. Dublin: Irish Academic Press, 2009.

Ottaway, Marina. " Islamists and Democracy: Keep the Faith." *The New Republic*, June 6 and 13, 2005. http://www.carnegieendowment.org/publications/index.cfm?fa=view&id=17037. Accessed January 13, 2011.

Panebianco, Angelo. *Political Parties: Organization and Power.* Cambridge: Cambridge University Press, 1988.

Pfeffer, Jeffrey. *Power and Organizations.* Marshfield, MA: Pitman, 1981.

Phares, Walid. "Liberating Lebanon." *Middle East Quarterly* 3, no. 4 (1996). http://www.meforum.org/418/liberating-lebanon. Accessed May 3, 2020.

Phillips, David L. *From Bullets to Ballots: Violent Muslim Movements in Transition.* New Brunswick, NJ: Transaction, 2009.

Pugh, Derek S., and David J. Hickson. *Writers on Organizations.* London: Sage, 1997.

Qassem, Naim. *Hizbullah: The Story from Within.* London: Saqi, 2005.

Rafter, Kevin. *Sinn Fein, 1905–2005. In the Shadow of Gunmen.* Dublin: Gill and Macmillan, 2005.

Ranstorp, Magnus. "Hezbollah's Command Leadership: Its Structure, Decision-Making, and Relationship with Iranian Clergy and Institutions." *Terrorism and Political Violence* 6, no. 3 (1994): 303–339.

Ranstorp, Magnus. *Hizb'allah in Lebanon: The Politics of the Western Hostage Crisis.* New York: St. Martin's Press, 1997.

Rapoport, David C., and Weinberg, Leonard. "Elections and Violence." *Terrorism and Political Violence* 12, no. 3 (2000): 15–50.

Richards, Anthony. "Terrorist Groups and Political Fronts: The IRA, Sinn Fein, the Peace Process and Democracy." *Terrorism and Political Violence* 13, no. 4 (2001): 72–89.

Ritzmann, Alexander. *Testimony on "Adding Hezbollah to the EU Terror List," January 26, 2009.* US House of Representatives, Subcommittee on Europe, June 20, 2007. http://internationalrelations.house.gov/hearing_notice.asp?id=846. Accessed August 30, 2009.

Robertson, David Brian. "The Return to History and the New Institutionalism in American Political Science." *Social Science History* 17, no. 1 (1993): 1–36.

Ross, Jeffrey Ian, and Ted Robert Gurr. "Why Terrorism Subsides: A Comparative Study of Canada and the United States." *Comparative Politics* 21, no. 4 (1989): 405–426.

Rowan, Brian. *Behind the Lines: The Story of the IRA and Loyalist Ceasefires.* Belfast: Blackstaff Press, 1995.

Roy, Sara. "Hamas and the Transformation(s) of Political Islam in Palestine." *Current History* (January 2003): 13–20.

Rucht, Dieter. "Movement Allies, Adversaries, and Third Parties." In Snow et al., *Blackwell Companion to Social Movements,*197–216.

Ryan, Mark. *War and Peace in Ireland: Britain and the IRA in the New World Order.* London: Pluto Press, 1994.

Saab, Bilal. "A New Hamas in the Making?" *The National Interest,* December 20, 2011. http://nationalinterest.org/commentary/new-hamas-the-making-6272. Accessed January 30, 2012.

Saad-Gorayeb, Amal. *Hizbu'llah: Politics and Religion.* London: Pluto Press, 2002.

Salloukh, Bassel. "Syria and Lebanon: A Brotherhood Transformed." *Middle East Report,* no. 236 (Fall, 2005): 14–21.

Sawyer, John Paul. "Ending Violence: IRA Monopoly Power and Market Closure in Northern Ireland." Paper presented at the International Studies Association Conference, 2009.

Scham, Paul, and Osama Abu-Irshaid. *Hamas: Ideological Rigidity and Political Flexibility.* Special Report. Washington, DC: United States Institute for Peace, June 2009.

Schenker, David. "Now Comes the Hard Part." *Weekly Standard*, June 22, 2009. http://www.washingtoninstitute.org/templateC06.php?CID=1293. Accessed November 1, 2010.

Schweitzer, Yoram. "'Divine Victory' and Earthly Failures: Was the War Really a Victory for Hizbollah?" In *The Second Lebanon War: Strategic Perspectives*, ed. Shlomo Brom and Meir Elran, 123–134. Tel Aviv: Institute for National Security Studies, 2007.

Scott, W. R. *Organizations: Rational, Natural, and Open Systems.* Englewood Cliffs, NJ: Prentice Hall, 1987.

Shikaki, Khalil. "Palestinians Divided." *Foreign Affairs* 83, no. 1 (2002): 89–105.

Shikaki, Khalil. "Peace Now or Hamas Later." *Foreign Affairs* 77, no. 7 (1998): 29–43.

Shikaki, Khalil. *With Hamas in Power: Impact of Palestinian Domestic Developments on Options for the Peace Process.* Working Paper 1. Waltham, MA: Brandeis University, Crown Center for Middle East Studies, February 2007.

Simon, Steven N., and Jonathan Stevenson. "Declawing the 'Party of God': Toward Normalization in Lebanon." *World Policy Journal* 18, no. 2 (2001): 31–42.

Siqueira, Kevin. "Political and Militant Wings within Dissident Movements and Organizations." *Journal of Conflict Resolution* 19, no. 2 (2005): 218–236.

Slavin, Barbara. *Mullahs, Money, and Militias: How Iran Exerts Its Influence in the Middle East.* Washington, DC: United States Institute of Peace, 2008.

Smooha, Sammy. "Control of Minorities in Israel and Northern Ireland." *Comparative Studies in Society and History* 22, no. 2 (1980): 256–280.

Snow, David A., Sarah A. Soule, and Hanspeter Kriesi, eds. *The Blackwell Companion to Social Movements.* Malden, MA: Blackwell, 2007.

Sobelman, Daniel. "New Rules of the Game: Israel and Hizbollah after the Withdrawal from Lebanon." Memorandum no. 59. Tel-Aviv: The Jaffee Center for Strategic Studies, 2004.

Soberg Shugart, Matthew. "Guerrillas and Elections: An Institutionalist Perspective on the Costs of Conflict and Competition." *International Studies Quarterly* 6, no. 2 (1992): 121–151.

Steinmo, Sven. "Historical Institutionalism?" In *Approaches and Methodologies in Social Sciences*, ed. Donatella Della Porta and Michael Keating, 118–138. Cambridge: Cambridge University Press, 2008.

Steiz, Charmaine. "Hamas Stands Down?" *Middle East Report*, no. 221 (2001): 4–7.

Stevenson, Jonathan. "Northern Ireland: Treating Terrorists as Statesmen." *Foreign Policy*, no. 105 (Winter 1996–1997): 125–140.

Stevenson, Jonathan. "Peace in Northern Ireland: Why Now?" *Foreign Policy* 112 (1998): 41–54.

Susser, Asher. *The Rise of Hamas in Palestine and the Crisis of Secularism in the Arab World.* Waltham, MA: Brandeis University, Crown Center for Middle East Studies, February 2010.

Taagepera, Rein, and Matthew Soberg Shugart. *Seats and Votes: The Effects and Determinants of Electoral Systems.* New Haven, CT: Yale University Press, 1989.

Tamimi, Azzam. *Hamas: A History from Within.* Northampton, MA: Olive Branch Press, 2007.

Terchek, Ronald J. "Conflict and Cleavage in Northern Ireland." *Annals of the American Academy of Political and Social Sciences* 433 (1977): 47–59.

Thompson, J. L. P. "Deprivation and Political Violence in Northern Ireland, 1922–1985: A Time-Series Analysis." *Journal of Conflict Resolution* 33, no. 4 (1989): 676–699.

UK House of Commons, Northern Ireland Affairs Committee. *The Financing of Terrorism in Northern Ireland.* Fourth Report of Session 2001–02. HC 978-I. London: The Stationery Office Limited, 2002.

Usher, Graham. "Hizballah, Syria, and the Lebanese Elections." *Journal of Palestine Studies* 26, no. 2 (1997): 59–67.

Usher, Graham. "The Intifada Two Years On." *Journal of Palestine Studies* 32, no. 2 (2003): 21–40.

Usher, Graham. "Letter from the Occupied Territories: The Palestinians after Arafat." *Journal of Palestine Studies* 34, no. 3 (2005): 42–56.

US Senate. *Palestinian Legislative Council Elections—Challenges of Hamas' Victory: Staff Trip Report to the Committee on Foreign Relations.* January 2006.

Van Engeland, Anisseh, and Rachel M. Rudolph. *From Terrorism to Politics.* Aldershot: Ashgate, 2008.

Van Voris, W. H. "The Provisional IRA and the Limits of Terrorism." *Massachusetts Review* 16, no. 3 (1975): 413–428.

Weinberg, Leonard, and Ami Pedahzur. *Political Parties and Terrorist Groups.* London York: Routledge, 2003.

Weinberg, Leonard, Ami Pedahzur, and Arie Perliger. *Political Parties and Terrorist Groups.* London: Routledge, 2008.

Weinberg, Leonard B. "Turning to Terror: The Conditions under Which Political Parties Turn to Terrorist Activities." *Comparative Politics* 23, no. 4 (1991): 423–238.

Weitzer, Ronald. "Policing a Divided Society: Obstacles to Normalization in Northern Ireland." *Social Problems* 33, no. 1 (1985): 41–55.

Wellhofer, E. Spencer, and Timothy M. Hennessey. "Political Party Development: Institutionalization, Leadership Recruitment, and Behavior." *American Journal of Political Science* 18, no. 1 (1974): 135–165.

Wiegand, Krista E. "Reformation of a Terrorist Group: Hezbollah as a Lebanese Political Party." *Studies in Conflict and Terrorism* 32, no. (2009): 669–680.

Wilson, James Q. *Political Organizations.* Princeton, NJ: Princeton University Press, 1995.

Winslow, Charles. *Lebanon: War and Politics in a Fragmented Society.* New York: Routledge, 1996.

Wood, Elisabeth Jean. *Forging Democracy from Below: Insurgent Transitions in South Africa and El Salvador.* New York: Cambridge University Press, 2000.

Zahhar, Mahmud, and Hussein Hijazi. "Hamas: Waiting for Secular Nationalism to Self-Destruct. An Interview with Mahmud Zahhar." *Journal of Palestine Studies* 24, no. 3 (1995): 81–88.

Zeid al-Keylani, Musa. *The Islamic Movement in Jordan and Palestine.* Amman: Al-Risala Institute, 1995.

Zisser, Eyal. "Hizballah in Lebanon: At the Crossroads." *MERIA* 1, no. 3 (1997). http://meria.idc.ac.il/journal/1997/issue3/jv1n3a1.html.

Zuhur, Sherifa. *Hamas and Israel: Conflicting Strategies of Group-Based Politics.* Carlisle, PA: Strategic Studies Institute, US Army War College, December 2008.

INDEX

Page numbers in *italics* indicate figures.